UNIVERSITY OF
WINCHESTER

Martial Rose Library
Tel: 01962 827306

To be returned on or before the day marked above, subject to recall.

Low End Theory

Bass, Bodies and the Materiality of Sonic Experience

Paul C. Jasen

Bloomsbury Academic
An imprint of Bloomsbury Publishing Inc

B L O O M S B U R Y
NEW YORK · LONDON · OXFORD · NEW DELHI · SYDNEY

Bloomsbury Academic
An imprint of Bloomsbury Publishing Inc

1385 Broadway
New York
NY 10018
USA

50 Bedford Square
London
WC1B 3DP
UK

www.bloomsbury.com

BLOOMSBURY and the Diana logo are trademarks of Bloomsbury Publishing Plc

First published 2016
Paperback edition first published 2017

Library of Congress Cataloging-in-Publication Data
Jasen, Paul C., author.
Low end theory: bass, bodies and the materiality of sonic experience/Paul C. Jasen.
pages cm
Includes bibliographical references and index.
ISBN 978-1-5013-0993-9 (hardback: alk. paper) 1. Music—Acoustics and physics. I. Title.
ML3805.J37 2016
781.2'32—dc23
2015029361

ISBN: HB: 978-1-5013-0993-9
PB: 978-1-5013-3591-4
ePDF: 978-1-5013-0994-6
ePub: 978-1-5013-0995-3

Typeset by Deanta Global Publishing Services, Chennai, India

For Olivia

Contents

Acknowledgements

My wife Sylvie planted the germ of this project; her partnership, insights, kind nature and patience are the book's foundation. I am also especially grateful to Paul Théberge who lent support, suggestions and encouragement from the very beginning. For their time, comments and enthusiasm along the way, many thanks to Jesse Stewart, Will Straw, Arun Saldanha, Brian Johnson, Chris Faulkner, Kyle Devine, John Shiga, Matthew Fuller, Michael Bull and Steve Goodman. I am particularly grateful to Ally Jane Grossan and everyone at Bloomsbury for their professionalism and their belief in this project, as well as the Social Sciences and Research Council of Canada for its generous support of my research. Many of the ideas in the following pages were first tested on dancefloors, at festivals and conferences, and in audio experiments and online discussions; respect due to the friends, collaborators and allies I've met through Riddim.ca, Deeptime.net, Artengine/Electric Fields, Blogariddims, Dissensus and Woofah Magazine.

To my parents and my family I owe an immeasurable gratitude for the love and support that made this possible. Thanks also to the friends I saw too rarely while writing. Lastly, I'd like to dedicate this book to the memory of Greg Jacobsen, my original myth-science collaborator, who left us too soon.

Introduction: Elements of a Myth-Science

Drifting in and out of the frame, a figure bathed in night-vision green investigates her newfound buoyancy. Her torso does slow half-twists in time with oscillating arms. Knees bent, she bobs in a stream of slow undulations. She's doing the vestibular skank – teased into motion by anomalies of the inner ear. Palms flat, she gently presses downward, over and over, seeming to nearly touch an invisible mass coursing around her. There's no suggestion of play-acting or pretending sound waves are water. But in the cyclic energies lapping from speakers, in the micro-barometric heaviness of bass-thickened air, there is something livably liquid about this dancefloor.[1]

This scene, is it something closer to reading or swimming? Construction or immersion? Mediation or modulation? If this figure were an actual swimmer, in the waves, at the beach, would we call her a consumer? Would we say she's performing her swimmerly identity? Or would we more likely call it sensuous play, as she feels her way through an unusual material relation? Liquid surroundings quite obviously alter what a body can do. Their speeds are different; their pressures are different. They impose their own rhythms and forces. In their undulant weight, we sense new constraints, but also new potentials. Ideas begin to arrive through the body, as habits of perception and movement are made to adjust. So we try things out: 'How will this feel ... ? How else might I move ... ?' We might intuit little repertoires of aqueous techniques that can be linked and elaborated. When we do these things together – devising games, forming groups – they acquire a sociality. A collective *aquatic body* begins to emerge.

Aquatic language is relatively common in depictions of low-frequency sonic experience, and it's easy to understand why. In order to be felt or heard, low tones must be many thousands of times more powerful than those frequencies involved in speech.[2] High-sound pressure levels condense air – noticeably thickening it, making it feel heavier. At these slower frequencies and higher amplitudes, sound waves are also more readily perceived in their cyclic undulations. We can watch them move through matter, or make the lightest things (paper, plastic, hair) dance and float. Their vibrations can buffet and wallop us. When they slide out-of-phase, we feel their drift or turbulence. They can also induce feelings of buoyancy, weight and flow, as they fill the inner ear and disrupt perceptions of motion and balance. This 'swimmingness' of perception can even spread to the eyes, which begin to oscillate and blur as they scan reflexively for invisible shapes. All of this considered, would it be fair to treat water–sound analogies simply as the tropes of auditory cultures? Or could we not more convincingly say that aquatic language is one route to putting thought in closer touch with the materiality of sonic experience, with the body's sonorous relations, and sound's a-signifying participation in culture?

* * *

The bass investigation that follows actually began before I quite knew it, in the throbs of an East London dancefloor, where I found myself being roughed up by the most powerful sound system I'd yet encountered. It was a shattering experience, physically, but also conceptually. Over those few hours, I had to learn to work with pressures that hummed me strangely, often hurt and made breathing a chore. At the same time, as two dozen of us shimmered together in the dark, certain habits acquired from cultural studies were also starting to shake loose. What became painfully obvious, in the most literal sense, was that for all our speculations about people's subjectivities and the value systems of (sub)cultural groups, we have had very little to say about how things sound and feel in these settings, even if this is largely why people are there in the first place. Bass, as vibratory force, rarely enters the discussion, except passingly as a signifier of something else, or a physical curiosity better left to science. This leaves us with no sense of sound's material participation in culture: how people engage it sensually, but also collectively and conceptually. Without this, we can never arrive at more provocative questions of sound's own structuring agency – its capacity to modulate developments in the social, quite independently of our ideas and intentions.

   This book starts from these concerns, along with the observation that, despite widespread, cross-cultural fascination with bass and its sometimes mysterious (sometimes dangerous) effects, we generally lack a language suitable for its investigation.[3] To develop one will mean beginning *in* the sonic encounter (rather than our discourses about it), asking what happens when waves mingle with fleshborne thought, and how these modulatory relations can work to catalyse developments along any number of axes. 'Bass' – as the common term for low frequencies more generally – is the ostensive starting point. But bass is a slippery thing to study. It quickly leads far beyond dancefloors, music and ears. It turns questions of musical sound to matters of extramusical vibration and extra-cochlear perception. The former opens onto the acoustics of bodies and buildings, inadvertent encounters with ambient waves, the unheard vibrations of infrasound and still more liminal events that can only be called sound-*like*. The latter points to whole intermodal worlds of sonic experience beyond audition, where perception is unsettled and synaesthetic overlaps make bodies re-imagine themselves and their surroundings.

This contingent, imaginative body that emerges in its sonorous relations, is what will be called the *sonic body*.[4] We'll follow it across many sites that are ostensibly unrelated when considered mainly in cultural terms (hauntings, laboratories, The Hum, burial mounds, organ workshops, studios, dancefloors, 'sound houses' and disused missile silos, among others), but which turn out to be kindred when viewed from the perspective of frequency, force and affective tone. As a term, 'sonic body' is already in circulation.[5] It likely entered this project via the closing lines of Julian Henriques' 2003 essay 'Sonic Dominance and the Reggae Sound System Session', which is notable for being, perhaps, the first scholarly effort to theorize the collective sensory experience of deep, powerful bass.[6] Since then, however, we have each developed the concept in our own ways. For his part, Henriques has very recently published the book *Sonic Bodies: Reggae Sound Systems, Performance Techniques and Ways of Knowing* (2011), which richly expands the themes first broached in 'Sonic Dominance'. There, the sonic body is understood as a route to knowledge, working as a transducer, of sorts. Here the notion of transduction is retained, but with the crucial difference that the sonic body will be investigated as a site of *un*-knowing. This is not to suggest the erasure of thought by sound, but to foreground how vibratory encounters can work to unravel self-certainty and recast our sensed surroundings, making us rethink what we can do and how we operate. The focus here is on the many ways this sonic body can be productively mystified by anomalous vibration (which works as an incitement to imagination, experimentation and invention), and how it becomes a bit of a mythic creature in the process.

The field: subjects without bodies

When this project was first conceived, it set out to bring the materiality of sonic experience more meaningfully into discussions of music and sonic culture.[7] Part of this strategy involves learning what we can about the sonic body from fields as varied as philosophy, acoustic science, anthropology, religious studies, paranormal studies, visual arts and Afrofuturism. However, it is also premised on an intervention in a group of linked tendencies that became normative in the wake of cultural studies and post-structuralism: the broad application of linguistic and literature-derived analytical models to all things (treating them as signs, texts, discourses and their effects, representations, dynamics of encoding/decoding, etc.), along with the dual assumptions that culture is the mediator of all experience (which is therefore only ever subjective, filtered, and relative), and that all the elements of experience, and their possible interactions, are always prefigured in their social construction, therefore holding no surprises, and having no world-making agency of their own.[8] Through the 1990s, these orientations acquired a commonsense status in the humanities. Graduate students quickly learn to speak the language and assume a stance of postmodern knowingness, in order to avoid the charge of 'naïve realism'.

Yet, when we step into the throbbing messiness of life, that language often rings false. An un-knowing starts to unfold when the world confronts us with non-discursive intensities that strain the constructionist premise and modulate us more than we mediate them.[9] Arguably, the greater naïveté lies in assuming we can really get a grip on it all. Without detracting from necessary efforts to undermine determinisms, essentialisms, hegemonic narratives and positivist interpretations of the social, we can also point to the problems that arise when work in this culturalist mould attempts to 'bracket' out aspects of material existence. This stance quite explicitly keeps nature and materiality at a remove, holding that they can only ever be encountered through our ideas about them, and generally denying the possibility of influence in the other direction. Similarly, despite the post-structuralist critique of Cartesian rationalism and its dualistic view of mind and body, the overriding tone, since the 'textual turn', has remained quite starkly cerebral, making everything a matter of interpretation and organization by the mind, whether individual or collective. 'Dumb matter' is generally left to the sciences where its cultural life is mostly ignored, leaving a vast and still largely unexplored region between the interests of the humanities and the sciences. This is the terrain of the sonic body, which operates as an itinerant between what Jane Bennett has called 'vibrant matter' and fleshy thought.[10] As such, it draws the overlapping fields of music, sound studies and sensory studies into the discussion, but it also helps reveal the ways that each tends to bracket aspects of experience and keep them at a distance.

The present work was provoked by the chronic elision of materiality in the study of popular music, even in scholarship that claimed to address the body, or which took as its object those musical cultures that most openly experiment with vibration and sensation. Jeremy Gilbert and Ewan Pearson begin from a similar premise in *Discographies: Dance Music, Culture and the Politics of Sound*, which presents an archaeology of Western thought on musical sound and bodily experience, since antiquity. They trace an ingrained distrust of materiality from Plato, through Descartes, Kant, Adorno and into the aesthetic theories of recent decades, arguing that these inherited predispositions have left popular music studies insensitive to basic facets of musical culture. Certainly, the field's scope is broad, spanning matters of industry, consumption, representation, power-knowledge, identity and community, resistance, policy and policing, authenticity, local/global relationships, technology, collective identity, space/place and the cultural specificity of localized musical practices. But, again, these myriad discourses on musical subjectivity rarely take into account the sonic-sensory conditions that often mean so much to participants. This remains largely true even of electronic dance music (EDM) studies which has yet to develop a conceptual language of its own, despite its focus on musics built around rhythms and forces more than texts, in any meaningful sense. The study of these musics has the potential to help force open a much wider discussion of the body and sensation in culture. However, the prevailing tendencies in the field have generally mirrored the political-economic and textual concerns that have preoccupied popular music studies as a whole.

Consider, for example, the enthusiasm for semiotic 'noise' since Jacques Attali's 1977 book *Noise: A Political Economy of Music*. In work on popular and experimental music, the notion of noise is often used to suggest a scrambling of sign systems, whether at the level of musical text, identity (treated as a network of representations) or social conventions.[11] In some cases, the parallel between these aspects of a musical culture and its sonic characteristics are fairly evident (the noise of punk, for example). Other times, the metaphor is more stretched, as in a series of studies that have made 'noise' and hip-hop virtually synonymous in academic discourse by punning on Public Enemy's track 'Bring the Noise'.[12] What gets lost in these 'readings', however (besides the fact that P. E.'s noisy sonics were the anomaly in hip-hop), is the song's opening line: 'Bass! How low can you go?' It's a challenge and a threat, built to issue from a bank of woofer cones in the back of a jeep.[13] If hip-hop has an overriding sonic profile – one that its makers and fans flock to, that its critics despise – it is neighbourhood-rattling bass. Yet this basic sonic-cultural fact has rarely been taken up in any sustained way.

When flesh enters these discourses, it is typically only by indirect means. The language of 'embodiment', for example, became popular in the 1990s, but too often, when it promises bodies, it only delivers their constructed, mediated, and discursive auras. There are raced, gendered, and classed bodies; consuming bodies; disciplined and resistant bodies; performative bodies; and so forth. This is the body as a cultural vector, but rarely as a sensate actor, or a *two-way* interface between nature and culture. Attention to dance does not necessarily move the discussion any further in that direction, when dominant tendencies in the literature still hold that 'as well as being a social, political, psychological, occasionally pharmaceutical and often economic activity, dancing is primarily a form of communication ... a performance'.[14] The implication (as Brian Massumi notes of embodiment discourses, generally) is that these bodies 'make and unmake sense as they might, don't *sense*'.[15] Moreover, the tendency to treat participants' descriptions of sonic experience primarily as metaphors or constructs (i.e. *just* discourse) precludes the possibility of bodily relations informing thought.[16] In the end, this leaves popular music studies, and scholarship on music generally, without much theoretical language that actually arises from the immanent conditions of the acoustic event. (Curiously, the 'old musicology', in the most traditional sense – e.g. organ histories – can sometimes show a greater willingness to let tales of sonic experience speak without debunking).[17]

In contrast, the following chapters make every effort to inhabit the sonic body, treating it as a conceptual event and looking for a language proper to it. Against the traditional emphasis on the social construction of sonic experience, we will investigate what might be called the *sensory production of the audio-social*, for both its affective and epistemological implications.[18] 'Audio-social' is Kodwo Eshun's term for collective sonorous spaces understood as sensory environments swarming with a-signifying forces that defy efforts to 'read' them and demand more relevant modes of thought. Eshun sets himself in opposition to tendencies within the humanities that keep sonic experience at a professional distance and, by accident or design, work to absorb affect's shocks through the language of mediation and construction.[19] 'You don't have to begin with the social', he argues, not to advocate politically ignorant writing, but rather to acknowledge just how much we miss in sonic culture (including questions of power and collective subjectivation taken up in the following chapters) if we ignore how it sounds and feels – how these dimensions are not only privileged by participants, but constitutive of thought and activity in these places. Eshun's book, *More Brilliant Than The Sun: Adventures in Sonic Fiction*, begins by demanding that, for once, we try to start the discussion from a different direction.[20] Writing specifically on electronic musics that target the moving, sensing body, he reasons: 'When it comes to dance music, it seems crucial to understand the weight of a sound – why does a break press on your arms, why does it seem to scuttle, or why do people describe electronic music as cold, why does it feel like your temperature has dropped?'[21] When the emphasis is nearly always on a communicative body and the meanings of sound, he says, 'these questions [go] completely unexplored'. This is perhaps the most crucial observation behind the present intervention which turns bass vibration into a vehicle for dislodging scholarly habits and discovering new strategies in their place.

If attention to sonic experience and the materiality of sound are largely missing from the study of music, then sound studies can be of help, although here too we need to be wary of tendencies that keep sonorous relations at a remove. The interdisciplinary field is rapidly becoming so diverse (overlapping with communications, music, film, media and technology studies, anthropology and various others) as to defy easy summary. We can, however, identify some broad tendencies and well-established orientations that have given it shape. There are histories of sound technologies, including the circumstances of their development and adoption, their social roles, cultural reception and adaptations. Also central, has been a concern with the conditions of sound reproduction, as a technological process and as a mediator of culture (through machines, as well as across time and between locales). This opens onto questions of listening which have comprised another major area of attention. Here, the focus turns to the language of sound, the meanings and values attributed to it in its various forms, as well as the cultural formations, techniques and norms that have emerged around specific varieties of listening practice, whether for the purposes of labour or pleasure. A related area of investigation examines questions of acoustic space, its sociality and sonorous politics and related noise/silence debates.[22] Diverse as they are, however, these modes of enquiry nevertheless tend to organize around common epistemological threads that are unaccustomed to thinking with sound's material agency. If there is a mainstream of sound studies, it remains most firmly committed to questions of sound's cultural interpretation and the social formations that organize sonic technologies and practices.[23]

For present purposes, it is also worth adding the general observation that sound studies, despite the amodal purview implied by its name (compared, for example, to visual studies), has been almost exclusively concerned with aurality, to the exclusion of other aspects of perception. A degree of 'cochlearcentrism' is understandable, when first turning to sound as an object of study, but, as an ongoing habit, this tendency is quickly problematized by the extra-cochlear, multimodal and intermodal dimensions of vibratory experience. In his book *Sonic Warfare*, Steve Goodman argues that the noise/silence binary that has preoccupied so much discussion of sonic culture has generally given little attention to those modulations that so explicitly implicate the rest of the body, and quite literally shake loose the culturalist mindset. In proposing an 'ontology of vibrational force', he writes,

> Of all frequency bands within a sonic encounter, [bass] most explicitly exceeds mere audition and activates the sonic conjunction with amodal perception: bass is not just heard but is felt. Often sub-bass cannot be heard or physically felt at all, but still transforms the ambience of a space, modulating its affective tonality, tapping into the resonant frequency of objects, rendering the virtual vibrations of matter vaguely sensible.

'Bass demands more theoretical attention,' he argues, noting that 'it is too often equated with a buzzing confusion of sensation and therefore the enemy of clear auditory perception and, by implication, clear thought. But for many artists, musicians, dancers, and listeners, vibratory immersion provides the most conducive environment for movements of the body and movements of thought'.[24] Grasping the sonic body means attending to these bass-induced movements of bodily thought, which, in turn, means giving greater attention to the role of sensation in sonic culture.

The present investigation, therefore, operates largely in a space where sound studies overlaps with the cultural study of the senses. The latter has a long and varied history, with notable twentieth-century contributions coming from phenomenology, experience-minded anthropologists and Marshall McLuhan, among others. More recently, the interdisciplinary field known as sensory studies has emerged largely around the work of David Howes, Anthony Synnott, Constance Classen and others associated with Concordia University's Centre for Sensory Studies.[25] In the last decade, much of this work has centred on the journal *The Senses and Society*, which has become a forum where body-related investigations from a range of disciplinary perspectives have been able to mingle.

In his introduction to *The Empire of the Senses* (2005), Howes summarizes sensory studies as a programme to 'recover a full-bodied understanding of culture and experience', arguing that the fixation on language and representation, in recent decades, has only worked to preserve the age-old distrust of the body by another name. This is very much the argument here, but again there are fundamental points of difference that can be traced back to this problem of culturalist overextension and its blind spots. Howes, for example, insists that sensation can only ever be socially constructed, that it always operates 'within the context of communal sensory orders' and never 'outside the symbol systems of culture.'[26] Even more sweepingly, he says that 'human nature is a product of culture.'[27] This may be true of ideas about human character, but nature is never reducible to what we make of it. As the basis of all things, it has an autonomy by definition. It always exceeds our knowledge of it, and concerns about its co-optation by deterministic discourses melt away when we recognize that its only essence is its capacity for variation and surprise.[28]

This outlook affords us a very different understanding of the body and its encounters. It also suggests that the humanities might devise more productive ways of critically engaging the sciences. For his part, however, Howes says that one role of 'the sensual revolution' is to 'recover perception from the laboratory', arguing that science has little to add to such analyses. Its findings are only ever relative and it is best kept at arm's length.[29] This habitual distrust of the sciences, while by no means unfounded, is also counterproductive because it risks cutting off vast areas of research from which theorists of culture might glean valuable insights, even if we do not accept the methodologies or conclusions. In *Parables for the Virtual*, Massumi makes a virtue of 'poaching' scientific concepts – that is, 'betray[ing] the system of science while respecting its affect, in a way designed to force a change in the humanities.'[30] This book works in a similar way. We learn what we can about the sonic body from empirical research in acoustics and perception, but a recurring theme is the deterritorialization of scientific systems and certainties by vernacular strategies, coupled with nature's innate (and much mythologized) capacity to mystify.

The theoretical kernel

This investigation relies on a small theoretical core, selected for its particular ability to think with the intensities of the sonic body. Massumi has written that Gilles Deleuze and Félix Guattari, 'almost alone among poststructuralist writers, reserve an important place in their thought for the concept of "sensation", and their work figures prominently here for the same reason.[31] They understand sensation as something 'pre-personal' – a matter of qualitative change in a body that precedes the interpretative work of perception. It strikes before cognition can make sense of it, and before culture can mediate it. The idea is not that it is separate from the social, but that it is *asocial*, that it retains an autonomy, and an agency of its own, having the capacity to redirect thought, action and collective organization. Never just a matter of experience privately 'had' by a discrete subject, sensation is understood in a more spatial or 'exteriorized' sense, as a 'block of coexistence' – a milieu shaped by the relations of bodies and forces that compose it. For his part, Massumi has built on this foundation, taking up questions of movement, affect and sensation in ways specifically meant to force self-reflection in the humanities.[32] The present investigation draws on his work, along with that of Deleuze, Guattari and William James, in order to theorize the sensory workings of various vibratory milieus.

Always in the background, however, is the seventeenth-century philosopher Baruch Spinoza and his *Ethics*, especially as synthesized by Deleuze, for whom it illuminated a dissident philosophical lineage that passes through the likes of Nietzsche and Bergson, and offers a remedy to Descartes and Kant's lingering hold over Western thought.[33] For the present purposes, there are several aspects of Spinoza's work that should be understood in basic terms. As an ontology, his *Ethics* is a monist one, taking the world and everything in it to be composed of a common, roiling, substance. This is what underlies the Deleuzian concern for relations of *immanence* (emergent connections, rather than transcendent unities), *exteriority* (the openness of things to mutual influence) and the *intensive* rhythms that texture blocks of coexistence (as opposed to the *extensive* slicing-up of the world, upon which notions of objective distance and separateness are premised). This has important implications for things held by rationalist thought to occupy distinct categories: matter/energy, nature/culture, mind/body. We ask instead about material-energetic tendencies, and the ways that nature and culture become one another. Similarly, Spinoza describes the essentially indistinguishable nature of mind and body – a 'parallelism'.[34] To speak of a living body, in this sense, is necessarily to mean a mind-body of thinking flesh. Moreover, he understood bodies in the broadest terms, encompassing those of creatures, but also the parts that compose them, as well as bodies of thought, collective bodies, 'inanimate' things, and any other assemblage insofar as it can participate in a block of coexistence. This includes bodies of sound. Finally, in assessing the relations between these bodies, ethics are distinct from morals in that their interest does not reduce to transcendent categories of Good and Bad, but ask instead how bodies impinge upon one another, how they augment or diminish each other's capacity to act (making it possible to imagine what an ethics of sonic experience might entail).[35]

This is the basic definition of *affect*, in the Spinozist sense, as adopted by philosophers since Deleuze, and more recently popularized by Massumi and others. Contra the term's commonplace usage as a synonym for emotion, these thinkers understand affect to identify a relational dynamic: a capacity to affect and be affected. The so-called affective turn of recent years has arisen largely in response to normative culturalism and textual fixations in the humanities. In *The Affect Theory Reader*, Melissa Gregg and Gregory J. Seigworth describe a field so broad (spanning Spinozist interpretations, to work in the tradition of Sylvan Tomkins and Eve Sedgwick, to developments in cognitive science and so on) as to make generalizations nearly impossible. The present text uses the concept in its Spinoza-Deleuze sense, but even still, a definition is elusive. For Deleuze and Guattari, 'affects are becomings', but also, 'affects are ... weapons'. Gregg and Seigworth note that an affect is a 'force, but not necessarily forceful' when it operates on infraempirical or subperceptual registers. Manuel De Landa neatly describes it as a 'capacity to interact', which echoes William James' emphasis on the *relationality* of things – not the individual parts, but the movements and responsivities that emerge between them. Similarly, for Massumi, affect is equatable with 'intensity', but it also denotes a transition, and therefore carries an aspect of futurity (which is the *virtual* component). Moreover, affect always has an autonomy, being not directly liveable but only ever grasped in its effects. For this reason, it is never reducible to language and something of it always escapes us.[36]

What unites these various definitions, say Gregg and Seigworth, is an outlook that can be called a 'processually oriented materialism'. It is processual because its focus is on the movements and *becomings* of things – the ways they *deterritorialize* (recompose) each other, as opposed to the relative 'situatedness' of objects understood to exist in discrete categories.[37] It is materialist, in a broad sense, because it concerns the ways things of all sorts impinge upon one another on a monist plane (e.g. the way vibration modulates thought no less than it does a violin string or a building). Deleuze and Guattari make the distinction between matter (whole, fixed, 'molar') and *materiality*, which is meant to convey this processual dimension and its 'molecular' processes – the way things move around, break down, mingle and coalesce into new assemblages, each with their own capacities to interact.[38] Materiality, in this sense, speaks less to concreteness, or the actual fact of matter, than to relationality, material tendency and capacities to affect and be affected.

To speak of sound's materiality, therefore, means considering the relational potentials of specific force–frequency combinations, asking what kind of modulatory compositions and transductive processes they might enter into. Similarly, to speak of the human body in its materiality is not to envision something fixed in either physiology or discourse, but to posit a contingent entity that is always adaptively recomposing (moving, adjusting, testing, imagining, anticipating) in the immanent relations of its worldly encounters. The issue, then, is not just corporeal matter, but the becomings of bodies. This view is called an *incorporeal materialism* because it also attends to the relational potentials of bodies – their 'yet-ness'.[39] This is the crux of what is being identified here as the *sonic body*, which is comparable to Deleuze and Guattari's *body without organs*.[40] The sonic body is the body impinged-upon by sound energies in ways that increase and diminish its various capacities, working unevenly on multiple registers to spark becomings-in-parallel of thought and flesh.

In these respects, *Low End Theory* also shares something with nascent modes of scholarship that have been collectively labelled 'new materialisms' for their efforts to grasp the self-activity of matter and account for the ways that non-human agencies operate in and on the social.[41] Manual De Landa's *War in the Age of Intelligent Machines* (1991) stands as an early example, while Jane Bennett's *Vibrant Matter: A Political Ecology of Things* (2010) has been a focal point of recent developments.[42] The latter draws, in part, on Deleuze's concept of 'a life' and Bruno Latour's 'actants' to investigate the agentic capacities (affects) of garbage, metals and stem cells. These and similar moves, along with the work of object-oriented philosophers like Graham Harman, Timothy Morton and Ian Bogost, are sometimes grouped together (though perhaps too neatly, given their divergences) as a 'turn to things' in recent scholarship. There is a strong element of this in *Low End Theory*, to be sure (in its bones, organs, organ pipes, rocks, rooms and so on), but the greater emphasis here will be on energetic tendency and 'capacities to interact' more than the 'thingness' of objects. A focus on sound makes this a necessity. Sound is most meaningfully understood as a relation, not an object. As mechanical vibration, its existence and character are always contingent on a medium and the ways its particles can be displaced, while in its travels acoustic energy undermines the apparent discreteness of the things it brings together in modulation. Thinking with vibration therefore requires conceptual tools that are especially attuned to matter-in-process and the circuits of responsivity that emerge between sonorous things.[43]

Myth-science

Also essential to the theoretical work of this project is the concept of *myth-science*. The term is borrowed from the American jazz musician Sun Ra, for whom myth offered the opportunity to unmake consensual reality and invent liveable futures.[44] (In this sense, it has a connection to J. G. Ballard's 'myths of the near future', as well as what members of the Cybernetic Cultures Research Unit (CCRU) have labelled *hyperstition*, or the becoming-actual of fictional quantities.[45]) Here, the term is put to specific work, being used to describe the myths and vernacular strategies that emerge around low-frequency sound's capacity to defamiliarize the world and inflect it differently. The concept will be fleshed out over the following chapters, but we can begin with a basic definition. On the one hand, myth-science is meant to encompass, but also expand, what Kodwo Eshun called *sonic fiction*.[46] When focused on sonic experience, sonic fictions can describe qualities of sound and tendencies in movement and perception (i.e. 'tales of becoming'[47]). They report, in language, what the sonic body already knows or suspects about a given relation. They also become repositories of speculation on the potentials of bodies, sound and machines. This is where sonic fiction overlaps with the other element of myth-science – what Deleuze and Guattari term *nomad science* (or sometimes *minor science*). Nomad science (vernacular and 'problematic') is set against Royal Science (official and 'theorematic'), although the two are essentially linked, diverging in tendency, but always feeding each other. While institutionalized science employs transcendent Method to extract generalizable laws from nature, a more ambulant science works intuitively and contingently, pursuing variation and anomaly, inhabiting materiality and following its singular flows.[48] (Here, we can also find resonances with what William James called *radical empiricism*, with its emphasis on immanence and relationality and its dual critique of rationalism and traditional empiricism.[49]) Where sound is concerned, it means following sonic materiality in signal, flesh, machine and space, intuiting what it can do, experimenting, pursuing anomaly and tweaking things towards qualitative change.

In this myth-science equation, sonic fiction thinks materially and intuits potentials, while nomad science, rather than attempting to solve something, sets out to intensify sonic experience, to rhythmically vary it, producing surprises and actualizing things previously only imagined. Sonic fictions theorize becomings and conceptualize affects; they attempt to find language for the mystifying feeling of affect's escape – the sense that one is caught up in more than meets the ear, and that reality doesn't quite add up. Their companion is an inductive science, comprising technical practices and techniques of *affect engineering*, designed to draw people out of themselves and into an unfamiliar relation.[50] Myth-science therefore has a world-making quality about it.

Trajectories of the sonic body

Chapter 1 starts to build on the theoretical kernel outlined above. It works towards what can be called an *ethico-acoustic* toolkit – a basic materialist framework that can be expanded, adapted and revised as we move though the various sites and sounds of the following chapters. We begin with a body undulating in the dark, investigating its capacities to interact in a sonorous space shaped by subbass pressures so great that they disrupt respiration, blur vision, induce phantom perceptions and resonate various bones and cavities.

The body, in these vibratory conditions, effectively turns into a series of questions: 'What's happening ... what's next ... how will I work with it?' Low-frequency vibration thus emerges as something more than merely physical or textual. As the agency that puts bodies at variance with themselves and their surroundings, it is a catalyst of becomings, both individual and collective. It turns bodies into conceptual events and exerts an organizing influence on the social. For the theorist, this raises a problem because predominant notions of social construction and cultural mediation cannot, by definition, adequately account for the 'becoming-cultural' of nature. This chapter re-theorizes sonic experience and its subjects with a view to affect, the incorporeal and the ways that sonic materiality can exert a modulatory influence in the social. The discussion ends by returning to the dancefloor and putting these ideas to work, in microcosm, as a loose guide for subsequent chapters.

Much of this book deals with powerful sound at frequencies and intensities that are hard to mistake or ignore. Many of the sonic milieus we will investigate have been purposely engineered to put bodies in uncommon vibratory relations. Chapter 2 steps back from these scenarios to focus on inadvertent encounters with unheard vibration, in the form of infrasound and other sound-like modulations, usually of natural or industrial origin. Broadly defined hauntings (infrasonic spectres and a global mystery called The Hum) are the focus, and a recurring theme is the confounding perception of *presence-absence* that can arise when sound escapes the ear but impinges on other registers, producing the unsettling feeling of activity by an unseen agent. This takes the discussion of sonic experience beyond audition, human intent, and even conscious awareness. As such, it has various implications for the theorist (of sound, no less than ghosts). First, it immediately frustrates culturalist frameworks and forces the adoption of better-tailored approaches. Relatedly, it also helps demonstrate how nature becomes culture, as unheard sounds (spectres) draw imaginations into bodies and begin influencing perceived reality (the emergence of a haunting). Finally, it offers an opportunity to explore the extra-cochlear aspects of low-frequency perception, and to examine the inherently synaesthetic nature of sonic experience as vibration spreads across the body, putting senses in conflict, and forcing the adoption of contingencies. The term *spectral catalysis* is proposed to describe how the right material-energetic conditions (the vibratory makeup of a given sonorous milieu) can work to deterritorialize the sonic body in ways that spark new trajectories in individual and collective activity. The discussion closely engages the scientific literature on infrasound and perception, finding it filled (though often obliquely) with accounts of peculiar neurophysiological effects, but also constrained by its unwillingness to pursue anomaly and its social life. In contrast, the present discussion learns what it can from science, but it stays with vibratory anomaly, in all its strangeness.

Chapter 3 begins from the observation that ritual bass-making technologies can be found the world over, and that tremendous effort, resources, and skill often go into their development and use. So it asks what low-frequency sound does that so many cultures find religiously useful. If we treat these devices and structures primarily in their cultural specificity, we risk missing material tendencies that cut across time and place. There is no suggestion here that bass carries some universal meaning, only that many disparate cultures seem to have recognized its ability to retexture felt surroundings and catalyse peculiar qualities of being. I argue that, in these settings, ritual bass emerges as a non-representational *strategy* used to temporarily alter the complexion of lived reality and modulate belief, in a process the anthropologist Donald Tuzin once called the *audiogenesis* of religious culture. Audiogenesis and nomad science become the organizing concepts for the remainder of the chapter as it investigates numinous strategies at work in a variety of settings. At the core of the chapter is what I call the organ-church assemblage. The discussion begins with the monstrous sonorities of the Medieval organ, asking how they may have contributed, materially, to a religious culture based largely on pedagogical violence. In the Baroque, we find a much more refined technology and an explicit programme of affect engineering that was coolly systematic in its efforts to seduce the flesh into belief. Finally, the Gothic assemblage is theorized as a total synaesthetic project in which liturgical practices downplayed the Text, while light, space, and extra-cochlear vibration were deployed in an effort to produce a 'felt-reality' of ascent.

The final two chapters are grouped together under the heading of 'Tone Science'. Now, attention shifts to predominantly secular creative practices of the last several decades that explore odd potentials in low-frequency sonic experience and take the sonic body as their medium. Chapter 4 identifies three broad tendencies within, but also (and importantly) cutting across, what would normally be called sound art and experimental music. The concept of *Cymatic Arts* is proposed to describe work aimed at 'hearing systems in nature,' 'seeing sound', or otherwise rendering sensible material-energetic rhythms that would normally escape human perceptual faculties. The term *Perceptual Abstraction* is borrowed from Op Art to draw connections between creative practices that work directly on the nervous system, producing anomalous circuits across the sensorium. The discussion also raises the possibility that arts traditionally divided by the modalities they address, may sometimes share more in common with each other, at the level of affective strategy, than they do with their formal relatives. Finally, the concept of *incipient dance* is developed through a number of installation projects that use powerful, low-frequency vibration (audible or not) to induce movement and bodily experimentation in collective space. The premise here is that the vibratory makeup of a milieu can be organized in ways that work to draw bodies into something that is not quite dance, but which might yet become it.

The last chapter organizes around the concept of *bass cults* – not referring simply to subcultures that enjoy a bit of weight in their music, but rather those scenes, or smaller sects within them, that make a myth-science of low tones and the sonic body. Bass cults are populated by people drawn to uncommon vibration. Their artist-technicians engineer sound and sonorous space to produce odd qualities of sonic experience and catalyse bodily motion along unfamiliar trajectories. This is the essence of *bass science*, the vernacular label for strategies, developed over decades, which treat sound and song as bio-aesthetic technologies. The discussion sketches a history of this science, identifying various *bass phyla* (machinic lineages of the low end), tendencies in sonic-spatial organization and recurring *drums-and-bass* moments, when musical machines are stripped to their basic kinetic elements, and re-engineered to do new affective work.[51] Finally, via Eshun's concept of the *rhythmachine* and Deleuze-Bacon's *logic of sensation*, we investigate three bass-led dancefloors, attempting to discern the musically encoded *physio-logics* that animate them.

As a myth-science ...

This book takes a less familiar route. It follows a nebulous 'sonic body' through ostensibly unrelated cultural sites, and also across disciplines that often share only a mutual disinterest, if not outright distrust. At each step, this means asking what this sonic body can do in a given relation, and where it might lead next. It also means patching together working concepts that arise from the singular qualities of each low-frequency milieu, each throbbing block of coexistence. At times we proceed by intuited leaps – prodding connections to see if there's anything in them, sometimes finding nothing (and adjusting), other times being surprised at the richness of a site (and adjusting). In these ways, the work is often speculative, but it aims to be rigorously so. Not meant to be definitive ('the final word on bass'), it strives instead to engender a mode of thought that draws sound-related scholarship into unfamiliar territory, and help nudge the humanities more broadly towards a greater appreciation of material agencies. Many of the writers who helped inspire this project (whether from philosophy, or studies of music, sound, the paranormal, etc.) make the point that we generally lack theoretical language suited to dealing with questions of (sonorous) materiality and sensory experience, not to mention affect and the incorporeal. This becomes a central concern here. Concepts are invented, borrowed, adapted and put to unintended uses. The idea is never to be clever or 'poetic' but to push language so that it might undermine engrained analytical habits in productive ways.

In the process, the discussion often slides between sonic-sensory description and efforts to engage it in theory, with the aim of interfacing the two as intensely as possible. There are several points to note about this strategy. Central to it is a rejection of metaphor, not only as a route to explanation but also as a rhetorical tool. Here, every effort is made to avoid writing figuratively. Instead of 'It's like ... ' we speak in terms of 'It livably is ... '.[52] The former is just simile and opinion, a comparison to the familiar that tells us nothing new. The latter attempts to conceptually inhabit an encounter and a process of bodily recomposition. It is an effort to plunge the reader into the logic of a becoming, at minimal remove. For our purposes this means writing affectively – sometimes at length, sometimes in almost lurid detail – in order to convey something of the vibratory event and its trajectories.[53] It need not be utterly 'right' or objectively accurate. It's doing its job if it manages to convey something of a milieu's affects, and their escapes, in ways that put theory more closely in touch with the sonic body. Similarly, if the theory seems to get a bit abstract at times, it should not be taken as cerebral detachment. Quite the opposite; it's an effort to deform thought and push it into the always complex, and often strange, traffic between nature and culture. Massumi, 'paraphrasing Deleuze again', notes that 'the problem with the dominant models in cultural and literary theory is not that they are too abstract to grasp the concreteness of the real. The problem is that they are not abstract enough to grasp the real incorporeality of the concrete.'[54] These are some of the broader stakes of theorizing bodies-in-sound.

1

The Sonic Body: An Ethico-Acoustic Toolkit

East London, 2005: *When bass wafted from the speaker cabinets, the air became thicker, heavier. Abrupt silences seemed to produce a vacuum effect. Most on the dancefloor just swayed with the shifts in pressure and vibration: the outward stillness of bodies danced by sound. Separated from the rest of the club by a heavy black curtain, the space was almost totally dark, leaving thoughts to focus on sound and sensation. Different tones drew different responses from various parts of my body – a chill, hums up the oesophagus, weight in the abdomen, shimmers over the skin – but the pressure in my chest was almost incessant. I could release it, I learned, by opening my mouth, although I wasn't always sure if I was breathing in, out, or at all. This confusion was intensified by textures designed to evoke the sound of respiration – synthetic gasps, strained exhalations, the room as rickety iron lung. Throughout the event, my nostrils fluttered and my vision blurred. I was buoyed, pulled, pummelled. Sped up, slowed down. Too much to grasp at once: just go with the flow. For long stretches, I could think of little beyond these streams of sonorous interactions, sometimes smiling at a sensation, sometimes nervously anticipating where it might be leading. Here and there, I retreated behind the curtain, half-fearing my eardrums might rupture from within. Entering again, there was a distinct feeling of energy in the dense air. Afterwards, myself and others in our party reported feeling as though we'd been part of a singular vibrating mass, all of us modulated by the same energy cycles, each grappling with the paradox of being made intensely aware of one's own body at the same time as it seemed to be dissolving into sound. Leaving the club someone handed me a flyer that read:* Come meditate on bass weight.[1]

A vibratory milieu; a field of sonorous relations shaped by the interactional capacities of volume, frequency, acoustic space, and sentient flesh.[2] The bass-drenched dancefloor is a laboratory for investigating the asymmetrical effects of low-frequency undulation as it alters the body's image of itself: tones and impacts felt strongly here, differently there and elsewhere not at all; vibrations that travel across the sensorium as their frequency shifts upwards or down; autonomic responses, anomalous perceptions, questions.[3] When bass moves bodies, it puts them at variance with themselves; new inflections of being are sparked in a stream of heterogeneous encounters. When bass permeates and modulates, it binds bodies together (putting them literally *on the same wavelength*), making the contingency and exteriority of their composition an intuitively felt-reality. The *sonic body* begins in material vibration, but it is always potentially the start of something more: an incitement to thought, movement, collective transformation. It is a transducer through which the bio-physical conditions of sonic experience are converted into various sonic-cultural trajectories (tales, experiments, strategies). Attending to it therefore entails an ontological shift and the engineering of new concepts informed by the sonorous fields they aim to address. It also forces a rethinking of some basic terms that are easily taken for granted. Body, subject and sonic experience all mean different things in a field of immanence.

Sonorous relations

We do not *have* experience so much as we are engendered by it, continuously. How, Deleuze challenged, could a subject transcend the always-recomposing relations that constitute its world? In this monist conception, experience does not arrive from outside to be mediated by an already determined subject. Rather, it is understood in its exteriority, as a field of intensities. It is a relational *milieu*, its shape and tendencies derived from the affects chaotically circulating therein.[4] But if the field in its totality is chaotic, it is also given to localized patterning, as idiosyncratic agglomerations (consistencies) emerge from its intensive rhythms.[5] The subject, in relation to experience, is therefore better understood as a trajectory, reshaped over and over through the infolding of heterogeneous intensities. This entering into composition with difference is key because newness can only emerge through relations of dynamic imbalance – a heterogenesis rather than a homogenesis.[6] There is no opening for the new in a world in which experience is always already prefigured in human culture. Here, it is important to remember that the French *expérience* means both 'experience' and 'experiment', and Deleuze and Guattari fully intend the pun. The experiential field is a zone of experimentation – of probing, intuiting, following, adjusting. It is in this sense that the material encounter with difference is also an incitement to thought and an opportunity for invention.

'Something in the world forces us to think,' Deleuze argues. 'This something is an object not of recognition but of a fundamental *encounter* [which] may be grasped in a range of affective tones'.[7] These 'encounters' are what Deleuze calls *events*. Events are the texture of experience. If experience is a field of immanent potentials, events are the instances of affective modification that differentiate it. They are the routes along which that potential is converted into qualities of lived reality, opening traffic between the virtual (what may be) and the actual (what is) or, in bodily terms, between the incorporeal (what a body can do) and the corporeal (the effective reality of a body). As instances of differentiation, produced through fleeting, contingent relations between divergent trajectories, events are considered singular and unrepeatable (The same act 'repeated' is always, in fact, singular, because the circumstances of its unfolding can never be exactly the same as before or after.). Events thus have an *individuating* effect, in the sense that they channel the unformed intensities of experience into specific, new qualities of a given lived reality. In these ways, then, events are also necessarily future-oriented, involving anticipation and the emergence of new modes of being and interacting. To grasp an 'affective tone' is to feel inklings of what-might-come-to-be, to sense tendencies, however discordant, that suffuse a given encounter.

From this, we can say that a synonym for the sonic body would be *the body as acoustic event*: the parallel modulation of flesh and thought in sonically-led self-variation. This eventness of the body, in general terms, has been theorized by Brian Massumi. Although sound does not figure prominently in his work, his depiction of the traffic between sensation and culture carries an acoustic connotation that makes it especially helpful to the present discussion.

The relationship, he argues, is one of *resonance* (a term which will recur with various implications in the following chapters). Resonance is a phenomenon of affection at a distance, involving transduction and a modulating-together, as the affected body takes on the energetic properties of the affecting one. Between them, there is not a void but a 'dynamic unity', a field of rhythmic intensities, feedbacks and emergent tendencies:

> With the body, the 'walls' are sensory surfaces. The intensity is experience. The emptiness or in-betweeness filled by experience is the incorporeal dimension of the body referred to earlier. The conversion of surface distance into intensity is also the conversion of the materiality of the body into an event. It is a relay between the corporeal and incorporeal dimensions. This is not yet a subject. But it may well be the conditions of emergence of a subject: an incipient subjectivity. Call it a 'self-'. The hyphen is retained as a reminder that 'self' is not a substantive but rather a relation. Sorting out 'self-reflexivity', 'self-referentiality', and self-relation' and, in the process, distributing subjectivity and its incipiency along the *nature-culture continuum*, becomes another major theoretical stake.[8]

The last point is an important one because it allows for traffic in both directions: becomings-cultural of nature and becomings-nature of culture. It is neither mediation nor determinism, but mutual modulation, and the eventness of the body is a conduit of these resonances.

Returning to sound, we can speak of: a *becoming-sonic* of the body; its conceptual dimension in attendant *becomings-in-thought*; these in their multiplicity as new trajectories of subjectivation (the *self-* of a sonorous relation); and those in their collective form as the emergence of a 'people'. 'Every becoming', Deleuze and Guattari argue, 'is a block of coexistence', an experiential milieu.[9] They use the term to describe an affective relation through which apparent wholeness and fixity are broken down (deterritorialized, or we can say *spectralized*) and potentials inherent in that relation are brought to life (the virtual/incorporeal made actual/corporeal). Becomings are, therefore, always a *becoming-other*, the fallout of the dynamic imbalance that characterizes the encounter with difference. The implication is not that a total, molar transformation occurs (we do not literally turn into a sound wave).[10] Nor is a becoming-sonic a matter of imitation or metaphor (i.e. play-acting or 'mere' discourse), and this distinction illustrates the difference between mediation and modulation.[11] Where sound and body interact, we can speak of 'an inhumanity immediately experienced in the body as such.'[12] It is a process of transduction, the sounding of a mind-body and a taking-on – even non-consciously or unwillingly – of certain affects of the impinging force.

In this way, we can say that powerful, low-frequency sound not only participates in culture, it has a material agency that can play an organizing role, putting matters of human agency and subject–object relations in question.[13] Here, a soccer analogy borrowed by Massumi from Pierre Levy is helpful. From Levy, he develops a notion of 'collective individuation around a catalyzing point',[14] or the emergence of a collectivity through shared experience, and the simultaneous internal differentiation of that group through the singular events that texture it. In the case of soccer, the field is the experiential milieu. Without it, there is no game. The game is organized by two polar attractors – the goals – which establish a directional tension according to which events will unfold. Ground, goals and bodies are *inducers* of play, while 'the ball catalyses it'. The ball is the *object and focus* of the game through which energies are channelled in the production of the event:

> The ball arrays the teams around itself. Where and how it bounces differentially potentializes and depotentializes the entire field, intensifying and deintensifying the exertions of the players and the movements of the team. *The ball is the subject of the play.* To be more precise, the subject of the play is the displacements of the ball and continual modifications of the field of potential those displacements effect.

So the ball is part-subject. It 'catalyses the play as a whole but is not itself a whole.' It 'moves the players.' If the ball is part-subject, then the player is part-object. Now the spectral aspect emerges: 'The ball does not address the player as a whole. It addresses the player's eyes, ears and touch through separate sensory channels … [which are] synthesized into an actionability.' In effect, it breaks a body down (its habit, organization) and draws a newly reconceptualized one forth. Deleuze called this the body without organs (not a denial of corporeality but recognition of its provisionality). 'No organ is constant,' he argued. Rather they are called into new contingent organizations through their encounters.[15]

Those encounters channel the asymmetrical pull of the virtual which is grasped in shifts of affective tone.

If we substitute the soccer ball for a bassline, a beat, an industrial hum, a singing cave, a singing iceberg, an organ blast, an infrasonic 'presence', an oscillating unknown ..., we can begin to imagine many ways in which low-frequency sound can function as the 'catalyzing point', organizing a collective sonic body as it modulates the intensities of the experiential milieu. It catalyses sonic becomings. This material agency is real, in the blocks of coexistence it engenders, whether the encounter is intentionally sought (as in a dance), unwilled (e.g. the effects of a sonic weapon) or even non-conscious (as can be the case with infrasound).[16] And these relations are ethical ones, in the Spinoza-Deleuze sense, of bodies affecting one another and increasing or diminishing each other's capacities to act along various axes.

When elements of style are introduced to the interaction, we enter a territory which Guattari labelled the *ethico-aesthetic*. Style is understood here not in a categorical sense akin to genre, nor in the spectacular sense familiar to cultural studies. Rather, it refers to operations done in the shaping, channelling and intensification of experience. It means finding new heterogenic rhythms and strategies for rupturing common sensibility.[17] More than just a means to an end, though, an ethico-aesthetics is the application of style to a modulation of affect. Guattari's ethico-aesthetic paradigm most directly refers to art practice, as such, but it has much wider implications.[18] On the soccer field, for example, Massumi calls style the freeness and 'modulatory actions' that play with and around rules, differently 'skew[ing] the potential movements composing the field'.[19] In life generally, it can describe modes of experimentation which take self-variation, or *autopoiesis*, as their aim.[20]

Tales and strategies

When an ethico-aesthetics proceeds additively – probing, varying, intensifying – it can be called a nomad science. A nomad science of the sonic body consists of catalytic strategies drawn from sonic experience, adapted and tweaked, then deployed back into the field. These are biological experiments in a sense, but ones aimed at generating unknowns rather than truths. This open-endedness makes it less a science in the traditional sense than a sort of applied science fiction. It imagines worlds and attempts to conjure them. Or it intuits potentials in the world and then sets out to mutate them. It operates very much in the realm of speculation. This is why myth, or sonic fiction, is its native discursive element.

Sonic fictions can be retrospective, serving as 'tales of becoming', or repositories of experiential knowledge. In the humanities, it is common to dismiss this sort of mind–body reporting on experience as more metaphor than fact, but this move, to borrow a critique from James, risks 'stay[ing] with the words – not returning to the stream of life whence all meaning of them came, and which is always ready to reabsorb them'.[21] If language lags behind experience, then sonic fictions are often an effort to invent more agile concepts. And these fictions can acquire affective resonances too, for example, when the more improbable-sounding elements of a tale begin to exert a pull on sonic practice. It can goad the artist-technician into attempting things seemingly beyond reason (and sometimes succeeding, in one way or, an unforeseen other). The language thus becomes more programmatic than figurative, and this is where the future-oriented aspect of sonic fiction emerges. It becomes part of a larger myth-science when it operates as a space for bio-aesthetic speculation and theorization of methods, cataloguing fragmented reports on technique and strategy, making them available for further elaboration. Often this can take the form of an *arcanum*, which serves a dual purpose.[22] On the one hand, it works to shroud the artist's secrets. But a secret, as a known-unknown, is also a deterritorializing force. It is something deployed as much as it is held because of its capacity to trouble and mystify.[23] When a secret is said to pertain to operations on one's own, or a collective body, it can play a modulating role by feeding anticipation or uncertainty into a milieu, thereby further charging and texturing its affective tone.[24]

There is, then, a back and forth between nomad science and sonic fiction, each informing the other, each drawing more out of the other as they work across the corporeal and incorporeal dimensions of audio-social space.[25] Again, simply describing these ethico-aesthetic discourses as expressions of culture misses the point. As conceptual vocabularies and strategies attuned to immanent relationality in vibratory fields, they are often better equipped than traditional cultural theory to follow the becomings of the sonic body, simply because they have a habit of taking these movements as their starting point.

With all of this in mind, we can begin to approach the breadth of sonic-cultural sites collected in the following chapters. We'll find them by looking for particular conditions of frequency and force. At times, the focus will be highly localized; at others, it will find consistencies across ostensibly disparate cultures, times and spaces. Sonic anomaly and its resonances will be central, as will those bodies of myth-science that accumulate around unusual vibratory milieus. First, however, it's worth returning to the dancefloor for a microcosmic example that can serve as a loose guide for the varied investigations that follow.

Myth-science in the vibratory milieu

South London, 2005: The *other* dark basement. A dim blue glow hangs over another swaying mass ('It's like having a rave on a sea bed'[26]). EQ-sharpened hi-hats slice the heavy air with a metronomic insistence, while heavy metallic judders reverberate in the distance. Gathering steam, the hats begin to shuffle and sloping subbass pulses echo the thuds of a lurching and raspy kick drum. Dubstep DJ/producer Loefah calls this track 'The Goat Stare', its name derived from the Jon Ronson book about alleged US military experiments with deadly ESP.[27] Conceptually, it plays on the experience of corporeal manipulation by an unseen force, and makes implicit links to the heavily mythologized field of acoustic weapons research. More generally, it capitalizes on popular mythologies of the sonic body that are widely held to be at least partly, or potentially, true: sound waves that can incapacitate, pulp organs, cause illness, trigger involuntary orgasms or bowel movements, and invade thought.[28] Ronson's book illuminates the role of the science fictional imagination in military research, but it is a small leap to see comparable tendencies in electronic music cultures that make an explicit project of conjuring new or altered realities via experimentation on the nervous system. The allusion, then, hints at a *modus operandi* of the artist.

The title is one sonic fictional entry point, but the track's sampled narration does more of the work. Over those tense opening bars, a voice prepares an audience for an experimental demonstration. The speaker's tone is steady, but a stray quiver betrays his nerves, suggesting the side effects he describes could be more dangerous than he lets on. The monologue is taken from the Cronenberg film *Scanners*, another story of weaponized telepathy. Lifted from its original context, it speaks more generally to techniques of affection-at-a-distance. Turned sonic fictional by Loefah, scanning has as much to do with the semi-mythical Dr Vladimir Gavreau – father of modern acoustic weaponry, a man who saw the body in all its exteriorized parts and wondered how he might selectively destroy them with sound.[29] Now, over Third Base sound system, the scanner becomes a multi-kilowatt sonic beam probing a field of bodies that have made themselves available for the bio-aesthetic experiment:

> *I'd like to scan all of you in this room. … I must remind you that the scanning experience is usually a painful one, sometimes resulting in earaches, nosebleeds, nausea, stomach cramps, sometimes other symptoms of a similar nature. … There's a doctor present, Dr Gatineau. … I know you've all been prepared for this but I thought I'd just remind you just the same. … There is one more thing: No one is to leave this room.*

The tendency in cultural studies and related fields would be to argue that these lines structure sensory experience, that they reflect collections of cultural norms and translate them into prescriptions for perceiving and interpreting the experience. But, this is a misreading. It misses non-representational intensities and their feedbacks. It precludes the possibility of an artist eliciting resonances where sound and imagination mingle at the material level and open onto strange horizons.

So rather than calling the narration a mediator, let's investigate it as a modulator of affective tone, an intensifier that follows from, and folds back into, sonic experience. It can be understood to have a retrospective element, in the sense that it serves as a provisional language made to resonate with conditions already emerging across the sensorium. But it also feeds forward, its speculative element working to charge the field. And, by making scanning an analogue of the subbass encounter, the monologue, though borrowed, is able to report vividly on the exteriorizing pulls of the sonic milieu. In these ways, Steven Shaviro's words on the film become relevant to the incorporeal materiality of the dance-floor experiment. He describes scanning as 'the direct linking of two nervous systems separated by space', arguing that the process 'disrupts the very notions of bodily integrity and of mental privacy, and hence upsets any concept of personal identity based on either of these'.[30] This is the spectralization of the individual sonic body and the priming of a collective one. 'In effect,' Shaviro writes, 'Cronenberg deconstructs Cartesian dualism by establishing an absolute Spinozistic parallelism between minds and bodies.'[31] What spoke to physically damaging telepathy in the film now describes skin that thinks and brains that dance ...

I'd like to scan all of you in this room ...

When Loefah calls what he does scanning, the filmic version becomes a loose guide for the musician devising his own strategy of catalysis. They're very different, but they both aim to organize a relational space premised on disquieting affection by an unseen force. Scanning becomes the speculative application of subbass energy to assembled human bodies, its plunging tone as directed energy beam. The sine wave cycling through the core of the track is clinical, sounding like the automated output of audio test equipment. Its perceptual effects can be striking. As it swoops through the lower end of the audible spectrum, bass vibrations expand unevenly across the sensorium, touching off bodily resonances and triggering autonomic responses, synaesthetic overlaps and strings of misperceptual adjustments. An eventness of the sonic body is catalysed.

I must remind you that the scanning experience is usually a painful one ...

The narration speaks to the all-consuming physicality of the sonic experience. It warns of unforeseen discomforts and involuntary reactions, highlighting that this is not just a musical text, this is a potentially damaging material encounter. It intensifies through coincidence, feedback and anticipation, as the physiological effects it describes partly coincide with those actually felt on the floor, while carrying the suggestion of more surprises to come.[32] In this way, it plays on the open loop of perception and assessment that defines the corporeal event: 'What is happening? What could happen? Am I all right? How do I work with this?' It also suggests that this is what constitutes the fundamental 'being there' of the event, that this music is made to be felt in particular ways, not just heard and interpreted. This has nothing to do with 'authentic experience', just the simple fact of its singular character. The comment that *no one is to leave this room* implies that the event is, in part, about endurance and passage, but it also denotes a very specific assemblage, comprising not just a music and a scene, but suitably capable sound systems as well. Dubstep, at this point in time, was still made primarily for either of two exceedingly well-equipped clubs in London – Plastic People and Third Base – so *This room*, had very localized connotations.[33] Yet it can also speak to portability: a sonic architecture encoded on vinyl waiting to be plugged into the right system.

There's a doctor present, Dr Gatineau …

There is another coincidence: the echo of Gavreau in Gatineau. Now the DJ/producer assumes the role of the doctor figure. As a scientist, he's part way between the technician and conjurer, holding secret knowledge of the sonic body. This is in-keeping with the Black Atlantic device of conflating science and mystification, the studio and the lab, sound and the cybernetic.[34] It would be easy to lump talk of the myth-scientist together with the sort of DJ-reverence – the DJ as shaman, rockstar, etc. – that has been noted and critiqued in the literature of electronic dance music, but there is something more interesting going on. The allusion to the doctor in the room is murkier. It suggests bio-technological experimentation, someone else in control of the corporeal event and where it may be headed.

I know you've all been prepared for this but …

This is the crucial statement for everything that follows. It is the crux of what has been called the sensory production of the audio-social, as opposed to the social construction of auditory culture. It tells us that whatever one's conceptions, expectations and rationalizations going into the event space, the dominant organizing factor will be the modulatory force of powerful and unsteadying low-frequency sound. It puts the emphasis on material agency and the autonomy affect, preventing us from collapsing the sonic-sensory realm into cultural mediation, thereby keeping open a rich conceptual field between the two. This is a key move towards the central concerns of this project. The guiding question is not so much what we make of bass, but what it makes of us: how does it undulate and unsettle; how does it incite; how does it invade the lives of people, drawing bodily thought into new equations with itself and its surroundings?

Spectral Catalysis: Disquieting Encounters

spectrum 1 a after Newton: a continuum of frequencies of electromagnetic radiation or mechanical vibration **b** any distribution (of parts, qualities, phenomena) across a population **2** in Goethe and Schopenhauer: retinal afterimage, a sensorial ghosting.[1] **3** for Lavater: "a substance without a body which, being hearde or seene, maketh men afraid."[2]

the spectral 1 topologies of wave energy **2** conditions of molecularity that open bodies to strange minglings **spectre 1** a presence-absence or half-felt agency; a phantom in-the-making **2** a nebulous potentiality on the horizon of experience.

haunting 1 a retrospective assessment: when spectral run-ins achieve a consistency and *what was that?* becomes a familiar *It,* acquiring 'habits' and apparent responsivity **2** this as the emergence of an operative reality and a collective assemblage (the haunter, the haunted, sympathizers, skeptics).

spectral catalysis 1 spectral-level events as inducers of odd becomings, however minute or partial **2** the swarming of spectral uncertainties toward new inflections of felt reality **3** a conceptual event that turns the body into a string of questions and forces adaptations (conceptual, physical, social).

The American author H. P. Lovecraft was especially gifted at finding terror in the spectral. His 'weird fiction' is full of protagonist-victims confronting strange materialities that push thought into uncomfortable new terrain by placing the predictability of nature in terminal doubt. The 'sensitives' and afflicted bodies that populate his work are haunted by uncanny agencies and half-perceptions that confound reason and force the adoption, however reluctant, of workable contingencies. His short story 'The Colour Out of Space' begins with a meteor strike on a remote New England farm – a place soon thereafter known as

The Blasted Heath and avoided by locals. From its core, the rock oozes a substance of hues so alien as to be deeply disturbing, a 'strange spectrum' that 'was almost impossible to describe; and it was only by analogy that they called it colour at all.'[3] The meteor itself dissolves quickly, but it persists insidiously in living things. Gradually, the farm is overrun by 'chromatic perversions' and 'strange colours that could not be put into words' because they diverge so sharply 'from the known colours of the normal spectrum'. 'No sane colours were anywhere to be seen … but everywhere those hectic and prismatic variants of some diseased, underlying primary tone without a place among the known tints of the earth'. What had begun as a spectral curiosity turns into a full-blown haunting, infecting the land and then the animals.

The farm's lone human occupants are plagued by half-felt modulations too: 'The entire Gardner family developed the habit of stealthy listening, though not for any sound which they could consciously name. The listening was indeed a product of moments when consciousness seemed half to slip away.' In time, the family becomes hyper-tuned to these deterritorializing *presence-absences* – things that insist in perception while also escaping it. Mrs Gardner is the first to disintegrate (mind, then body). Her last utterances reveal a terror rooted in the bodily perception of movement by unnamable actors, for 'in her ravings there was not a specific noun, but only verbs and pronouns. Things moved and changed and fluttered, and ears tingled to impulses which were not wholly sounds.' Similar sound shadows – 'faint, half-imaginary rhythms', a 'disturbing sense of vibration in the air' – recur elsewhere in Lovecraft when non-human agencies begin pushing into the lives of people.[4]

Faced with nature run amok, Lovecraft's scientists are always a step behind. 'Laws' fail them, while specimens act 'quite unbelievably in [the] well-ordered laboratory'.[5] The more systematic the scrutiny, the further answers seem to recede and unwelcome possibilities begin to form on the horizon. Yet they cling to reason and method, however unrealistically in the circumstances, and they arrogantly dismiss witness accounts with the sorts of assertions 'which puzzled men of science are wont to [make] when faced with the unknown'. The afflicted, however, have no choice but to go along with the felt-reality of the world they inhabit, and social marginalization only works to confirm their emergence as a people apart. In these circumstances, Lovecraft's sensitives find better allies in artists and folklorists anxious for whatever insights might reside in their stories.[6] This sense of affinity is not entirely different from that expressed for Lovecraft by the contemporary philosopher Graham Harman, who sees in these stories a rigorous attention to materiality and very necessary experiments with non-anthropocentric ontology. Playing on Lovecraft's usual categorization as an author of 'weird fiction'[7] and defending scholarship that proceeds by speculative leaps, Harman makes the argument that, in fact, 'Philosophy's sole mission is *weird realism*.[8] Philosophy must be realist', he says, 'because its mandate is to unlock the structure of the world itself; it must be weird because reality is weird.'[9]

The following proceeds by a similar logic in its effort to theorize cases of reality made weird by the silent modulations of infrasound. The hauntings described below tend to revolve around an incongruous sense of presence-absence that emerges when sounds felt but unheard seem to suggest the activity of an unseen agent. In these cases, there is an apparent link between a milieu's spectral makeup (its sonic materiality) and its affective tone, as anomalous sensation and deterritorialized perception exert a de-realizing influence on the scene, setting off new tangents of thought, bodily habit and social organization.

This has various implications for the study of sound, but also cultural theory in general. In the first place, it argues strongly for greater attention to a vibratory terrain that largely exceeds usual definitions of sound – what Steve Goodman has labelled 'unsound', or the 'not-yet-audible'.[10] By the same token, this means turning more attention to the extra-cochlear dimensions of sonic experience, which encompass all manner of synaesthetic interplay, misperceptions, microperceptions and other sound-*like* events. Encounters of these sorts can be mildly confusing, sometimes utterly bewildering, especially when they are inadvertent or non-conscious. When their effects are felt, but the cause of the feeling remains a mystery, they become an incitement to the imagination, one independent of intent or systems of representation, but nevertheless capable of exerting an influence on the social. We therefore need to think through the role of sound as a non-human social agency, whatever its source.

Here, Guattari's theorization of an 'a-signifying semiotics' can become a guide, with its radically expanded concept of enunciation being used to describe the transmission of affects by all things, living or not.[11] The aim is not to anthropomorphize the world by making it 'speak', but quite the opposite, to devise a non-anthropocentric cultural theory that can account for traffic in both directions along the nature–culture continuum. Somewhat similarly, Massumi uses the term 'insistence' to describe how material intensities are able to push themselves into perception and consciousness, and begin re-channelling memory, expectation and action. Insistence describes both the self-activity of matter and its ingress into the social.[12] Taken together, these perspectives allow materiality (including its incorporeal dimension) to be recognized as an active agent in the emergence of culture, rather than merely being mediated by it. The emphasis turns to those events that spark moments of self-variation (or becomings-other) which, alone or together, can catalyse developments in thought and social organization. From this basis, an enquiry into the unsettling effects of infrasound becomes a matter of tracing out the spectral relations of bodies-in-sound, tuning to their logics, listening to their tales and finding conceptual languages appropriate to them. What emerges is a richly nebulous mesh of myth and science that destabilizes inherited approaches to the study of sonic experience while giving inklings of the broad, and often weird, interactional potentials of sonorous bodies.

Spectres of the man-made unknown

Spectral subjectivities, of a sort, are the focus of Jeffrey Sconce's *Haunted Media*, as it investigates the persistent linking of telecommunicational space and the paranormal in the popular imagination. Sconce argues that contemporary notions of cyberspace as an electronic virtual are, in fact, traceable to the late nineteenth century, when proponents of spiritualism and emerging communications media shared a preoccupation with 'psychical connection in spite of physical separation'.[13] First, telegraphy introduced the paradox of discarnate communication, with its simultaneously present–absent participants and the implied possibility that electricity and consciousness might be mutually transmutable energies. This put human wholeness into question: if elements of it (ideas, emotions, voice) could be transmitted, what other part-beings might they tangle with on their way? How much further could the human be broken down? Later, radio's 'voices in the void' seemed to suggest that these relationships could become even more volatile.[14] The wireless released human communication into a boundless 'etheric ocean', its waves blanketing the terrestrial, traversing bodies and radiating their thoughts infinitely into the unknown. Inadvertent, and perhaps unwanted, contact – with the afterlife, the extraterrestrial – became a matter of intense speculation, both popular and scientific. At the same time, 'presence' took on a new meaning in a world evermore saturated by invisible waves. By the time television arrived, those waves were increasingly associated with subliminal control and Cold War fears of remotely triggered annihilation. Death rays and alien possession were their B-movie manifestations at a time when the arms race itself was acquiring an increasingly science fictional character.[15]

Sconce catalogues these speculative fictions. And he suggests that they often served a vernacular theoretical function, effectively asking what it means to be a human being permeated by weird energy and turned spectral. In a broad sense, then, it might be tempting to draw comparisons with the present discussion of mind-bodies carried away by infrasound. But beneath any thematic overlaps, the two projects diverge in ways which are more generally illustrative of the differences between culturalist tendencies in the humanities and the materialist investigation that follows. In the culturalist view, waves and current are significant only insofar as they carry information or become after-the-fact objects of discourse. Similarly, sound-making technologies are typically described in terms of their *re*-productive functions, with little thought to their roles in the production of singular, a-signifying intensities. Contrasting deployments of the term 'presence' speak to this distinction. Sconce uses it almost figuratively to describe a communicational coupling (sender–receiver, encoder–decoder) and the metaphors employed to represent it.[16] This is very different from a material encounter that produces a felt presence-absence, or the perception of an unseen actor's proximity and motion, along with the apprehension and grasping for contingencies that flows from those mismatched sensory cues. The latter opens onto the incorporeal, suggesting a still unexplored connection between events labelled 'hauntings' and other confounding brushes with the virtual. But the culturalist approach remains resolutely non-corporeal and insistent that the outcome of any encounter is always already prefigured in ideas about it.[17] This is unfortunate because so many of the cases described in *Haunted Media* read like tales of becoming in the electromagnetic age. Rich with material traces, they conjure an image of technologies going feral, exceeding our knowledge of them and producing surprising new terrains. What results can be called a dimension of the *man-made unknown* wherein heterogeneous energy fields produce unforeseen relations and unhomely resonances.[18] A cultural theory wary of 'metaphors of living media' might resist attending to such non-anthropomorphic agencies, but that risks obscuring the role of materiality in sparking odd becomings and modulating the social.[19]

'The Galaxy Being', a 1963 episode of *The Outer Limits*, helps to illustrate the difference between these approaches and their relative implications for theorizing tales of waveborne bodies. It tells the story of small town radio operator Allan Maxwell and his covert repurposing of the station's equipment to scan the cosmos for signs of alien life.[20] When Maxwell finally makes contact, he's faced with a luminescent being of vaguely humanoid form looming from his display unit. It fades in slowly, fluttering and shuddering. Not just an image, it has itself been transmitted (at least partly), and we watch it slowly come to grips with its alien surroundings. When it finally speaks (in the ring-modulated drone of Maxwell's translation computer), the Being describes an electromagnetic existence in which there is no distinction between energy, matter, life and consciousness. For it, radio communication and intergalactic travel are one and the same. This makes contact precarious, and tragedy inevitably strikes when a power surge draws the Being fully out of its own dimension and down through the radio tower. Stunned, the glowing figure drifts through town enveloped in winds of its own electromagnetic storm. At least one person dies in the ensuing panic, while the entity, having broken the galactic edict against human contact, is faced with an infinity in exile.

Altogether, the programme touches on various tropes often identified in media and technology studies: the isolated male technophile, the anxiety and superstition that surround new communication technologies, predictions of alienation, etc. Taking the episode figuratively, we can easily read the Being's call for intergalactic peace and cooperation as a plea for Cold War detente.

Meanwhile, Sconce proposes that the story works to represent a combination of anxieties around televisual experience and new frontiers at the dawn of the Space Age.[21] However, these various interpretations also ignore the most striking thing about the episode: the phantom-like figure of the Galaxy Being itself. It's an arresting sight, not only because of its unfamiliarity but because it is a body violently in process. We watch it undulate and contort with shifts in frequency and power. A blurry presence-absence, it fades in and out. The waves that transport it also break it down, meaning that from moment to moment its form and capacity to function hinge on the transceivers at each end of the transmission, along with any cosmic interference that irrupts in-between. (This relational precarity – a body suspended, at the mercy of indifferent forces – echoes the show's well-known opening sequence: the image of sine waves made to dance, collapse and stretch, while a cool voice punningly warns, 'We will control the horizontal. We will control the vertical ...'). What we see on screen is the modulation of a radically exteriorized body that is more contingent than concrete, more motion than fixity.

In these respects, does the Galaxy Being really represent anything? Or does it play on something that viewers' bodies might already suspect, intuitively, from daily (or occasional) brushes with the man-made unknown? Perhaps it points to a relatively new sort of haunting – one linked to the spread of ambient vibration since the Second Industrial Revolution. In his social history of ghosts, Owen Davies maps the changing character of English hauntings through the modern period, noting that we should be mindful of the ways 'changes in the environment over time have influenced the landscape of haunting'.[22] He describes, for example, a marked shift in the sorts of spectres being reported from about the late nineteenth century onwards.[23] Ghosts that spoke and took recognizable forms were on the decline. There were fewer troubled souls looking to right wrongs or warn family members of impending trouble. Instead, they were becoming increasingly mute, impersonal, formless or invisible. Reports of encounters more often centred on anomalous perceptual experiences that disturbed concepts of self, space and causation: an unidentifiable sensation, a vague presence, half-heard sounds, a chill. Though Davies himself does not make the link (preferring discursive explanations to material ones), the changes he describes correspond in time and place with the growth of heavy industry, mechanized transport and new communications technologies. One effect of these developments was the sudden emergence of a new and permanent vibratory environment textured by the wide-radiating, low-frequency emissions of blast furnaces, drop forges, motors of all sorts, ventilation systems and rail traffic (both over- and underground): waves travelling by air and ground; transmitted through sewers, pipes and tunnels; rumbling foundations, resonating the occasional room; and producing all sorts of localized harmonic mixtures. Eventually, air traffic, as well as military and industrial megaprojects, would add to the low-frequency din, while colonization of the radio spectrum presented a new focus for anxious speculation on wave–body interactions.

If industrial-era haunts increasingly manifested as anomalies of perception then we can reasonably speculate on the contributing role of industry in new sensory assemblages and new, bodily-held anxieties of affection by unseen forces. In short, new ways to be haunted. And in that case – if this is the material and imaginative terrain that produced the Galaxy Being – then the creature can hardly be understood in strictly figurative terms. I would argue that it operates on a different register, working instead to instil (or resonate with) a pathic grasp of the body impinged-upon by wave energies. And though the Galaxy Being may speculate on deterritorialization by electromagnetic means, I would say that it does its work synaesthetically, through the eyes of the sonic body.

Provisionally, at least, Deleuze's work on Francis Bacon can supply more suitable language for exploring this possibility. In Bacon's portraits of contorting bodies and faces, Deleuze saw a 'middle path' between figuration (representation) and abstraction (anti-representation), both of which rely on the interpretative function of an enculturated brain rather than attempting to work directly on and through the nervous system. 'They can implement transformations of form, but they cannot attain deformations of bodies.'[24] In contrast, Bacon's collected works display an obsession with sensation and deformation. In interviews, he explains his efforts to achieve shocks and singularities of experience which are inaccessible via narrative and intellect.[25] Inspired by fleeting monstrosities of human form captured in the photographic experiments of Eadweard Muybridge, Bacon's canvases freeze moments of transformation by invisible forces: 'the violent force of a hiccup, a scream, the need to vomit or defecate, of copulation, the flattening force of sleep'.[26] In these works, there is still a recognizable body but one in the process of its own abstraction: the body without organs, 'the deformed body that escapes itself'.[27] This is the non-representational middle route that Deleuze labels the *figural*. In Bacon, the Figure replaces the biography-saddled Subject and the storytelling of figuration. It is an abstraction but only to the extent that it aims to show a body at variance with itself, in the process of becoming-other. Rather than meaning, these works aim for feeling. 'Sensation is what is painted. What is painted on the canvas is the body, not insofar as it is represented as an object, but insofar as it is experienced as sustaining a sensation'.[28]

The effort on Bacon's part was to create a relational space, or a *logic of sensation*, between viewer and canvas. Rather than simply depicting a subject sensing, he aimed to implicate the viewer in that sensation, to render in painting 'the action of invisible forces' and make them sensible *in* the viewer. Used in this way, logic is distinct from transcendent Reason. Instead, it describes the immanent, or prevailing, logic of a given assemblage, how its affective structure invokes a spectral body which is drawn into new configurations and 'synthesized into an actionability'.[29] Singular rhythms of frequency and force, combined with a body's capacity to be affected by them, would constitute the most basic elements of a sonic logic of sensation (with an eventness of the body as its product).[30]

Visual arts, however, have to work by different routes, entering via the eye, but proceeding synaesthetically by what Deleuze calls a sort of sensual analogy.[31] He proposes the 'haptic', for example, as the sense of touch proper to vision. 'Painting', he writes, 'gives us eyes all over: in the ear, in the stomach, in the lungs (the painting breathes ...)'. The painting doesn't just 'breathe' metaphorically. It really feels to us, as creatures who breathe, who can sense breathing in others (which is neither a culturally specific, nor exclusive human, ability), as though we are witnessing respiration (an incongruous sentience?) in something supposedly inanimate. It may not be objectively the case, but through whatever fusion of light, paint, skill and perceptual quirk, it is both livably true and conceptually provocative, operating as a small rupture in common sense. In this way, painting can produce 'presences', or glimpses of the potentials that inhere in a relation, and that might turn into something more. Bacon amplifies this. Presence shifts to a 'hysterical' mode; things become '*too* present'.[32]

The Outer Limits sets up a logic of sensation between viewer and screen but it also plugs into that broader ecology of disquieting vibration that haunts industrialized life. It plays on those unsound presences of the man-made unknown (and low-frequency experience generally) – things that flutter, not-quite-sounds, disturbing rhythms in the air – that put us in suspense, and jolt us into an uncomfortable new awareness when they become too-present. The spectral Figure of the Galaxy Being works to render sensible a form of energy (electromagnetism) not usually considered available to the traditionally conceived sensorium, but which has long been the focus of anxieties over its potential neurophysiological effects (a debate which continues, decades later, having lately become entwined with similar questions about infrasound). To transmit this sensation, this logic proceeds by way of a sensual analogy that transduces radio waves into sound waves. It shows sensation by invoking the sonic body through what we might call the vestibular and proprioceptive sensibilities proper to vision.[33] Watching the Galaxy Being's modulations we can fathom the feeling. There is a pathic grasp that folds in sensation, memory of movement and anticipation of change, without the need for description or interpretation. The effect is similar to watching an empty plastic cup dancing on a bass bin, or a candle flickering in the imperceptible breeze of a subaudible wave. It is a way of seeing modulatory forces in their exteriority (spectral presences), and, by association, confronting the sonic body's own asymmetrical openness to affection (its own spectrality). Seeing vibration modulate is the eye's contribution to sonic perception, with or without the involvement of the ear, much as the haptic is a workable grasping of texture with or without dermal confirmation.[34]

Overall, we can take several things from this. The essentially synaesthetic nature of perception is reinforced again, while the concept of sensual analogy gives a clue to its workings. The scope of 'haunting' is also expanded. It moves beyond superstition and metaphor to describe material relations (which are historical and local) and associated sensorial ghostings. At the same time, the *logic of sensation* emerges as a productive and portable concept which can easily be adapted to describe the sonorous relationality of any given vibratory milieu. It is from this perspective that the remainder of this chapter investigates inadvertent encounters with the disquieting logics of spaces haunted by infrasound and other sound-like phenomena. (Later, we will turn to logics purposely engineered in the service of religion, art and dance).

Finally, as a tale of becoming, 'The Galaxy Being' also shows the importance of thinking beyond what could be called a figurative mode of analysis (rooted in notions of representation and mediation) if we aim to understand affect, sensation and non-human agencies operating in and on culture. A figural theory would be one that aims to think with deformation. But Deleuze is correct when he says the figural is a concept native to Bacon and painting, and that other logics will require their own language. The sonic body needs kindred concepts that arise more directly from its own experience. Aspects of 'the spectral' being developed here can, therefore, be understood to do similar work but in a manner more directly informed by the deformations of waveborne bodies.[35] As the above has attempted to show, part of what the figural/spectral offers is a means of finding tales of becoming in stories that might otherwise be taken only figuratively (as *mere* metaphor). Importantly too, it also becomes a tactic for rereading scholarship that misses the incorporeal (by accident or design) and extracting latent insights. The project then becomes one of scouring the humanities and social sciences for evidence of becomings and buried material traces, while also 'poaching' the natural sciences for disregarded anomalies and offhand observations about peculiar phenomena.[36]

Infrasound

In 1998, Vic Tandy and Tony R. Lawrence published 'The Ghost in the Machine' in the *Journal of the Society for Psychical Research*. It would cast a new light on more than a century's research by the British organization, while also adding to a newly emerging body of work that had already begun to trace connections between unhomely energies and other forms of 'hauntings'.[37] The article has since been disseminated widely, taking on a life of its own in those portions of the internet devoted to ghost hunting, New Age healing and conspiracy theories. Tandy's work now ranks with that of Vladimir Gavreau in popular mythologies of infrasound, but this should not distract from its importance as another component of a minor science of the sonic body.

In the article, Tandy relates an unsettling encounter he had while working as an engineer for a British medical equipment company. Soon after taking the job, he began to hear rumours that the large, well-lit, often noisy lab was haunted. He also noticed odd behaviour on the part of some co-workers: a night cleaner leaving in apparent distress, a colleague speaking to a presence he had sensed as Tandy, only to find himself sitting alone.

> *One night, Tandy was working on his own. As he sat at the desk, he began to feel increasingly uncomfortable. He was sweating, but cold, and the feeling of depression was noticeable. It was as though something was in the room with him. There was no way into the lab and all the equipment checked out fine. Tandy went to get a cup of coffee and returned to the desk. As he was writing, he became aware that he was being watched and a figure slowly emerged to his left. It was indistinct and on the periphery of his vision. The apparition was grey and made no sound. There was a distinct chill in the room and, as Tandy recalls: 'It would not be unreasonable to suggest I was terrified.' When he built up the courage to turn and face the thing, it faded and disappeared.* [38]

Spooked, and concerned for his sanity, Tandy called it a night. By the next morning, however, the event had largely faded from his mind, and he set out for work early, thinking ahead to a fencing match he had scheduled for that evening. The plan was to borrow a few of the lab's tools to modify one of his foil blades. Once there, he began by securing the blade in a vice before briefly stepping out. The previous night's terror came flooding back, however, when he returned to find the long, supple blade, flailing like a thing possessed, and with no apparent cause:

> *[This, and] his experience the previous night, prompted an immediate twinge of fright. However, as vibrating pieces of metal were more familiar to him than apparitions, he decided to experiment. If the foil blade was being vibrated, it was receiving energy which must have been varying in intensity at a rate equal to the resonant frequency of the blade. He placed the foil blade in a drill vice and slid it along the floor. The vibration got bigger until the blade was level*

with [Tandy's] desk, half way down the room. After the desk, it reduced in amplitude, stopping altogether at the far end of the lab. Tandy realized he was sharing the lab with a low-frequency standing wave! Quick calculation showed its frequency to be 19 Hz. Tandy said there were two questions to be answered: where is the energy coming from, and what does a 19 Hz standing wave do to people?[39]

The first question was essentially mechanical, answered easily enough when the lab's newly installed fan extraction system was switched off and the standing wave disappeared. That discovery is supported by various studies linking the production of powerful infrasound to industrial ventilation systems.[40] Moreover, the wave's peak appeared to be at its most intense at Tandy's desk chair, which would explain the spatial character of the experience and the way it seemed to recede when he moved from his spot. Still, the presence of unheard sound does not, in itself, explain how Tandy was induced to mild panic, becoming convinced that he'd either gained a companion or lost his sanity. How did an apparently straightforward corporeal encounter manage to transform, however briefly, his lived reality? What else might be possible? With this as its stake, Tandy's second question echoes the oft-repeated Spinozan adage *we still do not know what a body can do*, with all of its incorporeal ramifications and its suggestion of exotic resonances between nature and culture, discordant percepts and fleshy imagination.

Looking for answers in the scientific literature, Tandy happened on a collection called *Infrasound and Low Frequency Vibration*, edited by a W. Tempest. He found stories of other labs where workers complained of a strange or oppressive air in spaces where infrasound between 15 and 20 Hz was later found. There were reports of dizziness and refusals to re-enter the afflicted rooms, along with bouts of shivering, perspiration and inexplicable fear. Other studies found correlations between infrasound exposure and respiratory disruptions, nystagmus (ocular vibration), visual anomalies, piloerection (goosebumps), sudden chills and various other discomforts, ranging from the barely perceived to the intensely painful and the psychologically distressing. Panic attacks are an example of the latter and they point towards the potential for unsettling resonances to develop at the nexus of imagination and vibration. These episodes can be particularly alarming for the sufferer who perceives the physical symptoms of the attack (hyperventilation, dizziness, racing heart) as its cause, thus producing a troubling feedback between sensation and conscious thought about it, a self-compounding crisis that continues to flow from a catalytic event that has perhaps already faded or may never have been consciously perceived in the first place.

At most, Tempest and his colleagues only ever hint at the sorts of nature–culture resonances that might spring from such encounters.[41] Still we can glean clues about infrasound's haunting potential from among all the details of biology, acoustics and methodology. Themes begin to emerge when we read across the offhand remarks, hanging questions, outlier data and some of the book's shorter entries. Most telling, perhaps, is the acknowledgement – sometimes open, sometimes tacit – that low-frequency investigations can only ever give a partial account of a given spectral terrain; there are simply too many variables to measure, more than we can even grasp.[42] Put differently, there is always an 'excess of reality', something of which always escapes us.[43] Parsing the din becomes one of the acoustic scientist's biggest challenges, though it is typically at the expense of those singularities that texture experience. Add to this the related problem of individuals' own widely varying sensitivities to low-frequency stimuli. Vibrations that fail to register in most may leave a small spectrum of the population deeply shaken, and not necessarily in the same ways.[44] Such 'subjective effects' are typically ignored or mentioned mainly as curiosities in studies concerned with average tolerances and predictable neurophysiological effects. But what is a haunting if not an anomalous, unpredictable experience – a rupture in the quotidian? It is an experience of confounding liminality – just the sort of thing that science looks to avoid. But as Tandy's work helps to illustrate, it is that minority of anomalously tuned individuals who *make* a haunting, not in the sense of its construction, but in that they function as transducers of strange energies into social events. As with Lovecraft's sensitives, their affection by 'it', coupled with their conviction against reason that it is real, gives them a taint of monstrosity. This is the material encounter's insistence in the social.

What also becomes obvious in Tempest *et al.* is just how vague the categories of 'sound' and 'hearing' are, and just how much sonic experience entails intersensory crosstalk. Significantly, the authors undermine conventional notions of 'audible thresholds', or those *points* at which the perception of sound is often portrayed as simply cutting off. Instead of a lower 'limit' of audition, we are presented with a liminal region across which perceptual faculties break down and recombine while synaesthetic uncertainties flood in. Between about 20 and 25 Hz, for example, we lose the ability to distinguish between pitches, making it more difficult to identify a sound and imagine its potential source.[45] (Think, for example, of those moments when something low and uncertain is first sensed: is it a truck, a plane, an earthquake, a stereo, the furnace about to explode?) These lower frequencies are also more difficult to localize, leading to the sensory paradox of 'sounds that are not wholly sounds' seeming to come from everywhere and nowhere. Augoyard and Torgue call this the *ubiquity* effect, a perceptual short circuit that can quickly build into a panicked search for a cause, combined with a sense of 'powerless[ness] in the absence of possible feedback'. As if hinting towards the subject of infrasonic hauntings, the authors go on to describe how this dynamic can snowball, leading to the mounting 'perception of a harmful and voluntary intentionality ... directed toward oneself'.[46]

And Tempest's collection points to still more deterritorializing effects of potential relevance to infrasonic hauntings ...

Bodily resonances – The frequencies at which certain organs and bones can be caused to vibrate at high intensity by airborne waves.[47] Felt as a form of possession when induced at a distance and without an observable cause.

Vestibular stimulation – Vibratory effects in that part of the inner ear where motion, balance, and spatial orientation are gauged.[48] Linked to perceptions of heaviness, buoyancy and acceleration that are potentially at odds with other aspects of sensed reality.

'Sensory rearrangement' – Jumbled sensory inputs, in conflict with one another, and complicating the roles of memory and anticipation in the navigation of experience. 'When we expose ourselves to an atypical force environment ... this delicate harmony is artificially disrupted to produce a mismatch between signals communicated by the normally synergistic receptors'.[49] Results can range from confusion to nausea, as in motion sickness or filmic techniques that induce 'cinerama sickness'. The term 'atypical force environment' might be considered synonymous with an unsettling logic of sensation.

'*Pseudosound*' – A 'sensory rearrangement in which the motion signals transmitted by the eyes, the vestibular system and the non-vestibular proprioceptors are at variance not only with one another, but also – and this is the crucial factor – with what is expected on the basis of previous transactions with the environment'.[50] The authors focus on mechanical vibration perceived as airborne sound. We can ask how meaningful it is to separate sound and other forms of vibration in an environment that is either throbbing with audible sound or unsoundly pseudo-silent. Elsewhere, Geoff Leventhall discusses synaesthesia and studies which suggest 'that a transfer between sensory inputs can lead to a synaesthetic sound as a result of a visual input'. We can link this back to the Deleuze's 'ear that has become the polyvalent organ for sonorous bodies'.[51]

In the end, then, while Tempest and his colleagues set out to compile a comprehensive and reasoned survey of infrasonic knowledge to that date, the book also stands as a fascinating glimpse into everything strange and unpredictable about it. Read this way, *Infrasound* becomes a sort of arcanum of the sonic body. Certainly, for Vic Tandy, it seems to have contained more-than-enough evidence of sound's disquieting capacities to make a second experiment worthwhile.

Two years after his first investigation, Tandy published the results of a follow-up study conducted in the cellar of a fourteenth-century stone house in Coventry, England.[52] While the house was destroyed during the Blitz, the cellar remains, and now belongs to the foundation of a recently built Tourist Information Centre. In its new role as a historical attraction, the cellar receives a steady stream of visitors from around the world. The great majority pass through without incident, but the centre's staff report that a significant few leave in a panic, some too flustered to speak, others describing strange experiences suggestive of a paranormal encounter. The most commonly reported effect is an overwhelming sense of presence, described by some as a feeling of physical pressure on the body, and by others as an unseen entity seemingly in very close proximity. One visitor said she felt 'as if she were intruding, disturbing something'. Another found herself unable to cross the threshold because she felt something barring her way, yet her husband reported no effect. Still another left with the very strong feeling that a face had been peering over his shoulder. Other reported effects include the feeling of a sudden chill and the onset of piloerection.

This accumulation of reports, describing sensations associated with infrasonic exposure, from individuals apparently unaware of the cellar's growing reputation, led Tandy to speculate that, as in his own case, the cause might be infrasound. Indeed, measurements did find a notable infrasonic presence. And again, it was near 19 Hz (this time a room resonance), the same as the previous experiment and, significantly, just inside that liminal zone at the cusp of audition. Moreover, its peak magnitude was found to be located at the entrance to the room, precisely where the majority of encounters were reported to have occurred. Finally, Tandy also noted that the waveform was nearly sinusoidal – a smooth, S-shaped wave – meaning that it had very little in the way of harmonic noise, or higher frequency content which might be audible even if the fundamental was not. At the same time, the wave was modulated, to a significant degree, by several less prominent frequencies. Textured in this way, it would be sensed not as a single, undifferentiated tone, but at a fluctuating force, a factor identified repeatedly in the literature for its capacity to push, unsettlingly into perception. From this, and in combination with his earlier study, Tandy concluded that, under the right conditions, infrasound may well be a significant factor in some alleged hauntings. And while hesitant to discount other parts of the frequency spectrum, he suggests that that region around 19 Hz – just at the cusp of traditionally conceived audibility – may be of special concern.

There have been subsequent efforts both to prove and to discredit the premise of Tandy's work, but they have typically relied on reductive empirical methods that aim to bracket out the sorts of singularities that a haunting really needs in order to function.[53] They have tended to begin from the assumption that a haunting will be either of cultural origin ('all in the mind') or else something predictably and mechanistically triggered at the level of neurophysiology. Of course, these approaches will tend to obscure phenomena of a more complex and richly disquieting sort. But while controlled efforts to reproduce infrasonic 'ghosts' in the lab (and elsewhere) have largely failed, we need look no further than the now-extensive literature on low-frequency sound and vibration to find ample evidence of weirdly deterritorializing effects that might acquire a haunting character in the right circumstances. We can leave the strictly ghostly behind and investigate any number of other sites that can claim a comparable spectral character or where haunt-like accounts have accumulated. The issue is not ghosts per se, but a particular relationality of the sonic body. The real question is how to go about conceiving the becoming-cultural of those strange sonic materialities.

Unhomed

With Tempest's help, Tandy gives us tales of sonic bodies unsettled by feelings that put reason and sensed-reality in conflict. He makes an important link when he identifies infrasound as a source of confounding presences that can undermine our sense of the world and leave us grasping for clues as to how to adapt. When ghost stories emerge as a vernacular coping strategy, then it is a case of something mythic becoming actual (in the sense of being livably, if not objectively, true). Freud identified something notionally similar, when describing 'encounters in which the distinction between imagination and reality is effaced, as when something that we have hitherto regarded as imaginary appears before us in reality'.[54] This is the moment of apprehension that characterizes an uncanny, or *unheimlich* experience. Unheimlich loosely translates as 'unfamiliar', but most literally as 'unhome'. An 'unheimlich house' is a defamiliarizing space.[55] In this sense, it suggests a difficult confrontation with one's own exteriority – a body in a destabilizing relation. But this is largely lost in the Freudian sense which treats the uncanny episode in profoundly interiorizing terms, its shock deriving not from the *un*familiar but a dramatic moment of self-recognition as terrors repressed in infancy irrupt in a field of signs. Although he stresses passage between the homely and the unhomely as the generative tension behind the effect, Freud's schema works in the wrong direction (or, rather, only in one direction – a consummation rather than a resonance) by casting the unfamiliar as a 'sub-species' of the familiar. Any sense of newness or transformation attributed to the phenomenon is therefore illusory, while autopoiesis and the dynamics of subjective re-singularization remain untheorized.[56]

However, with some redirection, the unheimlich becomes a useful concept for a theory of the sonic body possessed by slow-cycling waves. Like the image of 'a haunting', it helpfully conveys an affective tone (a vexing presence-absence), a spatial relation (the unhomely milieu) and a sense of mystification that can never be entirely explained away (affect's escape). What is missing from Freud's usage, though, is the dynamism latent in the term. As an adjective it simply describes a fixed state, with no sense of how it came to be or how it works. As a verb, however, it takes on a molecularizing complexion and speaks to spectral tendency. Reframed in this way, with Freudian 'lack' recast as opportunities for strange connections, *unhoming* begins to resemble the deterritorializing forces that run through Deleuze and Guattari's theorization of affect, desire and the multiplicitous becomings of ostensibly whole entities. Deterritorialization can, then, be understood as the general concept, with unhoming as its more specific articulation regarding that incorporeal paradox commonly described as haunting. Unhoming by sound thus has several, linked inflections. In the spatial sense, a milieu is unhomed when its familiar vibratory composition is supplanted by an 'atypical force environment', or a strange logic of sensation. There are the unhomings of sonic bodies (individual and collective) like those described by Tandy, Lovecraft, Augoyard and Torgue. And we can also speak of the senses unhomed by spectral events that escape or short circuit them. In these various ways, unhomings are encounters that provoke bodies and shock something new into being.

Boo! (towards an operative reality)

Startles are unhomings, catalytic events that open a crack in the ordinary, allowing new vistas of experience to seep in. A startle, according to Ronald Simons, 'happens in and to the body, but it is more than that. When one is startled one's soul is troubled, and one's mind finds itself, if only for a moment, in a strange and surprising place.'[57] As a psychiatrist and cultural anthropologist, much of Simons' work has focused on so-called culture-bound syndromes, or group-specific conditions, which would tend to be considered more constructed than biological in origin. In contrast, he argues, the startle reflex is a cross-cultural, even cross-species phenomenon. He describes it as an 'override system', an autonomic refocusing of attention and a marshalling of problem-solving faculties to adapt to emerging, and potentially threatening, new conditions. If a survival instinct is at the root of the effect, then most startles are false alarms or misperceptions of innocuous stimuli, but they always involve unhomings and ontogenetic flashes that can develop in unpredictable ways.[58] This is the terror and the fun of startles.

Large startles, or accumulations of smaller ones, can give new inflections to reality, altering a body's sense of itself and its surroundings. They can acquire a cultural life through their ability to shock, amuse and bewilder, to incite the imagination and fill experience with anticipation. Yet they also retain an autonomy, being a reflex of 'inescapable physiology'.[59] Simons acknowledges that this may be a controversial statement, in his own field and beyond, but argues that an honest effort to understand the interpenetration of nature and culture has to begin by acknowledging that the latter is necessarily premised and constrained by the former.[60] What keeps this from sliding into biological determinism, however, is his conception of nature; hardly a guarantor of essence or fixity, Simons describes it as a realm of unpredictability and constant variation. Its relationship to culture is thus a modulatory one, not reducible to either determinism or mediation, but always injecting new rhythms and ruptures into experience. The nature–culture circuits thus engendered can become a source of newness in the social, catalysing developments in thought, habit and social organization.

Startle thus emerges as an 'interactional resource',[61] one made especially rich by its variability as a destabilizer of the known and expected. This is not to overemphasize novelty, however. Here, newness is better understood to describe singularities of experience rather than the arrival of something utterly without precedent, with Simons noting that although certain types of startles can become known through repeated encounters, 'every startle is a unique event'. The anticipated can be startling. One can startle oneself. We can be startled by our own reactions. Even rehearsed or stylized reactions – for example, the postures, gestures and vocalization of an extra-sensitive minority he calls 'hyperstartlers'[62] – speak more to a modulatory dynamic between nature and culture than to mere performativity. A familiar response is not, in itself, evidence that the new has been evacuated through repetition.[63] This last point is reinforced by his findings on the phenomenon of sensitization (the priming and amplification of responsiveness), which has a tendency to *increase* with repeated exposure, rather than dulling with 'familiarity', as is often assumed in the cultural theorization of repetition.[64] Moreover, sensitization very often co-functions with habituation, understood as learnt adaptation to the shock but without the capacity to limit the force itself. The result is an individual, or population, habitually 'on edge'. One need only think of London during the Blitz, or the residents of Gaza, to understand how accumulations of shocks, and the anticipation of more to come, can unhome a milieu and help engender a new collectivity.[65]

Comparable themes emerge in the work of folklorist David Hufford whose ethnographic studies of purportedly haunted sites have been ongoing since the early 1970s. Like Simons, his findings point away from culturalist assumptions of equivalence between repetition and recuperation, intention and mediation, leading him to conclude that haunting experiences are generally 'independent of the subject's intentions ... they are spontaneous rather than elective'.[66] This is the case, he argues, even when 'percipients' seek out the experience, because the feeling of being in the presence of *something* ultimately hinges on a confluence of forces rather than mere desire or superstition. So against those arguments that would locate hauntings 'all in the mind', or construe them as symptoms of discourses, Hufford describes the experience in less anthropomorphic and interiorized terms, arguing that 'the fact that an experience has been sought by no means proves that the seeker's intention *caused* the experience to be as it was (if I intended to get wet by jumping in the water, it is nonetheless the *water* that makes me wet, not my intention)'. Simply put, there cannot be a viable haunting without forces that exceed our grasp and control of them (much as we are unable to tickle ourselves).[67] Again, the question of non-human, or supernatural, agencies arises.[68] Hufford reinforces the point by citing the many cases he has seen in which similar haunt reports accumulate around a given site even though the individuals involved have no knowledge of each other or the site's reputation (as in the case of the Coventry basement investigated by Tandy). When 'the same perceptual pattern recurs in different subjects, those without

prior knowledge of it,' he says, 'then prior knowledge and intention cease to be explanatory options'.[69] In such cases, we need a conceptual framework that allows for non-human tendencies in the world to play an active role shaping the social.[70] To this end, he says, we need to pay greater attention to the stories people tell of being haunted.

According to Hufford, there is a crucial catalytic moment at the beginning of every paranormal experience when, in the face of mounting but nebulous evidence, the percipient is faced with the question: 'Am I haunted or hallucinating?' Neither option is especially palatable, but the latter at least comes with vernacular coping strategies in the form of existing legends (ghost stories, local lore, etc.) and the efforts of percipients to reach a workable understanding of their own becomings by articulating and sharing experiential accounts. Together, these tales constitute a form of 'unofficial knowledge' of particular places, types of experiences and variations in experience, and they operate much in the manner of a *minor literature* (in their deterritorialization of language) or a nomad science (proceeding by intuition and an immanent logic of experience).[71] Yet the scholarship on this minor science of the spectral too often treats it in metaphorical terms, or as a symptom of culture or psychology. 'Ignorance of the experiences from which many supernatural beliefs and narratives arise has often resulted in poorly founded speculations about meaning', he says. 'This problem is made worse by the common assumption that meanings necessarily precede and enter into shaping of alleged "supernatural experience" as well as narrative belief'.[72] By contrast, Hufford's ethnographic project treats legends and the claims of percipients much more in the manner of the tales of becoming being theorized here, as he attempts to find a language appropriate to the experience. (That these efforts often struggle, he says, speaks more to the ineffable qualities of the experience, and a lack of imagination on the part of listeners, than to the unreliability of the percipient.[73])

By attempting to meet these tales on their own terms – that is, according to the logics of sensation from which they arise – Hufford is able to extract myriad clues as to the becomings of those involved. The machinic conditions of a haunting can be glimpsed in descriptions of spaces (their age, location, construction, shape, size, layout, smells, acoustic qualities, visual character, occupants, their schedules and habits and so on) and events (the character of an unhoming deriving from distortions and strange circuits that develop in this ecology). Patterns of collective individuation and the passage from spectral questions to a declared haunting can be observed in stories that describe the accumulation, experience and cataloguing of strange events; patterns of reasoning and processes of coming into belief; and degrees of sensitization and habituation. Important too is the sharing and debating of evidence among those involved. This is when tales are checked against each other for consistency and signs of variation. Collective theorizing attempts to infer just what the entity is and what it might do next. Even disagreement plays a productive ontogenetic role, maintaining an air of unpredictability and illogic around the present–absent entity. The result of all of these interactions is the emergence of at least two new subjectivities: the haunter and the haunted. We have a full-blown haunting when spectral effects achieve a consistency, seeming to assume a personality (kindly, malevolent, aloof) and habits (a schedule, predictable acts). The haunted, it is important to add, are very often not enthusiastic about ghosts. Their coming into belief is often a wearily reluctant acceptance of evidence which defies reason but seems to offer no other explanation. Altogether, this accumulation of experiences, clues, speculations and collective decisions produce the haunted assemblage and contribute to its evidential force.[74]

What emerges, in Hufford's words, is an 'objective reality ... attested by the multiplicity of witnesses'. We might put this slightly differently, calling it the emergence of an *operative reality* that is livably true if not objectively verifiable. The concept of operative reality can be understood to build on Massumi's theorization of 'operative reason,' a mode of thought which

> is pragmatic rather than analytic. It doesn't master a situation with exhaustive knowledge of alternative outcomes. It 'tweaks' it. Rather than probing the situation to bring it under maximum control, it prods it, recognizing it to be finally indomitable and respecting its autonomy. Operative reason is concerned with effects – specifically countereffects – more than causes. ... Operative reason is inescapable from a process of trial and error, with occasional shots in the dark, guided in every case by a pragmatic sense of the situation's responsivity (as opposed to its manipulability).[75]

Massumi's 'operative reality' shares something with both nomad science and radical empiricism. Each, in their way, describes efforts to follow and work with the logic immanent to a set of relations, or an operative reality. Each describes a thought in-becoming, an emergent 'knowledge of sensible realities [that] comes to life inside the tissue of experience. It is *made*; and made by relations that unroll themselves in time'.[76] An operative reality emerges intuitively and pragmatically. The question is not 'is it true?' but 'does it work?' in the present circumstances.

That stark choice between haunting and hallucination is an example of a moment of rupture when contingent logic gets called on to paper over the cracks in reasoned perception. The cause of the unhoming itself, however theorized, is what James would call a 'terminus', or thought's conclusion. The many available routes to that conclusion he calls 'thought paths', which can often only proceed largely on intuition. In this way, we spend much of our time being 'virtual knowers … before that knowledge is verified'. Tales of becoming reflect this 'knowledge in-transit' and attendant transductions. Intuited realities become liveable when we are forced to 'commit ourselves to the current as if the port were sure'. 'Mainly', he says, 'we live on speculative investments, or on our prospects only', putting faith in the 'felt-reality' of our relations.[77] When strange materialities put experience and reason in conflict, they are not simply fictive because their reality is actually felt. There is little else we can do but try to get to grips with a workable, if not necessarily pleasant or predictable, reality.

The Hum

The Hum is a haunting for the Atomic Age – closer to the sort predicted by *The Outer Limits* than those recorded in standard ghost stories. Seemingly the product of unidentified wave energies, it unhomes spaces and produces still another type of sensitive/percipient/hyperstartler: The Hummer. Hummers hear/feel a spectral presence that may not be properly infrasonic, and may not be sound at all, but which insists in perception in a sound-like way. As its effects and tendencies reveal themselves, it seems to become an entity and an agency unto itself. 'There's nothing you can do', complains one Hummer. 'It's there ... It remains until it wants to'.[78] For the afflicted, but also their families, public officials and acoustic scientists, The Hum becomes an operative reality. Whatever its cause, it becomes collectively liveable. And with its rumoured origins in military–industrial megaprojects, it begins to look like a hyperstitional actualization of those wave–body mythologies that preceded it in science fiction.

Disparate reports of hum-like events date back as far as the 1940s, but it was in the 1970s that *The* Hum emerged as a widely reported phenomenon. Initially it seemed to be localized in the United Kingdom, but by the early 1990s, it had arrived in the United States. New Mexico's Taos Hum is perhaps the most famous example, while Kokomo, Indiana, has become another well-known case. In the years since, The Hum has continued to spread throughout the industrialized world, but only ever afflicting a small spectrum of the population.[79] Hummers describe the phenomenon in a variety of ways. It may be felt and/or heard. It is often, but not always, described as a distant rumbling (like idling trucks). For others it is a steady tone or a throb. These variations occur even within a group of sufferers associated with a single and mutually agreed-upon instance of The Hum. Some lab experiments aimed at matching the effect have suggested a fundamental frequency between 40 and 80 Hz and heavily modulated, giving it a pulsing quality.[80] Its effects on those who perceive it are profoundly unsettling. It may lurk at the edges of the senses, unavoidably there, yet not. Or it might rise to an unbearably high volume. It has been linked to insomnia, with sufferers often too tense to nod off, or having their dreams invaded by the sound before it jolts them awake again. Headaches, nausea, ear pain and body vibrations are also reported, and so is anxiety, caused not only by the noise itself, but by the memory and anticipation of it. Percipients are often left feeling helpless, depressed and isolated.

Hummers are another people habitually on edge. Like other sensitives they appear to be too finely tuned to a strange spectrum. Something in the world becomes all-too-present for them while escaping others unnoticed. Estimates put the proportion of those capable of detecting The Hum somewhere between two and ten per cent of the population. Treated with suspicion by scientists, engineers, doctors and public officials, they often band together to compare experiences and theories. They describe the vexing and ever wider searches that can end up dominating waking life: 'you look around the house ... can't find it ... but it's with you everywhere at the same loudness ... you can't deal with it because you don't know what it is.' You 'give up and lie down ... but attention is unwillingly drawn to sound that's ever-present ... though not loud, it disturbs sleep'. The typical search pattern often unfolds in three stages: search inside, search outside, give up. For some, this turns into a truly ambulant science, involving long, searching drives, mapping experiments, acoustic measurements, radio spectrum analysis and furtive investigations of potentially noisy industrial and military sites.[81] But failure seems inevitable. As a presence-absence that now reaches around the globe, it appears ever less likely that The Hum will be traced to a specific geographic location. It now seems to be both everywhere and nowhere. So, in the words of one noise consultant, 'if a source is located [it] is no longer "The Hum." '[82]

This would seem to raise two possibilities. Could there be a force, acoustic or otherwise, powerful enough to blanket the world yet be perceptible only by a small few? Or might The Hum be a single name for similar instances of something far more heterogeneous – for example, localized agglomerations of military-industrial din. Either way it becomes an insidious presence in the lives of Hummers. As elusive as The Hum may be out in the world, for sensitives it also becomes an inescapable bodily fact. In some cases there appears to be a stickiness about it, and despite its reputation as a geographically localized phenomenon it seems to follow an unlucky few. There are reports of some Hummers trying to escape it by moving or taking a holiday, but while they may find temporary relief, it often catches up with them. The spectral agency that began as something external and impersonal begins to feel possessive.

'And it was only by analogy that it could be called a sound at all ...'

Research on The Hum is still limited and potential causes are still very much open to debate. Frits van den Berg is one of those who believe its origins are primarily pathological. He labels The Hum a 'phantom sound' attributing it mainly to the anomalous perceptual faculties of a small minority. Media attention then amplifies their stories, which leads to the phenomenon seeming to take on a life of its own.[83] Citing a survey of low-frequency noise complaints (mainly surrounding wind turbines, other industrial sources and urban din) he hypothesizes that many low-frequency noise sufferers 'hear low pitched phantom sounds as other people would in a dead quiet place.' That is, they may have, or develop, heightened sensitivity to a normal, but often muted, peculiarity of human perception, whereby we hear 'sounds' with an internal, rather than external source. Van den Berg compares the effect to normal auditory experience in the acoustically dead space of an anechoic chamber, where 'within five minutes 94% of [subjects report] hearing a sound'. In another test, subjects were told that either light or sound changes would occur in a listening chamber. Neither occurred, but a significant portion of participants reported hearing sound variations when the light was alleged to be changing.

Like many of the effects described earlier, this suggests a fundamental co-functioning of the senses, rich with synaesthetic overlaps. It calls to mind Massumi's examination of the so-called Ganzfeld experiments, which aimed to isolate vision, only for subjects to report vivid hallucinatory effects as the bracketed senses flooded back in strange ways.[84] Van den Berg speaks of hallucination too when he draws a direct comparison between 'phantom' low-frequency noise and a visual effect known as Charles Bonnet syndrome (or visual release hallucinations) which afflict some sufferers of visual acuity loss. Recalling Massumi's claim that every sensory mode has a 'limit-field'[85] that reveals perception's synaesthetic underpinnings, van den Berg similarly suggests that there are varieties of phantom perception native to every sense.[86] This is the root of his claim that Hummers actually suffer from a form of tinnitus, which is to say the cause is internal to the sufferer. Or at least its physiological basis is. 'Fear is an important factor' too, he says, and noise-induced anxiety may increase the effect. He goes on to explain how the phenomenon can become a collective one, through the sharing of experiences and theories, whether different individuals all hear/feel the same sound or not. When picked up by the media, this can turn into a 'Hum', associated with a geographic place but without a known source, if one even exists. Then, as he puts it, 'a Hum is born'.

However, other researchers remain equally convinced that neurophysiological explanations alone fail to account for everything that is known about The Hum. Writing in *Applied Acoustics*, Vasudevan and Gordon conclude that it 'is very probably a real phenomenon and not imagined or self-generated'.[87] While in his survey of the evidence to date, David Deming purports to dismantle the case for tinnitus on several counts. Classic tinnitus, he notes, is a high-pitched ringing, usually between 3,000 and 6,000 Hz, and almost never below 1,000 Hz. Moreover, it is not associated with the sorts of physical discomforts and vibrations reported by Hummers. Tinnitus also fails to explain The Hum's geographic distribution. Why would groups of tinnitus sufferers be clustered in only specific countries, cities and towns? Similarly, if The Hum is purely a product of human physiology, how is it that many sufferers do in fact find relief through relocation. Given these questions, Deming concludes that the source 'must be external'.[88] The tinnitus diagnosis persists, he says, 'because it is the only option known to medical science'.[89]

If the source is 'external', then The Hum is better described as a logic of sensation that emerges between an 'atypical force environment' and anomalously sensitive bodies therein.[90] In Deming's view, the most compelling explanations actually suggest an electromagnetic cause rather than an acoustic one. Potential causes of The Hum would then range from electrical towers to far more exotic possibilities: submarine communication stations, the High Frequency Active Auroral Research Program (HAARP) project and another military venture called TACAMO (for Take Charge And Move Out).[91] The latter few could account for the global reach of the phenomenon, while HAARP's transmission patterns might also explain The Hum's very localized character. This view hinges on a small number of studies which seem to reveal a small percentage of the population capable of perceiving radio waves in a form that resembles sound. This raises the interesting synaesthetic prospect of *sound-like* experience that operates analogically in perception, like a non-mechanical version of pseudosound.[92] The Hum would therefore be attributable to radio waves – either collections of mutually modulating ones, or specific types of transmissions that travel around the globe only on very specific paths. For the extra-sensitive few capable of detecting them, their 'sound' would actually be closer to a high-pitched ringing than the rumble of The Hum.[93] But Deming points to some of the side effects recorded during the experiments: 'the perception of severe buffeting of the head, without apparent vestibular symptoms such as dizziness or nausea. Changing the transmitter, one can induce a "pins and needles" sensation.[94] If this is the case, then it points to something even more surprising than the strange prospect of 'audible' electromagnetism. It suggests that radio waves might be perceived by some in a way that evokes the extra-cochlear effects of low-frequency sounds that largely bypass the ears. That is, it may be analogically sound-like, but only insofar as it elicits varieties of vibratory perception *other* than hearing.

More Hum researchers, however, cling to acoustic explanations. In this scenario, the culprits would be major sources of mechanical vibration including the massive pipe and pumping systems involved in gas and water distribution. These sources could account for the strangely linear distributions of sufferers in the UK, for example, although utilities' refusals to provide maps of their networks make any efforts at correlation difficult. Moreover, the fact that The Hum is heard most often and most strongly indoors, in specific locations, points strongly to an acoustic explanation based on localized structural resonance. Simply put, unfortunately situated rooms or whole buildings might be hummed by nearby vibration sources. However, this explanation does not necessarily explain why The Hum seems to have spread over the last two decades, or the fact that many people around the world report very similar sonic characteristics.

Blinkered science

To the frustration of Hummers, answers and even clues remain elusive. But while there is certainly something inherently perplexing about The Hum in its spectrality, it also seems that investigations of it are chronically hindered by the limited purview and reductive tendencies that pervade much of the scientific research on low-frequency sound. Much of this work focuses only on the most pronounced and potentially damaging physiological effects of vibration. Or it aims to quantify the relationship between low-frequency 'noise' and vaguely conceived categories like 'annoyance' and 'performance'. The liminal and anomalous are systematically excluded. Norm Broner's 1977 survey sets the tone when it states that certain phenomena are simply 'not statistically relevant,' as when 'subjective response is vague'.[95] Similarly, he warns that tests using lower levels of infrasound produce 'mixed findings' and may be compromised by 'artifacts produced by faulty experimental procedures'. Nature outside the lab, however, is always complicated by artefacts. And paranormal, or supernatural, events are, by definition, anomalies of experience. The effort to normalize nature and see laws where there are none puts traditional empiricism at a disadvantage when it comes to haunt investigations. Following James, Massumi argues that, of course 'nature does not follow laws. *Laws follow nature.* What nature does is generate surprises and contracts habits. Laws come after. They formally model the already contracted habits of nature in a way that makes them humanly useful'.[96] But, extended beyond their useful limits, they begin to miss intensity. When variation and multiplicity are systematically excluded, he argues 'science misses nature by design'.

In Hum research, there is perhaps no more literal example of science missing nature by design than the persistence of a standard called dBA, or A-weighting, a filtering algorithm for acoustic measurement that aims to conform data to the sensitivities of the average human ear across the frequency spectrum (a standard known as an equal-loudness contour).[97] In other words, it excludes virtually 'all of the sounds we are not *expected* to hear', obscuring the activity of sound energy below 200 Hz (i.e. the entire bass range along with infrasound) and precluding any observations that might be made regarding the extra-cochlear interactions of low frequencies.[98] The problems with dBA weighting are widely acknowledged, including by the World Health Organization in its 1999 report on Community Noise.[99] There is a suitable alternative, however, in the dBC curve, which gives a much more even response at lower frequencies (although it too declines below 60 Hz, and more sharply below 30 Hz). And there is still another called dBG, which is specifically for infrasound, although it can be of limited use because it filters out virtually the entire audible range. Yet, researchers cling to dBA due to an engrained indifference to the extra-cochlear and because it is the standard according to which nearly all previous tests have been conducted. That the data may fail to account for wide swathes of sonic experience is of less concern than the ability to compare data across studies.

Add to this the other limitations typically imposed on low-frequency research. For example, pronounced modulation is often cited as a potentially crucial factor in sound's ability to put a body at variance with itself and disrupt perception. Yet, many studies base their claims about sonic experience on tests using only single, steady sine tones. As such, they miss movement, being unable to account for the relationality that emerges in rhythmic pressure variations. When such experiments are conducted using only headphones, it means that many potential effects beyond the ear, and perhaps the cranium, are excluded from the outset. When conducted in sealed chambers, on the other hand, they do allow for measurement of 'whole body effects' at varying degrees of force and subtlety, but they still give only so much insight into experiences of ambient low-frequency sound out in the world, with all of the spatial and harmonic variables that texture it. Moreover, the rational and traditionally empirical tendencies that guide this research keep the emphasis on the quantifiable, the normative and reproducibility of effects – that is, everything that anomalous experience is not.

Yet, if we are living in a world of evermore heterogeneous vibratory mixtures, then research that brackets out anomaly and liminal percepts is bound to miss the spectral things that unhome us. Haunting experiences are, of course, all about ambiguity and uncertainties of perception. It is surprise that keeps them vital; any haunting worth the name keeps people guessing. They work by striking a disturbing certainty in a small few who effectively become transducers of weird materiality into liveable, social fact. In this way, afflicted bodies become part of a haunting's evidential force, posing a conceptual problem for all but the most sceptical.

We still do not know what a sonic body can do ...

A 2001 survey of the infrasonic literature admits that there is still 'no agreement about the biological activity' of low-frequency sound.[100] What is clear, the authors say, is that it does *something*, but that its effects are quite variable and dependent on combinations of circumstance and individual sensitivity. Geoff Leventhall's 'Low Frequency Noise. What We Know, What We Do Not Know, and What We Would Like to Know' is even more candid in its acknowledgement of the mysteries that still haunt scientific knowledge. He concedes that 'it is also possible that there are subtle effects of low frequency noise on the body which we do not yet understand'. And he concludes with some very fundamental questions:

> Does the way in which we measure low frequency noise hide some of its disturbing characteristics? Is the ear in fact the most sensitive low-frequency receptor in the body? Alternately, is there a receptor mechanism in the body which is more sensitive than the ear at low frequencies? If so, what is that mechanism?[101]

In other words, he holds out the possibility of still-undiscovered, or as yet unrecognized senses. This is not so far-fetched. A 2009 study published in the journal *Pain* claims to have discovered a previously unknown, sensory system 'hidden in the skin'.[102] Even more provocative is the research of Thomas Heimburg and Andrew D. Jackson, which suggests that the long-held Hodgkin–Huxley model of neural transmission could be wrong. Their Soliton model proposes that nerve impulses are not, in fact, electrical but *sonic*.[103] If this were the case, how would it affect the way we approach questions of sonic experience (and its mediation or modulation)?

The purpose here isn't to find definitive answers but to indicate just how susceptible both scientific knowledge and cultural theory are to being unhomed by nature's capacity to surprise. Their own limit-fields are exposed by anomalies of experience, spectral agencies and the nature–culture resonances they engender. Because it highlights these complications especially vividly, infrasound, along with other unsound or sound-like phenomena, becomes an important entry point for discussions of the sonic body. Not only does it reveal a rich terrain of liminal sonic encounters (perceptual uncertainties, synaesthesia, etc.) that seem to accumulate around sonic bodies; it also poses the conceptual problem of sonic experience outside of audition, representation, intent and sometimes even conscious awareness.

This is where emergent myth-sciences of the sonic body become especially important – filling in where traditional frameworks falter. Their tales of becoming avoid transcendent Logic in favour of the immanent logics of vibratory fields, devising and repurposing conceptual language as needed. Sometimes too, this intuited grasp of sonic relations becomes the basis of arcane strategies designed to tease out odd vibratory potentials and intensify them in the service of larger projects.

Numinous Strategies

When streams of low-frequency vibration and perceptual anomaly draw the imagination into the body, they turn it into a string of questions: 'What is that ... what's happening ... how will I work with it ... ?' It's a small but important leap to begin asking, 'What can I do with it?' and, more importantly, 'What can we do *to* each other?' Bass emerges *as a strategy* when intuited potentials of the acoustic event become a matter of speculation, and the basis from which tools and techniques are devised to unhome bodies, spectralize subjectivity and retexture a collective assemblage.[1] Religious cultures were arguably the first to recognize the sonic body, make it a site of experimentation and develop repertoires of techniques for modulating it. The evidence is everywhere if we tune our thought to vibration and affect, but it easily escapes notice if engrained habits go unquestioned. This is true, for example, of dominant strands in the study of religious music where attention has centred on the musical work as an expression of belief. More recent interest in the sonority of ritual sites has brought the discussion closer to materiality, but still the analysis remains too firmly in the realm of representation and mediation. What both perspectives tend to miss are the ways that sonic experience can be generative of belief, not just reflective of it. That is, if anomalous vibrations are able to conjure presences, charge bodies and alter perceived reality, then they can also play a powerful role in the ongoing genesis of a religious culture. They can be sought out, exploited, technologized and reinvented.

Consider, then, the prevalence and diversity of powerful, low-frequency sound-making devices that play central roles in religious cultures around the world: drums, bells, gongs, voice, pipe organs, horns, didgeridoos, aerophones, as well as the multitudes of resonant structures (natural and man-made) that have been used to facilitate numinous encounters. Each has its own spectral character, each participates in its own culturally specific networks of ritual and belief. But taken together, these varied technologies also point to a vast, cross-cultural history – one in which bass is privileged for its material force and its a-signifying intensities. Bass emerges as a *numinous strategy* when people learn to 'play' the sonic body in ways designed to catalyse religiously useful becomings. This will be our focus. But first we need to step back, for a moment, and investigate what it means (and what it needn't mean) to treat the body as a sensate instrument.

Learning to play the sonic body

Lurking behind much of the low-frequency discourse in recent decades is the aforementioned Dr Gavreau, 'a key hyperstitional figure'[2] for bass-philic music scenes and bass-phobic anti-noise campaigners alike. From him we get the popular image of bass as either a blunt-force weapon or a subliminal unhoming ray. In a pre-echo of Tandy's ghost, the becoming-in-thought behind Gavreau's infrasonic gun was spurred by an encounter with a faulty ventilation fan which had left fellow lab workers complaining of perceptual anomalies and physical unease.[3] Rather than simply treating the phenomenon as an environmental curiosity, Gavreau saw the makings of a minor science, a field which could be mined for techniques that might be deployed to destabilize opponents and realign relations of power. His key innovation was to recast the battlefield in spectral terms, treating it as a population of resonant bodies (and bodies within bodies – i.e. organs, bones, but also rooms, pipes systems, etc.), each with their own natural frequencies that could be exploited to incapacitating or destructive effect. But his emphasis on 'pulping' organs and crumbling buildings has perhaps helped to skew much recent bass–body interest towards sound's most concrete, self-evident and violent effects. Gavreau's interest was in the production of a sonic totality, an overriding force that is transformative only insofar as it obliterates. (As such, his work may be ripe for sonic fictional mythologizing but, in practical terms, its application in sonic culture could almost only ever be metaphorical.) This is in contrast to work like Tandy's, which helps reveal the sorts of subject-object disruptions and heterogeneous affective circuits that can develop in strangely undulating spaces. These subtler deterritorializations can incite inventive tangents because, latent in them, is an image of the sonic body as a field of variable responsivity – a nervous polyphony which might be learnt and played like the most arcanely tuned instrument.

The nervous piano

Less exotic than Gavreau, but perhaps more helpful to grasping the body's bio-acoustic spectrality, is Hermann von Helmholtz, the nineteenth-century scientist and philosopher whose experimental research helped shape the modern study of thermodynamics, optics, acoustics and the biology of aural perception. In *On the Sensations of Tone*, Helmholtz offered the first comprehensive theorization of 'sympathetic vibration', or resonance: 'The tendency of a mechanical or electrical system to vibrate at a certain frequency when excited by an external force, and to keep vibrating after the excitation is removed.'[4] A structure's so-called natural frequency is a function of its size and shape, and refers to the frequency at which the space will be induced to oscillate by acoustic energy, amplifying it rather than dampening it. It is resonance that makes instruments and spaces 'sing'. It is at work in the body when a tune *hums you*, as when a particular bass tone throbs in the chest cavity. It can also be destructive when the energy induced is powerful enough, and prolonged enough, to shake the resonating body to pieces (the classic example being the opera singer whose voice shatters a wine glass). A so-called Helmholtz resonator is a tuned vessel, 'consisting of an enclosed volume of air connected to the atmosphere by a short channel or pipe',[5] that will begin to ring or hum when ambient sound approaches its natural frequency. (Blowing across the mouth of a bottle to produce a tone is another version of this effect.)

The principle behind Helmholtz-type resonators has actually been known since antiquity, and perhaps much longer, having been employed to shape the acoustic character of theatres and churches. It can also be observed in some drums and bells found around the world, and even in the shape of certain ritual structures, as well as in modern technologies like bass reflex speakers. In his foundational acoustic experiments, Helmholtz used incrementally scaled arrays of these resonators to isolate and observe minute slices of the frequency spectrum, both individual tones (produced by tuning forks) and the modulatory relations between multiple tones as they combine to produce harmonics. This was the beginning of mathematically precise spectral analysis of sound, which allowed the translation of musical scales and octave ratios into frequencies (cycles per second or Hertz). And it would form the empirical foundation of Helmholtz's theories of hearing and musical aesthetics.

This aesthetics is easily critiqued for its mechanistic linking of vibration, sensation and musical value. And certainly, Helmholtz can be seen as iconic of some of the most reductive and atomizing tendencies in nineteenth-century empirical science. Yet we can also read him for insights into the intuitive aspects of sonic experience – the ways in which sensed relations between sound and matter can evolve into working concepts and become the basis for new experimental techniques. It is in this sense that Helmholtz sees music as a laboratory: 'Musicians', he notes, 'are well acquainted with sympathetic resonance.' They encounter it, 'when, for example, the strings of two violins are in exact unison, and one string is bowed, the other will being to vibrate.'[6] Very early on, they learn to locate resonance, intensify it and vary it. They feel the increase in sound energy that makes octave ratios stand out from other tonal relationships. They notice that this note or that may draw sound from a vase, a window or a whole room. Helmholtz also explains how sonic knowledge can arrive visually, as in an experiment using a timpani (which he likens to the ear drum) covered with a thin layer of sand. Sound vibrations will cause the sand to move about the surface of the membrane, arraying chaotically at some pitches, while settling into kaleidoscopic shapes at others.[7] As Chladni and others had observed, the induction of a standing wave in the membrane can cause this patterning to assume geometries of such uncanny complexity that one would be forgiven for imagining the influence of an ordering intelligence.[8] What these shapes actually reveal, visually, are the nodal (or wave) patterns of the resonant body. Helmholtz explained that a well-trained singer 'who knows how to hit the tones of the membrane correctly', can learn to follow and tweak interactions in this sonic micro-milieu, 'easily mak[ing] the sand arrange itself at pleasure in one order or another, singing the corresponding tones powerfully at a distance.'[9]

However, it is in his theorization of what he calls the 'nervous piano' that Helmholtz most fully articulates a notion of music as the fine orchestration of corporeal vibration, at the interface of biology and acoustic technology. He starts with another experiment: 'Gently touch one of the keys of a pianoforte without striking the string, so as to raise the damper only, and then sing a note of the corresponding pitch forcibly directing the voice against the strings of the instrument. On ceasing to sing, the note will be echoed back from the piano.'[10] This 'echo' is not the original sound reflected back but, in fact, the same pitch emitted from the corresponding piano string. The two are brought into sympathetic resonance and they vibrate together in unison. When the singer stops, the string persists.

Helmholtz correctly predicted that the hair-like corti of the cochlea work in the same manner, each tuned to a very narrow band of the frequency spectrum. When sound energy in that range is present, the corresponding hair sings in unison. This discovery leads to further speculation:

> Now suppose we were able to connect every string of a piano with a nervous fibre in such a manner that this fibre would be excited and experience a sensation every time the string vibrated. Then every musical tone which impinged on the instrument would excite, as we know to be really the case in the ear, a series of sensations exactly corresponding to the pendular vibrations into which the original motion of the air had to be resolved. By this means, then, the existence of each partial tone would be exactly so perceived, as it really is perceived by the ear. The sensations of simple tones of different pitch would under the supposed conditions fall to the lot of different nervous fibres, and hence be produced quite separately, and independently of each other.[11]

Jonathan Sterne has written that this 'piano theory of hearing, which held sway into the twentieth century, is a curious combination of ... instrumental (in both senses of the word) understanding of hearing and an extension of the separateness-of-the-senses hypothesis.'[12]

There are three key ideas here that are worth distinguishing. One pertains to Helmholtz's construction of biology (the ear) in terms borrowed from contemporaneous technology (the historically situated piano), much as when the heart is described as a motor, or the brain as a supercomputer, with all the mixed metaphors implied by each. But in Helmholtz there is something more cybernetic than metaphorical at work because he effectively casts the piano, and other musical instruments by extension, as bio-aesthetic interfaces. From this perspective, whatever their involvement in musical texts and the symbolic functions of song, these instruments must also be recognized as technologies of the body, tools for sensory experimentation and modulating affect. They involve a becoming-biological of the machine and a becoming-musical of sonorous physiology. Helmholtz doesn't go this far, but the suggestion is arguably latent in the model.

The untenable aspect of Helmholtz's instrumental reason lies in his conviction that the relations (sensory, emotional, aesthetic) thus engendered would be rational ones, which might be orchestrated as precisely and predictably as an actual musical instrument. As we have already seen, sonic bodies vary widely in their sensitivities and responses, and logics of sensation are always fuzzy ones. We can speak of predictable physical effects to a real extent, but we are all tuned somewhat differently, and this still tells us nothing of all the heterogeneous factors and singular, incorporeal resonances that structure the acoustic event. So while we can very productively retain the concept of music technology as a nature–culture interface, the over-determination that pervades its supposed operation needs to be replaced with something more open-ended. We can instead understand nervous instruments to work by volatilizing the relations of sonic bodies in ways that may be culturally useful. To do this, however, requires one further step. As Sterne notes, Helmholtz's reductive empiricism assumes a strict separation of the senses. This obviates attention to their co-functioning and the role of synaesthesia and liminal perceptions in sonic experience. It also assumes that music operates exclusively in the domain of the cochlea. For Helmholtz, sound addresses the ear alone. Music has no other function and the outer edges of the audio spectrum are of little cultural concern.

This disinterest in sound's synaesthetic potential would seem to be behind his claim that 40 Hz (E_1 – the lowest note of a traditional orchestra) is the absolute, lower limit of musically useful sound. 'I think I may predict with certainty', he writes, 'that all efforts of modern art applied to produce good musical tones of a lower pitch must fail, not because proper means of agitating the air cannot be discovered, but because the human ear cannot hear them'. The lowest notes on a grand piano (27.5 Hz or A_0) or pipe organ (16.35 Hz or C_0) were merely there, he felt, to add fullness to the higher octaves. 'The musical character of all these tones below E_I is imperfect', he says, 'because we are here near to the limit of the power of the ear to combine vibrations into musical tones.'[13] While he is right that the ability to make tonal distinctions begins to break down in this region, he incorrectly makes the ability of the ear the sole criterion for determining what constitutes culturally active sound.

Writing on the 'Deep and Deepest Tones', he does come close to a fuller recognition of sonorous materiality, when he describes cycles low and powerful enough to be felt as individual pulses while straining the ear:

> The 16-foot C_I of the organ, with 33 vibrations in a second, certainly gives a tolerably continuous sensation of drone, but does not allow us to a give it a definite position in the musical scale. We almost begin to observe the separate pulse of air, not withstanding the regular form of motion. In the upper half of the 32-foot octave, the perception of the separate pulses becomes still clearer ... and in the lower half of the 32-foot octave we can scarcely be said to hear anything but the individual pulses, or if anything else is really heard, it can only be weak upper partial tones, from which the musical tones of stopped pipes are not quite free.[14]

We can imagine the scene that inspired the description: obscure progressions, rhythmic air pressure fluctuations, ubiquitous force, vibration separating from tones, not-quite-sounds, half-felt presences of indeterminate shape, perception confounded, imagination stirred. Helmholtz actually describes something quite confusing, quite haunting. Something potentially quite useful. But he leaves it at that. In the end, we have to look elsewhere to learn just what nervous instruments can do.

Numinous instruments

As a term, 'sympathetic vibration' seems ready-made for the collective sonic body implicated in a numinous assemblage: *resonating with divinity*. It is easy to imagine how vibratory effects like a conjured sense of presence, synaesthetic unhomings and the feeling of being surrounded and suffused by energy from

Table 1 Acoustic features of select ritual and numinous instruments

Instrument	Lowest Frequencies (Approx.)	Notes
Gongs (East Asia)	Infrasonic beats; may have a fundamental pitch as low as 20 Hz	Pitch dependent on size; shimmering, harmonically rich drone; modulated by an infrasonic 'beating' between 1 to 5 Hz.
Didgeridoo (Oceania)	60 Hz	Complex drone with similarities to overtone chant
Bullroarer (South Pacific)	20 Hz	A rotational aerophone; pitch is dependent on the speed of flight and can span several octaves in a single rotation.
Pipe organ (Europe)	32 Hz @ 16' 16 Hz @ 32' 8 Hz @ 64' (very rare)	Compass spans almost the entire range of human hearing. Lowest pipes straddle lowest audible region.
O-Daiko drum (Japan)	120–200 Hz	High volume, powerful impacts. Rolling, thunderous when used in combination. Originally used in warfare.
Djembe drum (Africa)	70 Hz	Produces bass, tone, and slap sounds. Body functions as Helmholtz-type resonator.
Great bells (Europe) Temple bells (East Asia)	Infrasonic beats; Hum tones range from near-infrasonic to 200 Hz and above.	Fundamental pitch ('strike tone') is largely dependent on weight; lingering 'hum tone,' one octave lower, emerges after.
Voice	Male: from 30 Hz Female: from 110 Hz	E.g. the low drones of Tibetan overtone chant and European Gregorian chant.
Dung chen horn (Tibet)	60 Hz	'Temple horn,' often used in conjunction with chant.

Sources: Thomas D. Rossing, *Science of Percussion Instruments* (Singapore: World Scientific Publishing Co Ltd, 2000), pp. 174–6; Noam Amir, 'Some insight into the acoustics of the didjeridu', *Applied Acoustics*, 65 (2004), pp. 1181–96; Ingo R. Titze, *Principles of Voice Production* (Upper Saddle River, NJ: Prentice Hall, 1994), http://www.gcna.org/data/GBGreatBells.html and http://www.gcna.org/data/Weights.html (accessed 9 January 2011); Ingo R. Titze, 'Tibetan Chanting and Harmonic Singing', *The Journal of Singing* 53/2 (1996), pp. 31–2; and Brian Pertl, 'Some Observations on the "Dung Chen" of the Nechung Monastery', *Asian Music* 23/2 (1992), pp. 89–96.

an invisible source, might be put to use by religious cultures, not merely to denote Godly presence, but as an incorporeal catalyst of belief, re-energizing it and lending it evidential force. Anthropologist Donald Tuzin has suggested that 'sound making-devices comprise the most universal and preferred category of ritual facilitators'. And, given the range of sounds available to be created, it seems significant that 'only a few [types of sound] have been repeatedly selected for ritual elaboration'.[15] Bass, it turns out, is foremost among them.

The drum is perhaps the most familiar bass-producing instrument around the world. It is certainly the most symbolically loaded, linked for centuries in the Western imagination with primitive abandon and the threat of subliminal control. The low-frequency throb of ritual drumming – carried by air, invading bodily rhythms – perplexed and offended European sensibilities in colonial Africa. Conrad distilled those anxieties in *Heart of Darkness* through a narrator increasingly haunted by ambient percussion – the 'tremor of far-off drums, sinking, swelling, a tremor vast, faint; a sound weird, appealing, suggestive, and wild' – until he could no longer distinguish the jungle's pulse from the beating of his own, 'darkening' heart.[16] Similar anxieties were behind the suppression of drumming in the Americas over fears that they might rouse slaves and Indigenous peoples to revolt. And it was an inherited blend of disdain for, and exoticization of, the corporeality of the beat which tainted early ethnomusicology and early treatments of African- and African-descended musics so severely that researchers outside of the sciences effectively abandoned sound–body questions for several decades thereafter. Subsequent moves to treat beat and body as 'text' made way for a critical archaeology of those earlier discourses and the racialized essentialisms underpinning them. But as the culturalist stance became normative – quarantining discussion of corporeality and demoting tales of becoming to the status of *mere* discourse – they became insensitive to the cultural life of the sonic body. And in conflating their injunction against biological determinism with a more generalized disbelief in the capacity of biology to participate in culture (except as an object of mediation), they relinquished the means to imagine numinous soundmaking as a bio-aesthetic project.

The problem of such approaches stretched beyond their useful limits is well illustrated by their inability to adequately account for the material agency of thunder in many religious assemblages and their sonic practices. Dozens of thunder gods populate the world's belief systems. And a survey of literatures describing the various types of instruments employed in numinous ceremony reveals a strikingly pervasive tendency among those who use and encounter such devices, whatever their background, to relate the vibratory effects to those of thunder.[17] But the tendency among twentieth-century observers has been to treat these tales of thunderous experience and thunderous instruments in primarily symbolic terms. Among ethnographers of recent decades, this has often meant a highly localized focus and an emphasis on the cultural specificity of any given group's thunder-related discourses. In this model, thunderous tales are treated primarily as symptoms of a situated cultural outlook. This relativist approach is designed, in part, to avoid the sorts of transcendent claims that had tainted earlier work. Tuzin, for example, points to the earlier predominance of psychoanalytic approaches with their readiness to cast social relations the world over in Freudian tropes.[18] But is the reduction to metaphor a sufficient, or even plausible, approach if peoples around the world, and through recorded time, have routinely drawn on thunder to describe varieties of sonic experience and practice? Tuzin takes the position that whatever stories may be devised around it, the fascination with thunder must begin in its materiality, in the catalytic strangeness of thunder as a bodily event.[19] Certainly, before thunder may be said to *represent* the power and majesty of the divine, it simply *is* bodily-felt power.

If we turn attention instead to the materiality of thunder, we are suddenly faced with two important points that representationalist accounts may miss. First, it raises the possibility of thunder as a conceptual catalyst – an opportunity to glimpse possibilities in sound, and to begin intuiting its potential uses. As such, it operates as an invitation to experiment and invent. In this way, thunder would be seen as the inspiration, arriving from nature, for the technological development of bass-making devices. But second, and perhaps more to the point, if it were merely enough to *represent* divine grandeur, there would be many simpler ways to go about it than by attempting to synthesize one of its greatest sonic expressions in nature. The acoustic production of large-scale, low-frequency force is always a tremendous undertaking.

Bells illustrates this well. 'A part of almost every culture in human history', their largest incarnations have been called the heaviest instruments on earth, and the lengths undertaken to cast and hang them have often been phenomenal.[20] Lists of great bells (tower bells and temple bells weighing at least four tonnes) compiled by The Guild of Carillonneurs in North America give a sense of the scale involved: among thirty-seven great bells in the British Isles, there are ten weighing over 20,000 pounds, the largest being 'Great Paul' of St Paul's Cathedral, at over 37,000 pounds; an 'incomplete' list of great bells around Europe describes almost fifty instruments ranging from 20,000 pounds to well over 40,000 pounds; of fifty Russian bells, five weigh more than 100,000 pounds, with the largest at 362,000 and 436,000 pounds, respectively; while among a list of two dozen Asian temple bells, there are seven over 100,000 pounds.[21] The largest of these is Burma's 655,000-pound 'Bell of Dhammazedi', cast in 1484, which was lost before it could be hung, and now sits on a riverbed in Rangoon.[22]

Casting bronze and copper instruments on this scale is difficult enough, but the process of transporting and hanging them is even more laborious. George W. Bird's *Wanderings in Burma* (1897) offers the following on the early life of Burma's 195,000-pound Mingun Bell:

> It was cast on the opposite side of the river, on an island called Nan-dau-kyhn, and was brought over on two boats to the Mingin side. Canals were cut for the passage of the boats to the present site, the mouths of which, after the entrance of the boats, were dammed up. The level of the water in the canals was then raised by partially filling them in, and the bell brought into position between the immense posts and beams which were erected for its support. After the huge beams had been passed through the shackles the dams were removed, the boats subsided, and the bell remained suspended.[23]

Once hung, however, these resonant giants present entirely new sets of problems, as Satis Coleman describes in his 1937 survey *Bells: Their History, Legends, Making, and Uses*:

> It has often been observed that the vibrations of a large bell ringing in a tower can be felt in the masonry near it, and serious accidents have been caused by such vibrations. In 1810 the spire of a church in England fell while

the bells were being rung for morning service, and twenty-three people were killed. In most church towers the bells are hung in a framework which, as far as possible, is kept clear of the walls.[24]

What is unclear in Coleman's account is whether the destruction was an effect of the bell's pendulous motion (if it was in fact swung rather than struck) or the acoustic energy it emitted. Engineering questions aside, however, the ultimate sonic-cultural fact would seem to be that these buildings were imperilled by a collective desire for *heavier* sound.

The pitch of a bell is closely linked to its mass. If the instrument's history seems to suggest ongoing efforts to cast heavier and heavier bells, then this has been primarily in the pursuit of deeper and deeper tones. The deepest of Europe's great bells have pitches in the mid- to upper-bass range, between about 200 Hz and 400 Hz, with Great Paul being the lowest in Britain at 317 Hz (E^b_4).[25] Frequency information relating to other bells can be difficult to locate, but we can make broad inferences about the larger instruments in Russia and Asia from reports which suggest that heavier specimens have pitches nearer 100 Hz and even well below.[26] However, the nominal pitch, or strike note, of a bell can be deceptive. This is literally so, in that the strike note is understood to be a psychoacoustic effect, rather than a physical fact. It is an example of the so-called missing fundamental, a presence–absence effect whereby the ear infers a fundamental pitch from mathematically related harmonics that imply it.[27]

More significant for our purposes, though, is the so-called hum tone. The hum is the lowest of those harmonics, typically one octave below a bell's stated pitch. This means, for example, that Great Paul's lowest tone would be 158.5 Hz (E^b_3), while the 53,350-pound Petersglocke bell in Cologne, with a strike tone of 252 Hz (B_3), would have a hum at around 126 Hz (B_3). Meanwhile, Beijing's 102,000-pound Yong Le Bell is reported to hum at a nearly infrasonic 22 Hz.[28] In practice, the hum is that deeper drone that emerges after the initial strike and lingers long afterwards. It seeps and radiates. It suffuses the things it encounters and occupies them. Its contribution to a numinous assemblage is its ability to materially implicate a collective sonic body in a haunting sensory logic. In this way, the bell's hum can be understood to function as an acoustic membrane, a spectral territory that gathers a collective sonic body in its unusual modulations. As such, the depth of the hum tone is arguably the ultimate measure of a bell's acoustic capabilities.

But beyond these heroic efforts to achieve sheer low-frequency force, bellfounders around the world have also devised many more subtle techniques for shaping bells' spectral characters and operating on human perception. For example, modulatory effects may be systematically elicited or excluded, as a means either of injecting rhythms into bodies or, alternately, smoothing sound so that it persists with an unnatural-seeming degree of tonal steadiness and purity.[29] The latter can be observed in the hums and other lingering tones of European bells, which tend to have a steady quality, without the sort of modulations, known as *beats*, that might indicate imperfections in the instrument's casting. Helmholtz summarizes this concern: 'If a bell is not perfectly symmetrical about its axis, if, for example, the wall is a little thicker at one point of its circumference than at another, it will give, on being struck, two notes of very nearly the same pitch, which will beat together.'[30] A recent dissertation expresses the same concerns in a section labelled 'The Problem of Doublets', warning that 'this warbling spoils the tone of the bell if too pronounced'.[31]

Yet, many Asian bellfounders have actively pursued these very same rhythmic effects, making a minor science of teasing 'warbles' and beat patterns from their instruments. They do this by adding decorations to the exterior design of the bell, thereby introducing minor asymmetries that ever so slightly unbalance an otherwise acoustically 'perfect' bell. This produces doublets – vibratory modes, just out of sync – which will be felt as a slower or faster pulsations, depending on the number of frequencies separating them. Rossing notes, for example, that 'in large Korean bells, the slow beating (typically about 1 Hz) is considered to be a desirable characteristic.'[32] In that instance, then, the effect on a long-lingering hum would be a tremulous fading – about once per second – in and out of perception (auditory, vestibular and otherwise). This means, too, that the decorative dragons and other figures extruding from the walls of these instruments actually perform a vibratory function ahead of any symbolic work, being, quite literally, the metallurgically encoded rhythms of a numinous strategy.

Rossing also points to the use of a *eumtong*, or chimney, in Korean bells, 'which is said to act as a low-pass-filter, favoring (in the case of the King

Seongdeok bell) frequencies below 300 Hz'.[33] At the same time, many such bells also have a 'circular depression in the ground or pavement beneath them, that, together with the volume of the bell and the chimney, at the top, creates a Helmholtz resonator'.[34] Staying with the example of King Seongdeok, we can therefore find at least three components of a vernacular bass strategy, beginning with the enormity of the bell (approximately 38,000 pounds), and continuing in the efforts first to filter away the higher-frequency content of its upper partials, and then to intensify its resonance by extending its interior acoustic space by almost a metre underground. The aim of all of this, as explained by an inscription on the bell itself, is for its 'clear sound [to reverberate] across the country [and] teach without preaching'.[35]

Religious audiogenesis

If bass-making devices are common, even essential, to a large proportion of religious assemblages around the world, it suggests that low-frequency force is widely valued for its capacity to produce religiously useful resonances. The need then arises for greater and more varied attention to the materiality of ritual sound in the study of religious culture. Since the 1980s, anthropologists have made some initial steps in this direction, with a small but growing faction combining interests in sonority and sensation in their work. This varied field includes the 'archaeoacoustic' investigations of Iegor Reznikoff (1987; 2006), Craig Wright's sonorous history of Notre Dame Cathedral (1989), and elements of a broader 'anthropology of the senses', as initiated by David Howes and members of Concordia University's CONSERT working group. Notable, too, is Steven Feld for his introduction, in the mid-1990s, of the concept of acoustemology, or a working relational knowledge of place as derived from sonic experience.[36]

Often forgotten, though, is an idiosyncratic article by Donald Tuzin, published several years before sonic and sensory concerns had properly taken root in the discipline. 'Miraculous Voices: The Auditory Experience of Numinous Objects' (1983) is important not only for its uncommon attention to low-frequency sonic experience, but also (and in some contrast to both the title and the preoccupations of much sonic-cultural scholarship since) for Tuzin's very deliberate shift away from the cochlear, and questions of musical text, representation and mediation. What he describes instead is a complex ecology, textured by confluences of myth, meanings, weather conditions, energy fields, technologies and vernacular techniques, terrain, season, song, the actions of humans and other creatures and so on. Ultimately, though, 'sound is the catalyst', and it leads less by signification than mystification. What Tuzin attempts to understand is how ritually-produced bass might operate as a modulatory strategy, one that posits the sonic body as a transducer, turning weird energy into belief[37]:

> My thesis is that a certain type of naturally occurring sound has a perceptual effect on some, possibly many, animal species that is *intrinsically* mysterious and thus anxiety-arousing; that this sensation is humanly interpreted and its accompanying anxiety cognitively resolved by referring it to the mystery that is allegedly inherent in the supernatural realm; and that certain kinds of ritual sounds capitalize on this iconic resemblance by simultaneously mimicking, as it were, factual and artifactual mystery, thereby summoning the senses to bear witness to the noetic truth of the sound's religious meaning. ... As a frustrated perceptual impulse, this anxiety can be resolved only by attaching it to an object; and if no object can be found, if our perceptual apparatus is not equal to the task, then one must be created. The argument here will be that certain sound stimuli may produce such an experience and that *religious culture stands at the ready, so to speak, to provide an interpretational object*.[38]

Tuzin labels this process the *audiogenesis of religious culture*, in recognition of the sonic body's ontogenetic role. Here, he sounds something like Vic Tandy and David Hufford when each speculated that anomalous perceptual encounters – including an unsettling sense of 'presence' – can leave us grasping for workable explanations, which, even when discomforting, at least provide something of a contingency plan – that is, an operative reality. Tuzin similarly depicts a catalytic moment – a spectral unhoming – but one that is (a) purposely engineered and (b) meant to be 'answered' by religious reasoning. Answered but not captured (that is, depleted through mediation): its charge still resides in a certain ineffability, an escape of affect. Its evidential force, and capacity to produce and sustain belief, lies less in what can be explained about it, than the degree to which its incorporeal oddness exceeds meaningful words.[39] Audiogenesis works by mystification.

This raises an important question. It can be argued that the production of religious subjects is quite the opposite of a becoming-*other*, tending not towards the molecular (openness to influence), but interiority and Logos (The Word) – that is, the very definition of molarity.[40] If this is the case, then what is the role of low-frequency sound? What of the deterritorializing and catalytic effects that we have thus far attributed to unhomely low-frequency encounters? Is it still relevant to talk of incipient subjectivities in such, apparently, over-determined circumstances? The argument here is not that audiogenesis 'makes' or cements the fully formed and compliant subject of religion, nor that it carries inherent meaning or value. This would be to overestimate sound's abilities and to mistake it for a moral force. Rather, audiogenesis should be considered an ethical-affective strategy and nothing more, pertaining only to material relations and a-signifying forces. Its role is, in fact, to volatize subjectivity, unsettling it and putting it in a strange place, thereby putting it up for grabs and making it available for modulation and channelling by religious culture.[41] In this way, it is a priming of belief through the sonic body. Or perhaps more accurately, it is the production of a bodily-felt belief in *something*; religion's role is to give it a story. This is its contribution to keeping a religious assemblage vital, to re-singularizing belief. But it is also where unpredictability creeps in because sonic experience, however carefully organized, is only ever a condition of possibility. Effects may be predictable within certain parameters, but anomalies, individual variations and the singularities of experience mean that results are never guaranteed. Unhomings can easily take unexpected, even inconvenient, turns; they might reveal sensitives or inspire mystic cults – that is, mutant, and potentially dissident, subjectivities that carry a deterritorializing threat of their own.[42] (This is why warnings against music riling 'the passions', despite their usual resort to moralizing language, are nevertheless worth investigating for potential neuro-affective insights.) For these reasons, audiogenetic strategy has often lived in uneasy tension with normative religiosity.[43] The challenge for the organizers of religious culture is therefore to find a compromise between the spectral and the molar in what will always be an unbalancing call-and-response.

Numinous sound design

As a concept, audiogenesis can be likened to what Massumi passingly labelled 'synaesthetic ontongenesis', or mixed-up sensations as an incitement to becomings-in-thought.[44] In 'Miraculous Voices', Tuzin's focus is, ostensibly, ritual 'musical' practice among the Ilahita Arapesh, of Sepik, Papua New Guinea. Yet, his account is more notable for its attention to sound's extra-musical functions, as a generator of acoustemic distortions, synthetic entities (animals, deities) and ontogenetically rich psychosensory effects. Following his depiction, we may in fact find it more relevant to speak of 'sound design' among the Arapesh as they employ techniques and tools devised for the purpose of fashioning a sonic-spatial environment. Their apparent function is to temporarily reshape lived reality, producing an experiential milieu that is conducive to the modulation of belief. In other words, it is the acoustic synthesis of an operative reality – with bass as its driver. As he puts it, 'the sounds we do not hear can potentially evoke a feeling which, by virtue of its inexplicable character, we are taught to construe as "religious." ... this feeling and this reality are objectively one and the same within us and ... it is the system of religious ideas which arguably forms the response'.[45]

Tuzin outlines various types of instruments employed to this end by members of a secret men's cult among the Arapesh. This includes drums, slit gongs, panpipes, flutes and trumpets used for partly-representational purposes. Some are modified, using techniques known only to the cult members, to 'impersonate' the voices of spirits. Others are used to mimic various types of birds, which perform an especially important role in Arapesh cosmology, as itinerant entities whose travels put them in contact with both the human and spirit worlds. Important among these are cassowaries, which, despite being among the largest birds on earth, lead a relatively secretive life, preferring to lurk out of view in the dense vegetation. Their presence is felt, however, in the shape of their low, booming call, with its fundamental tone of about 23 Hz.[46] The sounds of the cassowary, therefore, operate in that liminal zone of human audition where tonal and directional perception break down, and ubiquity effects can bloom. This adds a curious inflection to the Sepik sound world: the moving modulations of an invisible sentience, the unhoming tones of a familiar but unpredictable presence. And this is just one part of the acoustic environment that Arapesh sound technologies are built to engage. Of the animal-like instruments in general, some are said to be quite faithful imitations, while others are described as less 'realistic' in more or less subtle ways.[47] But this lack of fidelity may be quite intentional and appropriate if, rather than considering the latter a failed copy or an impressionistic representation, we think of it as a tactic for de-realizing the sonic environment – not pure hallucination, but an unhoming of the norm, or difference-in-similarity. In this way, we can understand these instruments as carefully tuned tools for confounding ingrained perceptual habits by selectively magnifying or blurring elements of everyday sonic experience.

Driving the event, however, is another class of devices that remains closely guarded by the all-male secret society. 'Designed to mystify', they work through the sonic body, flooding acoustic space with low-frequency force, and triggering various sorts of perceptual anomalies, including powerful feelings of presence-absence. 'These sounds are so weirdly disturbing, so arresting in the local auditory environment that one is sorely tempted to agree with believers who maintain, against all reason, *including their own*, that they are not of this world.'[48] The sources of these sounds are a whirling aerophone-type instrument (essentially a wooden slat at the end of a length of cord) called a bullroarer (or 'thunderstick') and a collection of 'large amplifier pipes', which, together, produce a disorienting low-frequency din. The bullroarer's contribution is a slow-beating drone layered with the rougher timbres of wind coursing over the airborne slat. The sound swirls and envelops, its pitch rising and falling with the rate of rotation. Spun at high speeds the bullroarer acquires a 'piercing, eerie' quality, while at a relatively slow 1-2 cycles per second it takes the character of 'a loud pulsating growl', almost respiratory in its ebbing and swells.[49] At these speeds, the fundamental pitch slides through the synaesthetically rich range of 20–150 Hz, teasing the limits of an auditory apparatus straining to keep up. Added to the throb of the bullroarers is the drone of the powerful amplifier pipes, described as bamboo tubes about 13 feet in length and inserted into large 'hourglass'-shaped drums.[50] Each is powerful in its own right, but Tuzin describes events in which twenty to thirty of the amplifiers are used together to startling effect. 'To liken it to that of a pipe organ would not do it justice, for combined with the organ-like majesty of the sound, there is a barely distinct (better, subliminally felt) presence of a chillingly immense, almost human *voice*.'[51]

The combined output of the bullroarers and amplifying pipes is said to 'generate an experience so unusual as to validate belief in the supernatural.' Here, Tuzin draws on research into the perceptual effects of low-frequency sound, particularly its capacity to produce experiential anomalies, altered mental states and vestibular effects associated with feelings of movement, weight and buoyancy.[52] And closely echoing our discussion of infrasonic hauntings, he argues that central among these unhoming effects is a bewildering perception of presence-absence, a sense that there is more here than meets the ear. This leads him to believe that 'we are dealing, then, with the possibility that certain sounds – perhaps, most crucially, those which are not "heard" in the usual sense – affect the brain in a manner that arouses feelings of the uncanny, the preternatural, *deja vu, jamais vu,* and other mysteries commonly indicative of "religious experience"'. He likens the incipience of such moments to those 'verge of mind' experiences, described by William James in his *Varieties of Religious Experience,* concluding that 'the mysteriousness of the experience is inherent in the fact that its source lies just beyond the working of our psychosensory apparatus – just beyond, as James said about the allied mystery of music, 'the operations of our understanding'.[53] Again, we come back to the mystifying perception of affect's escape.

If the Arapesh claim that the bullroarers 'speak' might be considered a complication of this view, Tuzin warns against reductive 'readings'. The source of the comparison is the bullroarer's ability to approximate certain of the phonetic envelopes, or formants, that are used in human speech (specifically the production of vowel sounds). Through a linguistic coincidence, and the careful manipulation of the bullroarer in flight, the player can shape the sound in such a way as to draw from it the Arapesh words 'Ai tembi- tembineiii' ('I am a great, great man'). Rising as it does through the deep vibrations, it gives the impression of being spoken *through* the collective sonorous body.[54] But Tuzin says that, for him, learning the words did not somehow deplete the singularity of the experience:

Thereafter, I was able to 'hear' what the 'voice' was saying, but this only shifted my perception from utter bewilderment (expressed in the startle reaction 'What in the world is that?') to taut ambiguity: the message was now clear, but the medium retained an undiminished aura of wonder and mystery, especially when heard during the jungle night.[55]

Wary of any effort to reduce this linguistic coincidence to social construction, or recuperation of materiality by the symbolic, Tuzin is quick to point out that these sounds 'do not pretend to imitate *anything* – natural or supernatural'. To the Arapesh, 'Quite simply, their productions *are* the cult spirits.' This is to say that a particular quality of sound energy, produced by the instruments, and known in the first place through thunder, is recognized to be one and the same with the spirits. To conjure it is to conjure them, as such.

Finally, if Tuzin provides a starting point for investigating uses of low-frequency sound in numinous assemblages, then he also hints at how we might also open the discussion to account for the spaces of ritual sound, along with the machinic relations and vernacular practices that emerge therein. This is broached through his discussion of thunderstorms and their possible role, even exploitation, in Arapesh sonic practice. Storms are very common to the rain forests of Papua New Guinea, becoming especially violent and incessant during the wet season, leaving many people 'uneasy, some actually frightened' (again, it is helpful to remember that habituation and sensitization are not mutually exclusive). However, these conditions also make it impossible to perform most ritual activities, which are instead saved for the dry season. For a portion of that time, he observes, the 'spectacular light displays' of faraway storms can still be seen along the southern horizon. Interestingly, these spectral storms coincide precisely with the ritual nights of the secret men's society. 'At these times, Sepik is literally bathed in infrasonic waves of very great intensity – greater in their effects than actual thunderstorms, since they are free of the mask of audible concussions and distracting winds and rain.' This leads Tuzin to suspect that this is no coincidence, but rather an alliance, actively forged between sonic-spatial strategy and atmospheric–electrical activity.[56] This is plausible, if we admit research that suggests a link between far-off storms and road accidents, or less specifically (and less contentiously), documented links between infrasound exposure and effects on cognition, wakefulness and psycho-motor skills.[57] In any case, if calm-before-the-storm effects are indeed exploited by Arapesh affect engineers, it is 'little wonder that when Nggwal is at hand, [according to] informants, you cannot mistake the feeling of his presence'.[58]

Playing the resonances

The space of ritual sound is the central concern of archaeoacoustics, which proponents describe as a subset of an emerging 'archaeology of the senses'.[59] Archaeoacoustic investigators argue that the sounds of past cultures have been too readily given up for lost, following the logic that, even where evidence of musical instruments would seem to exist in the archaeological record, we have no way of knowing what sorts of tunes they produced, nor what cultural meanings were attached to them (nor, for that matter, if they were even designed for music making at all; perhaps the resemblance to known instruments is merely a coincidence). Similarly, they note that the musical prehistory of the voice has also been neglected under the assumption of its archaeological invisibility. What archaeoacoustics aims to do is piece together the sonorous conditions of the past, if not its musical 'texts', traditions or meanings. This requires new investigative methods. Cautiously assuming that surviving instruments carry little intrinsic information about prehistoric sonic culture, archaeoacoustics aims instead to discover the acoustic relationality of ritual spaces, looking for evidence of intent and engineering in the material features of ritual sites and, where possible, in the traces of human activity found therein. At its worst, archaeoacoustics can tread too closely to New Age pseudoscience.[60] At its best, however, it is rigorously speculative, acknowledging the impossibility of proving intents and uses beyond question, at such a distance, but arguing for more inventive efforts to deduce what we can, while providing a necessary supplement to overextended ocular-symbolic models.[61]

Foundational to the field are a series of investigations conducted by Iegor Reznikoff in ten French caves well known for their prehistoric paintings.[62] Through extensive spectral analysis of these sites, Reznikoff found a recurring coincidence between acoustic characteristics and the placement of wall art, with paintings tending to cluster in those parts of a cave complex where strong resonances could be found. 'In the cave of Niaux in Ariège', he notes, for example, 'most of the remarkable paintings are situated in the resonant Salon Noir, which sounds like a Romanesque chapel'.[63] Not only does this pattern suggest a ritual interest in the phenomenon of resonance, he says, but also the possibility that palaeolithic visitors to these caverns had devised techniques for finding their most excitable recesses and putting them to use. By the same token, it also means that the paintings may have performed functions beyond the ocular and the symbolic.

Still more striking, however, was Reznikoff's explanation of small red dots that have been found in remote, cramped and less accessible parts of the caves, and for which no symbolic function has ever been established. Through exhaustive acoustic measurements and blind trials, his team was able to find an overwhelming correlation between the locations of dots and points of maximum resonance in the caves. The results of repeated tests were unequivocal, all but ruling out coincidence, and pointing strongly to prehistoric purpose and intent.[64] This has led Reznikoff to conclude, beyond a doubt, that the markings were intended as acoustic sign posts for early humans using the caves. As sonic instructions, they carry a 'sound-resonant meaning' for anyone seeking to elicit the strongest acoustic response possible from the caverns. He argues that the discovery of these points must have been an entirely inductive process, not a matter of ancient acoustic theory, but more or less blind exploration of a sonorous topology. Humming might have been used 'as a kind of sonar', using the reflections of the dark cave – mottled here, clearer and stronger over there – to gauge the unseen spaces that lay around them. Indeed, this is how Reznikoff proceeded, noting the pull of those most excitable spots: 'Reaching the location of maximum resonance (the acoustical main antinode) is very impressive', he writes, 'the whole tunnel resonates to a simple *hm* and the sound can be heard outside the tunnel, in the main cave.'[65]

By establishing sonic experience as a material–spatial concern, Reznikoff's work undoes the assumption of sound's fleeting immateriality. And by recognizing it to be inseparable from the acoustics of specific sites, he puts it within the purview of the archaeological record. This means that, where those sites still exist, visitors can encounter the same sorts of material-energetic conditions that prevailed there millennia ago. Time and cultural distance may render formal and symbolic details of prehistoric music inaccessible, but archaeoacoustics foregrounds *sonority* – the relationality of acoustic space – rather than music proper. In this way, it can be said to have an ethico-acoustic orientation at its core.

Tellurian organs

Half-buried, and sometimes lost for millennia, megalithic mound structures are a proto-architectural link between the cave and latter-day temples. As such, they also represent a pivotal moment in ethico-acoustic thought: an elaboration of the exploratory ethic described above (unearthing and eliciting odd sonorities in the natural world) towards strategies for organizing acoustic space and channelling sonic experience.[66] Following Reznikoff, a number of archaeoacoustic studies have examined those purpose-built structures that would seem to translate the ritual importance of unusual vibration into vernacular construction practices.[67] This includes a pair of investigations (Jahn, Devereux and Ibison 1996; Watson and Keating 1999) into the remarkable acoustic features of prehistoric earthworks – cairns and passage tombs – that can be found, bulging just below the surface, across the British Isles.[68] From the outside, the more discreet mounds are easily mistaken for naturally occurring hills, a single, stone-lined entrance being the only clue to the hol(e)y space inside.[69] The earthen portion of these structures may be nondescriptly round and sloped, but it harbours an arrangement of megaliths that divides the burrow into two very distinct regions: a wide central chamber (often branching into several sub-chambers), and a much narrower entrance passage of some length. While these sites, and their geometric engravings, have long been of interest to archaeologists, those investigations have typically followed the lead of cave studies that proceed mainly along ocular-representational lines. This despite the strikingly odd sonic ecologies often found inside.

When wind blows across the entranceway, or a voice inside hits just the right pitch, a mound may begin to *hum*. In fact, many mounds are deeply resonant structures, and spectral analysis has confirmed what acousticians had already guessed from their bottle-like shape: the ancient tombs are effectively giant Helmholtz resonators. They are bass-making devices on a massive scale, and the similarities between them suggest this is more a product of numinous strategy than structural coincidence. In 1996, Robert G. Jahn, Paul Devereux and Michael Ibison published a study of six earthworks across Britain and Ireland, noting that 'although many shapes and sizes of chambers were presented', the dominant resonant frequencies of these far-flung sites all clustered firmly in the bass range, spanning 95–120 Hz, with four of them at or near 110 Hz.[70] Significantly, this is within the peak range for vestibular effects, meaning that discordant perceptions of motion and balance could be expected to occur.[71] The authors themselves suggest that these frequencies were perhaps favoured because the male voice can 'generate a relatively high intensity in this range, and the human ear can detect it sensitively and comfortably.'[72] However, they also point out that this 'is not a range that contributes to speech intelligibility to any extent.'[73] This is to say that if there is an acoustic strategy at work in the mounds – as in the cave and the cathedral – it would seem to be one concerned with qualities of vibration rather than content of speech.[74] Were language or the representational functions of song the priority, we would expect these obviously engineered auditory environments to dampen sound in the service of communicative clarity. Instead, we find the opposite – a throbbing hollow, tuned below the registers of meaningful speech. As an acoustic space it is highly excitable but, as Jahn et al. note, it also shows evidence of careful attention to sound's shape and movement. Referring to the mound at Newgrange, Ireland, they say: 'Equally if not more remarkable' than the resonance effect itself, 'was the pattern of standing waves sustained along the entire length of the entrance passage ... with 12 antinode/node pairs', produced in the reflections between precisely oriented stones, and 'extending over its full length from chamber to outside entrance in a classic sinusoidal pattern akin to that of some gigantic wind instrument.'[75]

Somewhat more speculatively, a follow-up study by Aaron Watson and David Keating also raised the possibility of using the structures to produce powerful infrasound. Their survey of eight earthworks in Scotland, Ireland and Wales, revealed strongly defined resonant modes ranging from 1 to 7 Hz.[76]

These frequencies are well below the range of the human voice and the tones of musical instruments, but the authors propose two other potential sources. One is wind as it passes across the passage entrance. Infrasonic wind effects could certainly add a haunting quality to the space, but they might be too irregular to be of ritual use. The other suggestion is that these frequencies may have been synthesized by drummers, who could have learnt to synchronize their tempo to the number of cycles per second required to elicit Helmholtz resonance in a given space (e.g. a 4 Hz resonance could be excited by drumming at four beats per second, or 240 beats per minute). The process would have been an inductive one, with performers learning to follow the resonances, developing an awareness of the tombs' lowest resonant modes and their potentials for interaction. Whether the frequencies produced would be neurophysiologically perceptible is still a matter of debate in the infrasound literature. However, it is quite reasonable to imagine infrasound being exploited for its ability to exert strong modulatory effects on higher-frequency content (song and chant, for example) in the acoustic space, working much like a low-frequency oscillator (LFO) in an analogue synthesizer.

Striking as they can be, however, these powerful resonances are far from the only sound effects to be found in these megalithic earthworks. Bass, it would seem, was meant to participate in, and perhaps drive, a project of sonic-sensory de-realization (itself part of a still larger project of ritual affect engineering). As Watson and Keating describe, a mound's interior acoustic space may be textured by unpredictable echoes, 'microtonal disturbances' and strange modulatory effects caused by arrangements of stone, the movement of bodies and interactions between sounds. Sounds are transmitted in curious ways around the chamber and along the passageway. They may 'unexpectedly intensify, change in pitch, and develop vibrato', while voices may become so distorted as to develop 'extraordinary harmonics'. Exploration of the space will often reveal distinct acoustic regions where standing waves are trapped or very localized harmonic mixtures occur. In some spots, even tilting one's head can produce arresting shifts in volume and tonal mixtures. Altogether, this leads the authors to conclude that 'these places may not have been simply a technology for producing visual and acoustic experiences, but a means of creating different worlds altogether'.[77]

The organ-church assemblage

Much the same could be said of the alliance, between the organ and the church, since the Middle Ages. In combination, the pair represents perhaps the most sustained, and highly elaborated example, of sonic and spatial practices co-functioning in audiogenetic strategy. Their shared history is one and the same with the spread of Christianity through Europe, the return of musical and intellectual life to the West after the Dark Ages and developments in science and technology (no less than alchemy and magic) that would both trouble the church and drive development of an instrument that would eventually become its greatest sonic advocate.

The organ has been described as 'a complex synthesizer, not an electronic synthesizer, but an acoustic one'[78] capable of spanning almost the entire range of human hearing, but always measured by its largest bass pipe (often called the Principal) from which the rest are scaled. In its presence, one is readily struck by the realization that this ancient machine has been designed as much to project physical force as to emit musical notes. In fact, one of its most common pre-Christian uses was in the amphitheatres of Greece and Rome, producing music and sound effects as accompaniment to gladiatorial combat, its role being 'not so much to please the unexacting crowd as to accentuate the rhythm of the various movements of the combatants'.[79] According to one account, these early organs would have been 'fitted mainly with heavy reed pipes capable of filling the arena with their music [and they] likely struck up some martial air' to whip up the crowd during the last throes of a battle.[80]

From the outset, the instrument was associated with harnessing power and experimenting with the physicality of sound. The first organ – the water-driven *hydraulis* – was, in practice, the laboratory through which Ktesibios of Alexandria (ca. 285–222 BC) worked out the principles of hydraulics, the science of water pressure (while his wife, Thais, became the world's first organist).[81] Philo of Byzantium (ca. 280–220 BC), and then Hero of Alexandria (ca. 10–70 AD), turned sound into a material concern when they discarded the classical concept of *the void* and theorized air as a substance (composed of molecules, in latter's description). This founded the study of pneumatics, and led Hero to propose a bellows-driven organ, which was elaborated by Vitruvius, and later became the model for the massive, wind-driven instruments that began to spread through Europe in late Middle Ages.[82] Throughout this history, the preoccupation with sonic force only seems to have increased. Efforts to devise more powerful organs, and harness ever greater quantities of wind pressure, were ongoing. The result was certainly greater volume but, even more so, deeper bass, as it is only the lowest frequencies that require such tremendous pressure. On this, Jean Perrot has written: 'It is remarkable that the history of the organ, starting from the high-pitched syrinx, has seen a steady extension of sound towards the lower register until, by the end of the Middle Ages, the compass reached four octaves below middle C [i.e. 16 Hz] on the 32 foot pipes.'[83]

The evocative names bestowed on the machines' largest pipes are indicative of this bass-reverence. They also give clues to their sonic character and hint at the extramusical functions envisioned for them: Subbass, Infrabass, Sub-Octave and Grossunterbass all pertain to a sound region *below* bass; Untersatz loosely translates from German to mean 'under the text'; (Gros) Bourdon – derived from 'Bourdonner', meaning to buzz, hum or drone – is a name shared with great bells. Others, like the ominously named Bombarde – a 16' reed stop, kept in isolation because of its disturbing vibratory effects on the other pipes – carry a more sonic fictional tinge in-keeping with the air of mystery that surrounded the organ for centuries.

The Arcanum: an ambulant myth-science

The early history of the organ is also one of migration, passage into myth and hyperstitional return. It disappeared from the West, along with instrumental music and so much of intellectual life in general, after the fall of the Roman Empire, becoming 'completely forgotten' by the eighth century (by which time Gregorian chant had emerged and the meanings of *organum* had become diffuse).[84] Organ building is said to have spent the Dark Ages 'hibernat[ing] outside Europe', being preserved by artisans, scholars and players in Byzantium. And it was a gift from Byzantium to Pepin, in 751 that marked the machine's 'dramatic re-entry' into the West, making it an important symbol of the revival of art and learning in the Carolingian period. At the same time, the organ's reappearance, after centuries of absence, was also steeped in mystery and hermeticism. Its legend had been conflated with stories of other mythic devices, like Muristus' hydraulic siren, said to have been used in war, and audible for sixty miles, with 'a loud and terrifying sound, so violent as to tear at the hearts of its hearers' who required ear protection lest they 'swoon or lose their hearing'.[85] These tales arguably drove the rapid fascination with the organ in the Middle Ages, and teased builders into drawing evermore improbable mutations out of a technology that had remained largely unchanged through much of the previous millennium.

More broadly, though, this was also the period during which classical texts, along with the works of Islamic scholars, were beginning to trickle, and later flood, back into Europe from the East, where they had been translated and preserved. This included many hundreds of what came to be known as 'books of secrets' – long 'lost' works of ancient philosophy and experimental science, as well as alchemical texts that compiled artisanal techniques (e.g. metallurgy, glass staining and ceramics), medicinal recipes and other forms of 'practical magic'. Vitruvius' *De Architectura* was among these, as were Philo and Hero's theorizations of pneumatics, and fragmentary translations on the hydraulis that may have been derived from Ktesibios' own writings.[86] On the their arrival in the West, these texts were treated variously as the 'wisdom of the ancients' and the esoteric knowledge of Eastern magi. They were understood to reveal the secrets of nature, along with occult techniques for its manipulation, and they were held securely in monastic workshops where they became foundational to the eventual emergence of modern science.[87] This was the intellectual climate into which the Byzantine monk Georgius ventured in the ninth century, when he became the first organ builder to visit Europe in five centuries. Georgius' students spread across the continent in the following decades, establishing a network of organ-building centres and helping to initiate an alliance between the machine and an often suspicious church hierarchy.

As the esoteric preserve of wandering monks, early European organ building was quite literally an ambulant, or nomad, science. It is very close to what Deleuze and Guattari had in mind in their theorization of nomadology, and their identification of an itinerant mode (of which the metallurgist is exemplary) that works by contingent, or operative, logics and shuttles between disorderly smooth space and the striation of the State. Certainly Georgius, his colleagues and his descendants were itinerants many times over: between East and West; between the church and Islamic scholarship; between monastic outposts in a still Darkened Europe; between performer and technician (for centuries, the builders of organs were often their players[88]); and between the disciplines of mathematics, metalworking, woodworking, music, pneumatics, architecture and theology. They also participated in the deterritorialization of scholastic, or 'Royal', science (astronomy, optics, mechanics, medicine), by the emerging experimental sciences (e.g. chemistry, magnetism, electricity and metallurgy), whose empirical pursuit of nature's secrets was perpetually exposing the limits of theorematic knowledge.[89] This was the germinal moment of both modern engineering and empirical science, but it is important to remember that for the authors of *secreta,* as for their readers, ' "empirical" meant both "derived from experience" and magical.'[90] William Eamon writes that the contemporaneous 'distinction between the two kinds of knowledge was essentially that between *scientia* and *magia*, the knowledge of the cause of natural phenomena, and magic, consisting of techniques by which nature is controlled, manipulated, and made to serve human ends.' If we look past the alchemist's boasts of mastery over nature, then practical magic begins to look very much like what we have called a minor science of testing relations in nature, creating *problem-events* (experiments, encounters), and devising techniques for catalysing becomings (in biological systems, inorganic materials, etc.).

Following the flow of materiality and conjuring something from it: this is the other essential feature of the itinerant mode, the mode of the alchemist and the artisan. In Deleuze and Guattari, it is the metallurgist, networked with prospectors and merchants, who works the ore, extracts the metal, melts it down, stirs the alloy, forges it, quenches it and so forth. In Massumi, it is the woodworker, covering ground, locating suitable material (*content*), following its grain and giving it shape (*expression*) through the application of technique (*force*). For the organ-builder, the task is to follow the flow of sonic materiality, pursuing qualities of sound (pressures, vibrations, mixtures, resonances, reflections) and shaping them for the audiogenetic project. This is what is meant by *The Arcanum*, a term that recurs widely in the literature to describe the 'deep, secret wisdom' that constituted the 'art and science' of organ building, scaling and voicing. The Arcanum can generally be understood to describe the mixture of theorematic knowledge and intuited detours that defined the builder's relationship to a machine that is, itself, mystifying in both its technical complexity and its sonorous effects.

The practice of pipe-scaling speaks to this well. On one level it is a relatively straightforwards undertaking, in that one begins from the Principal and scales upward according to Monochord ratios, whereby the physical length of a resonant body is halved to produce a tone one octave higher.[91] Following this 2:1 ratio, a 32-foot pipe produces a tone a C_0 (16 Hz), while a pipe half that length will produce C_1 (32 Hz) and so on. Other harmonic intervals are produced by following similarly simple physical ratios. But, in practice, that process is deeply complicated by factors as diverse as the singular features of a given acoustic space and the whims of the local climate (and made more so by the advent of equal temperament). As Poul-Gerhad Andersen says, we know much about vibrating metal and resonance in tubes, 'But concerning the interaction of all of these details, vast numbers of additional factors assert themselves, and theory becomes hopelessly inadequate for any additional applications.'[92] This is true even of the more specialized elements of the craft. For example, the architectural–acoustic question of bass management is so perplexing in itself that a 'well-known organ theorist' describes a formula 'so complicated that it was already unsuitable for any practical purpose'. For Andersen, then, it becomes clear that the sonic body performs the crucial itinerant function in organ building, being the affective vector through which all other factors pass. For him, 'the secret, the "Arcanum", was the organ builder himself.'[93]

Elsewhere, though, The Arcanum seems to have referred to very specific techniques. And again, bass experience was a central concern. By the time Georg Andreas Sorge published *The Secretly Kept Art of the Scaling of Organ Pipes*, in 1764, books of secrets had lost much of their mystery, being closer in status to popular science and how-to texts, while the 'secrets' themselves were increasingly being formalized as industrial patents.[94] Sorge doesn't reveal his secrets in the text (which operates, in part, as an advertisement for his services). But he is known, along with Romieu and the violinist/composer Tartini, for discovering the phenomenon of combination tones – also known as Tartini pitch, the missing fundamental, or the phantom fundamental – whereby a pair of higher frequencies combine to create the psychoacoustic perception of a harmonically related, lower pitch.[95] Augoyard and Torgue liken it to a 'sonic hologram',[96] the inverse of the present–absent effects described above, because it exploits a cochlear curiosity to elicit the perception of low-frequency vibration where it may not physically exist (leaving many still-unanswered questions regarding cognitive response, in the form of intermodal anticipation of, and neurophysiological adjustment to, illusory vibration).[97] Histories of acoustic science have noted that these effects 'were soon well recognized by organ builders' who could offer the perception of deeper bass to those who lacked the space or money for larger ranks (or those who simply wanted to further bolster the perceived force of already large instruments). This was achieved, 'for example, by using two organ pipes, one 16 ft sounding C_1 ($f = 32$ Hz) and another of 10 ft 8 in. sounding G_1 ($f = 48$ Hz), the (difference or) combination tone resulting from sounding them together is C_0 ($f = 16$ Hz), which can otherwise only be obtained from a much larger, 32-ft single pipe.'[98] If, as Perrot says, the history of the organ to modern times has been one of steady extension to the lowest registers, then Sorge and others managed to extend it even further, finding still another route along which imagination could be made to resonate with anomalous perception. For his part, Tartini spent much of his life experimenting with the technique in composition, claiming it had been revealed to him in a dream by Satan.[99] Perhaps fittingly, it has since been adapted for use in sonic weapons systems.[100]

The nervous organ

And if you desire to torment your listeners until their spirit is softened and their body grows weak, then open the holes of the upper pipes on all three skins (those of the high notes) and those of lower pipes on the three skins (those of the low notes), that is to say the stoppers M, F, Sh, X,R, Kh. Then you will see something marvelous, for this complex effect is alien to man's temperament, since, hearing it, a man does not grasp what we have just described.

–Muristus[101]

Early European reactions to the organ varied. Some complained of the 'loud bursts which may be heard from far off' and the violence of 'organs, in which a bellows is tortured into belching forth blasts of air.'[102] Others weighed personal distaste against the machines' mystical value: 'I do not delight in the organ's modulations ... [but] organs are a good thing, if we regard them as mysteries and derive from them a spiritual harmony.'[103] Among the most widely repeated accounts to have survived from the Middle Ages is a poem by the monk Wulstan describing a tenth-century organ at Winchester, an instrument so monstrously noisy that one contemporary mockingly claimed it was 'audible at five miles, offensive at two, and lethal at one.'[104] It took two organists to play this unwieldy machine, and because it had no stops with which to regulate and direct the flow of air, the instrument simply blew all of its pipes at once in an inharmonious roar, leading later chroniclers to conclude that whatever its role in church ceremony, 'such an organ could scarcely be used to accompany the singing.'[105] Wulstan writes:

> *Above, twelve bellows are set in a row;*
> *While fourteen lie below.*
> *Their alternating blasts supply vast quantities of wind,*
> *Worked by the might of seventy strong men,*
> *Labouring with their arms, running with sweat,*
> *Each urging his companions to force the wind up*
> *With all his strength, filling*
> *The wind-chest's vast cavity that it may rumble ...*
> *Like thunder, the strident voice assails the ear,*
> *Shutting out all other sounds than its own[106];*
> *Such are its reverberations, echoing here and there,*
> *That each man lifts his hands to stop his ears,*
> *Unable as he draws near to tolerate the roaring*
> *of so many different and noisy combinations.*
> *The music of the pipes is heard throughout the town,*
> *And their winged fame goes forth through the land.*[107]

Wulstan describes the enormous effort that went into operating this mammoth, and musically hopeless, instrument which, he says, required dozens of men to pump its bellows. Some writers have been quick to dismiss Wulstan's claims about the scale and sound of the Winchester organ, but there are historians of the instrument who argue that it should be taken more or less at face value. There was, after all, a near-contemporary machine of comparable size, at St Sepulchre-without-Newgate in London.[108] And while the reference to seventy blowers working the bellows might be easy to read as poetic licence, it has also been called entirely plausible 'if we imagine that there were a number of men in reserve to take the place of those exhausted by the labour at the twenty-six feeders.'[109] Consider, for example, the organ at Nicolai Church, Leipzig, which, until 1890, required a team of four acrobatic men to pump the bellows: 'Each man ran up a little staircase ... and jumped on to one of the levers, which slowly fell with his weight',[110] repeating the cycle continuously until the music ceased.

Andersen similarly warns against treating Wulstan's account as an exaggeration, arguing that it is in 'perfect agreement' with reports of other provisional medieval European organs and the monstrous sounds they emitted. With so many blowers 'competing to produce the highest possible wind pressure', he notes, 'the result [would have been] a tremendous noise and nothing more. The stability of the wind pressure and tuning would be thrown into absolute chaos by that type of bellows operation.'[111] For comparison, he points to a steam-driven hydraulic organ ('*aqua calefactae violentia*') built in Rheims in the tenth century, and those described by Praetorius, notably a large one at Halberstadt. The latter, Williams argues, would have been 'typical of the organs in most cathedrals in the fourteenth century'.[112] With a 32-foot Principal, an Octave 16' and two Octave 8' pipes, its sound was described by Praetorius as a 'deep rough roaring and horrible grumbling ... an extremely violent sound ... an atrocious screaming'.[113] Little wonder, as the act of playing the instrument was almost as violent as the turbulent air within, its large keys 'requir[ing] great force on the part of the pulsator organorum ("striker of the organs")' who 'played with the clenched fist or the elbows'.[114] Then there is the twelfth-century account of St Aelred, then the Abbot at Rivaulx Abbey, Yorkshire. Aelred's broadside sums up the complaints of those members of the clergy who wondered just what liturgical purpose the organ was supposed to serve. However inadvertently, though, his description also hints at an answer:

> During all of this [distorted singing] the people, standing trembling and speechless, are amazed by the throb of the bellows ..., the jingling of the little bells ..., the harmony of the flue pipes ... . It is as though the crowd had assembled, not in a place of worship, but in a theatre, not to pray, but to witness a spectacle.[115]

In the end, the Abbot asks: 'What use, pray, is this terrifying blast from the bellows that is better suited to imitate the noise of thunder than the sweetness of the human voice?'

'What use?' is the question. There is a tendency in parts of the literature to treat these devices as failed instruments or, more generously, as primitive (and overblown) renditions of a technology still centuries away from its full realization. Wulstan's poem, for example, has been widely repeated, but it is often treated as a curiosity of little practical significance. This view is inevitable if traditionally conceived 'musicality' is the primary concern, with accurate reproduction of a musical text understood as the organ's singular function, and the history of the instrument treated as a progression towards this ideal. But why build larger and larger machines, involving greater amounts of uncontainable wind pressure, if musicality were the only concern? Craig M. Wright has suggested that, even as late as the fourteenth century, the organ was valued more for its extramusical functions than for the quality of the music it produced. 'Clearly,' he says, 'the very sound of the organ *per se* was far more important than musical style or idea. The power, brilliance, and, to a great extent, the mechanical capability of the instrument reduced intrinsic musical worth, as judged by the standards of plainsong, to a secondary consideration.'[116]

It would seem reasonable, then, to suggest that these early machines served another purpose quite effectively, if fear, bodily unhomings and even pain were considered important components of the religious event. That is, we gain a different perspective on the early organ if we consider its audiogenetic function, its role in catalysing religiously useful becomings, transducing energy into belief and briefly reshaping ritual space. In that case, we might adapt Julian Henriques' term 'sonic dominance' to describe the condition it engenders, not so much to indicate the displacement of the visual by the sonic, but to describe a sonically-led, and violently intermodal, overfilling of experience.[117] Its dynamic is not so simply defined as one of power and subjugation, but, closer to Henriques' vision of the Jamaican dancehall, a collective submission to the sort of shattering encounter that works to open people up and keep belief vital. Moreover, as it boomed and rumbled beyond the walls of the church, the monstrous organ would have had a partially exteriorizing effect, turning the Christian ritual space into a seeping, pulsating membrane. Less subtle than the hum of a great bell, it would radiate a force that needn't stand for anything because it was felt so unmistakably in the body. In the same way, and paralleling the sonic conditions of other ritual environs already described, it would also have confronted non-participants and non-believers – those not in the church but in its proximity, permeated by its modulations – with a striking perceptual encounter combined with the promise/threat of something altogether more transformative 'inside'.

Attempting to imagine the organ's sonorous relations in the medieval Christian assemblage requires us to draw what information we can from disparate sources. This might seem an especially difficult task, as medieval religious culture and its music are typically understood to have 'spurned' or 'despised' the corporeal. This is summed up by St Augustine's oft-repeated ideal of a music 'free of all body' (*De musica librisex*) and his assertion that music is ultimately a 'science of measuring well'. In this respect, Augustine is symbolic of the hold that the Monochord, understood to reveal the divine mathematics of Creation (the Music of the Spheres), had over the Western imagination for centuries. Yet, in *Music, Body, and Desire in Medieval Culture*, Bruce Holsinger has provocatively argued that the body was hardly ignored by medieval thinkers. In fact, it was a matter of obsession, looming largely in texts from the era, but also figuring centrally in music-led pedagogy, through which it was physically targeted. 'Music and bodily violence coexisted intimately in the religious cultures of the middle ages, so much so that in many cases music *is* violence for all practical purposes.' Violence, he argues, was at the root of the development of church song, Gregorian plainchant, for example, having once been inseparable from the threat of 'Gregory's whip'.[118] The beatings of choir boys, self-flagellation by the devout, the terrorization of the congregants by all available means – all were a pedagogical reality for several centuries, but one 'that many Christian writers [sought] to deny or conceal'. This contradiction is quite evident in the immensely influential writings of St Augustine, yet most accounts and surveys of Western aesthetics avoid it, focusing on 'his vision of the beauty residing in number, proportion, and measure.'[119] If anything, he says, recent scholarship has actually exacerbated this tendency by over-emphasizing textuality and medieval mathematical concerns.[120]

In contrast, Holsinger finds in St Augustine, as in Gregory of Nyssia, a strong if uneasy belief that music offers a more direct route to God than text possibly could, because it works through the body, directly. The unique capacities of sound to touch and move the body were seen as a necessary addition to pedagogy and liturgy, doing what words and images could not. And so it is in this sense, in *City of God* 22, that an ageing and less cautious Augustine imagines musical sonority as '"tumultuous," "seething," a Christian weapon that achieves a stark material agency as it penetrates a human body and wages an inner battle against a possessing demon.'[121] Holsinger's project aims to reveal this countercurrent of bodily thought as it participated in music and religiosity of the period. To this end, his 'musicology of the flesh' searches for sonorous, material clues in writing as well as art. (Important to this undertaking is a recognition of the twofold medieval usage of 'flesh', meaning a meaty body on the one hand, but also bodily *tendency*. That is, nature not as fixity, but in its inherent mutability). Holsinger argues that this necessitates a different approach to metaphor, as the term is commonly, and rather reductively, used to describe accounts of bodily experience. Rather than treating these tales as pure fiction or construction, they should be 'culled for that residual kernel of bodily practice and material circumstance.'[122] This includes a re-examination of the grisly depiction in medieval art and writing of 'the musical body in pain', conceived not-so-figuratively as a quivering instrument that could be dissected by sound, its various parts turned into pipes and drums, its sinews plucked.[123] In other words: a spectral body, a resonant assemblage, the body as acoustic event.

A glimpse into how this might be translated into ethico-acoustic strategy appears in the writings of Notker Balbus, a ninth-century Benedictine monk at St Gall, who compiled a set of instructions for the performance of his order's book of chants. For Holsinger, the notes give a rare sense of the *sonority* of the musical event, something almost entirely missed by musicological approaches that focus only on 'the work', in the abstract. Notker's sonorous instructions

– each one represented by a letter of the alphabet which could be added at any point in a score – would seem to have been conceived, at least in part, with a view towards the disturbing. Reprinted in McGee's *The Sound of Medieval Song*, it contains the following guidelines:

> 'F' furiously demands that the note shall be begun with a harsh sound or the sound of gnashing teeth.
>
> 'G' genuinely grants that a note is to be gargled gradually in the throat.
>
> 'H' heralds that one aspirates on the note itself in the manner that one does when pronouncing this letter.
>
> 'I' indicates a lowering of the sound with the heaviness of the letter 'g'.[124]

Elsewhere, the letter 'K' called for a 'ringing sound' and 's' stood for 'sibilance'. 'When Notker explains the letters accompanying the notation of chant from St Gall,' says Holsinger, 'he is instructing his readers – medieval and contemporary – in the effective deployment of the body in chant.'[125] We can imagine that, were these instructions carried out, the effect would have been quite removed from the pleasant sheen of most contemporary Gregorian chant recordings. Taken to its least pleasant conclusions, it could have been closer to the rather more nightmarish vocal performances of the monk-cloaked doom/drone metal band Sunn o))): low, droning, guttural and pained.[126] Finally, and perhaps significantly, it is worth noting that Balbus was also known as Notker the Stammerer, leaving us to wonder whether a life of observing others' reactions to the troubled sonorities of his own speech might have influenced his affective programme.

Taken on their own, Notker's instructions might be seen as a curiosity specific to a localized version of plainchant. But these extramusical guidelines actually had a much wider influence, becoming 'an integral part of the singing style' around Europe.[127] McGee notes that, although opinions of appropriate performances practices varied widely, numerous manuscripts up to the twelfth century 'use these expressive letters rather liberally.'[128] Notker's instructions therefore stand as an early effort to systematize techniques of affect engineering. Moreover, their wide influence, and the apparent readiness with which they were accepted in many quarters, further reinforces the idea that music and religion were allied in a project of developing and intensifying belief through the sonic body. What, if any influence, these developments in plainchant may have had on ideas about the organ is still largely a matter of mystery. (Curiously, Holsinger is among those who dismiss Wulstan's poem as hyperbole, and a passing reference to Winchester is the book's only mention of the instrument.) Certainly, the roughly built organs of the era were incapable of the subtle modulations of mood imagined by Notker, but this would change over the coming centuries. In time, it would begin performing a far more varied role in liturgical practices, as they themselves made a transition from the outward brutalism of the Middle Ages, towards a new emphasis on God's radiant beauty, and the seduction of belief via the senses.

Baroque affect engineering

The organ-church assemblage is not a stable one. If medieval audiogenetic strategies were characterized by an alliance between blunt sonic force and pedagogical violence, their early-modern articulations arose from newly emerging tendencies that cut across religious culture, musical practice and the emerging sciences. For its part, the organ evolved rapidly during this period, assuming a form familiar to contemporary ears by the end of the Renaissance, and nearing the peak of its pre-industrial size and technical sophistication by the end of the Baroque. Its sound had become far less noisy and more refined thanks to improved construction techniques and materials; more efficient pneumatic systems delivered greater air pressure with less leakage, while developments in pipe-scaling and voicing honed their tonal and timbral qualities. Better keyboard mechanisms and the gradual inclusion of more, and more varied, ranks offered finer control over a greater complexity of tones. Range was increased too, as increasingly commonplace 16- and 32-foot pedalwerks, combined with the wind chests necessary to drive them, continued the steady push towards lower tones in organ design, performance and composition. These machines were capable of more delicate operation and subtler effects, offering greater control over the lowest frequencies, which could now be more artfully modulated. As organs became more refined, the idea of pummelling the sonic body into submission was giving way to something altogether more spectral, inspiring visions of more precisely orchestrated bio-aesthetic strategies than had previously been possible. Moreover, while medieval and classical approaches purported to deny the body, and the Renaissance placed a new emphasis on musical text, the Baroque saw a new emphasis on sonority and perception in an explicit effort to control nature in the service of God. 'It was now the listener and not the text that had become the object of the composition.'[129]

In Germany, this took the form *Musica Poetica* (*Affektenlehre*), or music-rhetorical techniques for religious edification. Commonly known as the *Doctrine of the Affections*, it was a specifically Lutheran approach to sonorous affect engineering.[130] Contrary to the Reformation's reputation for hostility towards music (of which the destruction of organs is iconic), Luther himself was a strong advocate of music in the church and he derided those who argued otherwise. For him, 'God was the author and source of the natural phenomenon of sound, including the world of tones' and he embraced the 'affective and formative power' of music. 'The act of hearing music, of listening to ordered sound', he argued, 'is to resonate with Creation' (Creation being understood as a condition of ongoing genesis rather than something fixed in the past).[131]

It is important to note that 'affect', used in this context, does not carry quite the same connotations as it does in Spinoza(-Deleuze), but nor is it closer to that modern tendency to make affect a synonym for individual emotion or a socialized 'structure of feeling'.[132] It is instead a curious mixture of the two: moralizing and qualified, but by Creation rather than culture, allowing it to also be pre-personal and exteriorized. Bartel cautions that 'the subjective expression of a personal sentiment or feeling, so familiar to us through a nineteenth-century aesthetic, is quite foreign to this understanding of music. The intended affection remains an objectively conceptualized state of mind.'[133] Indeed, it was against the humanist tendency to regard music as a product of individual self-expression that Luther envisioned a means of sonic communion through direct, pre-personal and material impingement on the body. It is in this sense that German theorists of the affections conceived music as an 'active agent' and an 'ethical force', and that we can call *Affektenlehre* an ethico-aesthetic project. The aim was to sonically induce and modulate collective states of being with sound. If a systematic knowledge of these sound–body relations could be compiled, it was reasoned, then it could be strategically deployed in composition. In theory, the Doctrine's rationalist and idealist tendencies lead to a circumscribing conception of affect, imagining for it only a limited spectrum of already known and neatly separated categories, each mechanistically linked to particular qualities of sound and, therefore, obviating questions of affective escape. Yet, in practice, there was also always a strong empirical component to the project and, in this respect, *Affektenlehre* can indeed be called a minor science of the sonic body. In aiming to produce affective resonances in more or less predictable ways, it relied on a repertoire of techniques intuited, accumulated and developed over time.[134] Further, its teachers also advocated that composers train themselves in the close observation of human behaviour, emphasizing that particular attention be paid to the relational patterns through which various responses could be elicited, and that thought be given to the means by which this responsiveness might be intensified and varied. These observations were to be interpreted through theory and then applied in composition. All of this, said Johann Mattheson, was 'calculated in cold blood'.[135]

Many of *Musica Poetica*'s theorists were organists and cantors and they advised their contemporaries to commit 'all available resources' to the project of edification.[136] As in other religious cultures, this often meant more power and more bass – a fact reflected in the Baroque emphasis on the lower registers, in both musical composition and the technical aspects organ building and installation. This priority is perhaps most evident in the near universal use, in Baroque music, of *basso continuo* structures, whereby compositions are built upward from a strong, consistent bassline which forms the foundation of the music. Played on the organ in a large church, the effect can be one of body-humming envelopment, as the long waves of the lowest pipes unfold and accumulate in space, slowly building into an undulating presence that lingers long after each note is struck. The importance of the low end is also evident in the technological demands of the organist-composers of the era. Both Buxtehude and Bach are known to have worked as consultants on the construction of new organs and the renovation of old ones to bring them in line with these requirements. Andersen notes Bach's especially detailed suggestions for the organ at Blasiuskirche in Mühlhausen, which included the addition of a Posaune 16' and a stopped Untersatz 32' to the pedalwerk (to give it 'dignity'), along with an enlargement of the bellows, and the careful examination and reconstruction of the wind chest. The latter was meant to dramatically increase the force of the organ, while also increasing its precision by carefully regulating the flow of air, in part to allow for more forceful *tutti*, or full organ, effects, in which all stops are opened to produce a tremendous roar. Similar demands were being voiced by organists and composers throughout Northern Germany and Northern Europe in the decades after the Thirty Years War as organ construction resumed. Among the most prolific builders of the era was Arp Schnitger who, over the space of forty years, supplied nearly 150 organs said to be characterized by their 'deep and impressive' sound.[137]

The influence of this audiogenetic moment was profound, and we can trace it well beyond the affective strategies of early Protestantism. In Catholic regions, the Counter Reformation responded with its own appeals to the senses. In part, this involved a minor trend towards a more total vision of sonic design, with organs incorporating various automata and sound effects. This included mechanical drums and *vogelsang* (birdsong) effects, as well as efforts to simulate human voices (*vox humana*) and thunder, the latter through dissonant combinations of larger pipes.[138] *Birds, Bells & Thunder* is the fitting title of an album documenting the massive and peculiar Gabler organ at the Benedictine Abbey in Weingarten, with its battery of 16- and 32-foot pipes.[139] According to Andersen, its 'tremendous mixture "roar" [is] the most characteristic quality of this organ.'[140] Even two centuries later, the bass-favouring approach of the Baroque continued to influence developments, most dramatically in Britain, where organ building had lagged well behind the Continent since the Civil War, when nearly all of its organs were destroyed. According to myth, this all changed with Mendelssohn's visit to the Victorian Court, when 'he had to explain that he could not play Bach nor his own compositions on most of the English organs, and for a very good reason – they had no pedal werk.' The response was frenzied: 'After that, it seems as if all resources were concentrated on creating not only pedal werk, but an organ type corresponding to the authority and power of the Empire.'[141] Indeed across Europe, in the nineteenth century, there was a concerted effort to bring reason, advances in acoustic science and the tools of industrialization to bear on the practice of organ building. The latest machines were larger and engineered with a new precision to be more efficient and, therefore, even more powerful. Bass pipes proliferated. Later, the bombast of the nineteenth-century instruments would be combined with the older sound effect technologies in the massive Wurlitzer organs of the silent film era (while their players – cinema's first sound designers – were provided with performance manuals derived from *Affektenlehr*[142]).

But during this time, church organists and many builders began to raise concerns about the direction of the craft. In the preceding decades, inherited methods rooted in experience and intuition (i.e. *The Arcanum*) had been 'violently attacked'. The efforts to rationalize the machine had led to a belief that 'now the standards of excellence had been scientifically established, and consequently there was no reason either to think or hear any more. ... There was nothing else to be done except making shapes according to' formulae and diagrams.[143] But the difference was audible, becoming such a concern by 1926 that the Freiburg Organ Congress was organized to determine whether organ builders should rely strictly on ' "sacred numbers" in calculating organ scales' or be given 'the full freedom of their "artistic intuition" '.[144] This was an early moment in what became the Organ Reform Movement, which ultimately took the Baroque organ, with its intuitive foundations, and all of its tonal and structural idiosyncrasies, as its ideal. In other words, the hold of Royal Science over organ building lasted for just over a century out of the instrument's 2300-year history.

The Gothic assemblage: applied synaesthetics

It would be difficult to overestimate the marvel of the Gothic assemblage in late-Medieval and early-Modern Europe: stone turned sinuous, shaped into sky-piercing spires and light-filled lattices; liturgical strategies aimed at overfilling the senses while promising transmutation, communion with a higher order and ascent to a higher existence. In its vision and scale, Gothic was a project for which we have no contemporary parallel, outside perhaps the imagined scenarios of science fiction. Hundreds of churches were built across Europe at phenomenal cost, and construction times were typically measured in centuries. This makes any simple periodization of Gothic difficult, particularly in relation to the organ's own Gothic period. Many churches begun in the late-Middle Ages would have been completed during, or not long before, the period when organs were assuming more or less modern form, size and capabilities.[145] By this time, the lighter, thinner-sounding Gothic organ was becoming obsolete in many parts of Europe, giving way to more powerful Baroque organs and their successors. Indeed, Perrot speculates that it was the enormous scale of Gothic architecture that forced organ builders to devise instruments which were 'more complex, more sonorous', and more capable of filling the church with suitably impressive sound.[146] If the acoustic space of the church drew more out of the organ, organ builders responded by attempting to exploit church acoustics to their fullest.

More than an architectural style or a holy aesthetic, what Robert A. Scott calls 'the Gothic Enterprise' was a melding of materiality and belief aimed at cultivating divine energy itself.[147] It was a myth-science in many respects, its methods combining Christian and Classical doctrines with alchemical science and vernacular techniques of sensory mystification, working in combination to serve God and to create conditions conducive to belief. Its aim was to embody Heaven on Earth – the building conceived as a 'vector' drawing divinity Earthward and projecting believers Heavenward.[148] Georges Duby has called the Gothic church a 'monument to applied theology',[149] a distillation of divine mathematical harmony (*musica universalis*), of which music (*musica instrumentalis*) was considered its highest human expression, and architecture a concrete application thereof. To this end, the 2:1 octave ratio of the Monochord 'permeates the entire edifice', becoming the 'genetic code' that determines every material–spatial relationship therein (and, more pragmatically, driving the iterative construction process as it unfolded – literally on faith – in the absence of comprehensive blueprints or sophisticated equations).[150] In this way, the church was understood as an 'image' of heaven, but Scott notes a very different usage of the term: 'To us an image is a visual representation of an object that inherently entails our personal interpretation and perspective.' The Medieval theological view was very different, not symbolic, but referring to actual presence and embodiment.[151] It was understood that sacredness could be acquired by material objects, that it would imbue them and radiate from them. And, so went the fear, it could also be depleted and lost. There was a strong sense, then, that every means should be harnessed to preserve and regenerate this numinous energy.

However, while God's presence might be invited by pleasing ratios, it could only acquire evidential force through the senses, and Gothic affect engineering used myriad tactics of mystification 'not only to accommodate a divine presence, but to heighten the impression that the divine was indeed there.' The entire assemblage was designed for affective modulation, as widespread illiteracy required 'a kind of involvement which strongly emphasized the sensorial aspects. Visual art, the solemnity of rites, and the enveloping character of the music all contributed to achieve this aim.'[152] Following the classical ordering of the senses, medieval theologians considered light the most noble natural phenomenon, its radiant immateriality making it 'the medium par excellence through which physical objects became capable of revealing their divine properties.'[153] Light was, therefore, a central concern of Gothic architects as they set out to replace the dark and heavyset Romanesque church with a new, internal luminosity made possible by a skeletal structure of soaring vaults and external supports.[154] The exterior was considered mere 'backstage' support for the sensory conditions of the interior, where space was opened and walls replaced by vast windows which had the effect of 'subtracting mass and giving the impression of weightlessness'.[155] This was the de-realizing effect of the architecture itself. As Scott says, it was important to 'make the task *seem* more difficult than it actually was, to create the illusion that the building itself defied the laws of nature and had come about through an act of magic. One of the defining qualities of the Gothic style is that it made the doable seem impossible.' One favoured technique was to make stone seem to float, while the relatively new technology of stained glass would have intensified the unreal the luminous conditions. Scott notes that, while many windows have since been replaced with uncoloured glass, the originals were single-toned, usually in deep, primary colours. The mixtures they produced would have divided the internal space of the church into rich and distinct zones of unnaturally tinted light.[156] Not just an ocular effect, however, this would have worked in alliance with the massive buildings' unique sonorous textures – their 'long reverberation times and poor speech intelligibility ... melting timbres and envelopment of sound'.[157] With their extended naves, Gothic churches, more than any other, gave the lowest frequencies ample space to mix and accumulate, allowing each note to hang in the air for as much as ten seconds, or more, after being struck. The result was a reverberant haze that could mingle with the tonal play of the weirdly luminous interior.

If these techniques were meant to unsteady and blur the senses, others were more directional and propulsive, seemingly aimed at turning low-gravity illusions into an operative reality of bodily motion. 'Thrust' is a term commonly used to describe the trajectories of the Gothic church, with its flying buttresses and soaring vaults. Deleuze and Guattari write that while 'Gothic architecture is indeed inseparable from a will to build churches longer and taller than the Romanesque churches ...

> the difference is a not simply quantitative; it marks a qualitative change: the static relation, form-matter, tends to fade to the background in favor of a dynamic relation, material-forces. It is the cutting of the stone that turns it into material capable of holding and coordinating forces of thrust, and of constructing even higher and longer vaults. The vault is no longer a form but a line of continuous variation of the stones. It is as if Gothic conquered a smooth space, while Romanesque remained partially within a striated space.[158]

The implication is that stone, turned projectile, is less a formal ideal than a trajectory of becoming (of stone, of engineering, of perception, of belief), producing a church that 'escapes itself' under the influence of an invisible attractor. There is an unmistakable skyward tendency about Gothic – a vertiginous pull that draws the visitor inward and up – and everything about the interior space, including the sonorous engine at its core, is oriented towards an ultimate flight.

We need to ask, then, what more the organ might have contributed to the affective strategies of the Gothic project. If the aim of Gothic was to produce transmutational encounters, this certainly would have been amplified by an instrument that could flood church space with low-frequency force, touch bodily and structural resonances, and spark presences across the sensorium. But if thrust was a central concern of the Gothic assemblage, then we have to consider still another important sonic effect – the non-auditory stimulation of the vestibular system – in greater detail. The vestibular system is that portion of the inner ear which has no direct role in audition but through which we derive our sense of motion and spatial orientation (the posterior and superior canals sensing rotation, the otoliths sensing linear acceleration). It adjusts muscular responses to help control balance and posture, and it works with the eye to maintain focus on a fixed point while a body is in motion (known as the vestibulo-ocular reflex).[159] Because it is a bilateral system, it can also be thrown out of balance when overstimulation of one ear puts the pair in disagreement. This can result in nystagmus effects, beginning with the eyes' slow drift away from the overstimulated side, followed by rapid saccadic vibration as focus oscillates between two points. More profound inner ear disturbances include vertigo and Meniere's disease.[160]

We have already noted that frequencies within the bass range are especially likely to elicit vestibular feelings of buoyancy, weightlessness, heaviness and movement in an otherwise still body. And it has been suggested several times that we might be able to infer vestibular collusion from the audiogenetic strategies of various groups. Gierke and Nixon speak strongly to the inner ear's capacity to unhome, suggesting that these can be among the more startling effects of exposure to low-frequency sound, noticeable even at fairly low amplitudes, and capable at higher levels, of producing disorientation, nausea and disrupted balance.[161] A more recent study, measuring sound-induced head acceleration and ocular-vestibular muscle responses (oVEMP), has suggested that the frequencies of about 100 Hz are most capable of exciting those effects in humans (with the still very prominent effects noted at 50 Hz). Elsewhere, neuroscientists have suggested that the unsteadying effects of inner ear disruptions are a major factor in the enjoyment of loud, amplified concerts ('the rock effect') and bass-heavy nightclub musics even more so.[162] Crucially, they cite the vestibular role in producing 'sensations of *self-motion*', that is to say, self-variation with a sense of directional thrust. If sound has a role in none-too-figurative feelings of 'being moved', then its potential religious applications become obvious.[163] In *Neurophysiological Bases of God Beliefs*, Michael Persinger writes: 'Few people appear to acknowledge the role of vestibular sensations in the God Experience. However, in light of the temporal lobe's role in sensation of balance and movement, these experiences are expected.' Reading 'literature concerned with the God Experiences' for tales and traces, he finds them 'full of metaphors describing essential vestibular inputs. Sensations of "being lifted," "feeling light," or even "spinning, like being intoxicated," are common. A more general experience is flying or leaving the body.'[164]

In every respect, the Gothic church is a promise of ascent. It's all lightness and thrust – the same sorts of feelings that an organ so aptly induces in the vestibular system with the right modulations of force in the lower registers. So we should reasonably be able to speculate on the apparently prominent place of the inner ear in liturgical strategy, especially in an assemblage where speech intelligibility was, for centuries, subordinated to reverberant envelopment, and the organ was valued more for it sonorous-affective functions than its musical abilities.[165] If stories of flight to an alternate plane were woven with levitational sensations and the feeling of 'becoming alien' to oneself, then we may have another version of what Eshun called 'abduction by audio'. For Eshun, abduction described the mnemonic-affective tangents of sample-based dance musics, recombining words and atmospheres (felt places) from cinematic sources as a means of drawing bodily imagination into discordant new environs ('You're abducted into this world, distributed along its dimensions – but this world leans into yours.'[166]). For us, abduction describes entry into a logic of sensation – that of the 'vestibular organ' (the pipe organ and the inner ear to the extent that they comprise a bio-technological machine). The felt-reality of this sonorous relation is *actual motion*, the body becoming ever-so-slightly ethereal and glimpsing ascent; not full-blown flight, obviously, just a tilting of bodily imagination in the direction of flight, feeling it on the horizon of potential. It is a catalytic moment, however small, and swarms of these moments can accrue evidential force. Experienced in a group, these perceptual tilts can catalyse a collective audiogenesis. Not simply the mediation of experience by belief, but the modulation of belief by sound – it is the sort of material encounter with another reality that makes, and keeps, the idea of the numinous credible, and gives meaning to words.

Tone Scientists I: Vibratory Arts

Patently, art does not have a monopoly on creation, but it takes its capacity to invent mutant coordinates to extremes: it engenders unprecedented, unforeseen and unthinkable qualities of being. The decisive threshold constituting this new aesthetic paradigm lies in the aptitude of these processes of creation to auto-affirm themselves as existential nuclei, autopoietic machines.[1]

If low-frequency strategies and tools were long the monopoly of religious cultures, then recent times have seen a vernacularization of the means of mystification. Tools and strategies for producing unusual sonic milieus have proliferated, while gradually becoming more portable and accessible. The concert hall and the cinema have been two important sites of expanded sonic experimentation, as have various modes of art practice since the advent of amplification and electronic recording and sound generation. The following takes up the latter to examine experiments of recent decades that specifically investigate the autopoietic potentials of low-frequency sonic experience. In many ways, such projects are extensions of the mix of nomad science and sonic fiction that pervades many religious cultures' sonic practices, but in this secular context the emphasis shifts. It is still a matter of audiogenesis, but instead of becomings-other being channelled in religiously useful ways, now they are investigated in their own right, pushed to new intensities and elaborated into uncertain existential territories. They ask: *what more* can a sonic body do? The following identifies three broad tendencies in modern, low-frequency sonic practice, labelling them *Cymatic Art*, *Perceptual Abstraction* and *Incipient Dance*.

Wherever possible, the voices of the artists themselves figure prominently. This follows Deleuze's argument (echoed by Eshun) that we don't listen closely enough to artists and what they have to tell us about the world.[2] The point is not that we should treat these utterances as definitive, but rather to engage them as theoretical orientations in their own right (inherently different from, but no less valid than, those of philosophy and science) and as opportunities for further invention. Pervading many of the statements collected here is an interest in probing the inherent provisionality of the sonic body (individual and collective), the ways it can be unhomed and remade through its encounters. There is, therefore, an emphasis on the emergence of new subjectivities through vibratory experience. What these bodily reorganizations also reveal, however, is the somewhat arbitrary grouping of arts by sensory modality. There is an argument to be made that certain, seemingly disparate, practices (e.g. one visual, one sonic) may share more in common with each other, as strategies of affect engineering, than they do with formally kindred works. What emerges then is a transversal conception of art practices that finds vibratory tendencies cutting across notionally distinct creative fields. Similarly, when we start to consider all the synaesthetic dimensions, and potential transductions, of vibratory phenomena, then the parameters of 'sound art' begin to dissolve.

Cymatic arts

A German animated short called *Das Rad* follows a day in the life of two piles of rock overlooking a valley. Clouds whirl rapidly in the grey-blue sky. Vegetation swarms over terrain. Lichen darts over the rock companions, collecting in spots that are hard to scratch: 'Awww, Nein! Just when the Ice Age is over, you're happy, the sun is out ... whack they're back again.' When human life appears, it moves so quickly – picked up only as faint blurs by the camera – that Hew and Kew can perceive it only in its material traces (wooden huts, a mud road, waste). Only during a brief interlude, when the shutter speed shifts to a biological pace, does the viewer glimpse human forms toiling at a familiar speed, the rocks now inert. Back to geologic time: Hew and Kew watch a sudden burst of activity with apprehension. The sky darkens, vegetation evaporates and the huts are devoured by a wave of concrete and glass that hurtles towards the pair in a matter of seconds. Then, a pause, the lights go out, and it all comes crashing down. Human time is over. The rocks exhale. Vegetation sweeps in again and the pair return to lichen-grooming.

Spanning a geologic age in eight minutes, *Das Rad* plays with relative speeds in order to glimpse an inhuman temporality and the 'life' of seemingly inanimate matter.[3] In this way, it can be called an experiment in non-anthropocentric art, as it seeks to nudge human sensibilities towards a pathic grasp of things alien to them. A similar encounter, reached from the opposite direction, can be found in a promotional video for Fluke Corporation, which specializes in tools for visualizing and measuring industrial vibration.[4] The video shows the striking of a cymbal, shot at 1,000 frames per second, and stretched to nearly a minute and a half.[5] What it reveals, in extreme slow motion, is a momentary liquefaction of the metal. In the immediate aftermath, the once rigid disc looks more like a jellyfish in rough water, seesawing slowly in space while internal waves deform its now flaccid surface. So while *Das Rad* finds long rhythms in compressed time, the Fluke videos find micro-rhythms in stretched time. We could, therefore, say that each aims to render visible an order of periodicity that would otherwise remain imperceptible, even as it participates in the rhythms of lived experience. For this reason, we can say that the two videos share a *cymatic* orientation.

First proposed by Hans Jenny in 1965, cymatics is the study of periodic systems in nature. It takes its name from the Greek *ta kymatika,* meaning 'matters pertaining to waves'.[6] The classic cymatic experiment involves a speaker cone, laid horizontally, connected to a tone generator, and filled with a non-Newtonian fluid – that is, a liquid that becomes more viscous, even approaching solidity, when agitated. (A cornstarch and water mixture is the preferred medium, but paint, gelatin, custard and blood have similar properties.) When a signal is passed through the transducer at a high enough volume, waveforms begin to take visible shape in the tremulous goop; different frequencies produce different geometric patterns, often of uncanny complexity and symmetry. These are the same sorts of patterns revealed by Chladni, and then Helmholtz, when they used violin bows to induce vibration in panes of glass coated lightly with sand, but there are important differences.[7] Chladni's 'figures' could only ever be frozen moments of vibration – a captured image of sound. The fast-fading energy from the bow made it impossible to observe variation over time.

In this way, the static shapes thus produced fed a conception of the acoustic wave primarily as a form, more than something kinetic and relational.

Cymatics, on the other hand, adopts a more *figural* orientation, made possible by the tone generator's capacity for continuous signal output and frequency variation.[8] This meant that processes of transformation and intermodulation could now be observed. By altering the frequency and shape (sine, square, saw, etc.) of the signal, the experimenter could bring about ever-shifting streams of modal patterns in the energized liquid (a visible, material expression of the kaleidoscope geometries first predicted by the Monochord). This is the same phenomenon that can be observed in water when a cup is vibrated, but the slowness and higher surface tension of a non-Newtonian fluid produces something more properly three-dimensional and less fleeting. 'Sculptural shapes are actually formed', says Jenny. 'It sometimes seems as if one is vouchsafed a glimpse into the origins of Baroque.'[9] Equally, or more striking is what happens when the speaker is overdriven and the fluid's tension-limit is strained. Now, the orderly geometries dissolve into a chaotic sloshing, through which new shapes begin to emerge. The congealing liquid whirls and tumbles over itself, and uncanny, golem-like forms rise, morph, dissolve back into it: 'the mass flows up into the figurines, circulates, flows down, pulsates. But the shape of the figurine persists in spite of the turnover of material.'[10] These cymatic figures are provisional bodies, (de)formed in, and danced by, vibration. Watching them, one might begin wonder: 'me too?'

Cymatics is often called the study of visible sound. But in conceiving 'a general cymatics in the widest sense', Jenny's project encompassed the full breadth of vibratory systems in nature, from the molecular to the cosmic.[11] This includes wave activity of all sorts – electromagnetic, liquid, acoustic, seismic – but also many, less obvious periodic systems. In living creatures, it means observing the systole/diastole of the heart, the cycles of respiration, serial nervous impulses and so on. Cymatic processes can also be observed in the growth of geometric structures: the lattice patterns of vegetable tissues; galactic spirals; the crystalline growth of minerals.[12] For Jenny, the sea was 'cymatics in its native element', but by slowing perception, he argued, we can observe similar dynamics at work in orogeny, or mountain-formation (i.e. deep-time rhythms in the geologic sea).[13] However, he also argued that the concern should never be limited to the waves themselves. The real question is how their effects participate in the vibratory makeup of things, how they intermingle to produce heterogeneous or 'polyperiodic' milieus, across which unforeseen relations might emerge. Contrary to New Age co-optations of cymatics, Jenny never claimed to have discovered a deep, underlying order to the universe.[14] His concerns were closer to those driving the related fields of chaos theory and systems theory, with their shared interest finding organizing patterns in reality's irreducible excess.

Cymatic experiments were designed to at least make visible processes that exceeded measurement or comprehensive description. 'With these selected methods', he said, 'the vibration of complicated bodies can also be rendered visible. The vibrations of structures whose mode of vibration cannot be calculated at all, or only approximately, can in this way be made accessible to experience.'[15] This is the sense in which cymatics sought to 'fertilize perception' and conceptual invention.[16] And this is its connection to arts concerned with vibratory relations and the opening of nature–culture conduits. When Jenny said the goal of cymatics was the 'formation of a perceptive organ sensitive to periodicity', there was an echo of Paul Klee's claim that the role of art is 'not to render the visible, but to render visible' (i.e. not to represent a known thing, but to create a logic of sensation).[17] This is developed further in Deleuze-Bacon, where 'sensation is vibration' and the 'rhythmic unity of the senses can only be discovered by going beyond the organism', towards the spectral, and the body without organs. For them, the questions facing the artists are: 'How to render sensible forces that are not themselves sensible? How to render the nonvisible visible in painting, or the nonsonorous sonorous in music?'[18] For Jenny, speaking to the artist and the philosopher, as much as the scientist, this was always an ambulant project. In proposing cymatics as a methodology, he reminds us that the Greek, *methodos*, means 'to go after', to follow intuitively, rather than being restrained by norms or reason. 'As scientists we cannot taboo the mysteries confronting us and forbid ourselves to investigate them.'[19]

With all of this in mind, I would suggest that any radically empirical project aimed at 'hearing systems in nature' or 'seeing sound' can be collected under the heading of *cymatic arts*. The term is meant to describe work that attempts to follow rhythms in materiality, to make them accessible to experience, and to devise tools (conceptual and technological) capable of plugging into their affects. Cymatic arts may be documentary or speculative. As projects aimed at rendering the insensible sensible, they may work by amplification, transduction, transposition or analogy – whatever works to draw the sonic body into a meaningful modulation. As Jenny himself argued, cymatics is the study of becomings, conceptual and collective, as much as material.[20]

Documentary practices

'The same thing that leads a musician to discover the birds also leads him to discover the elementary and the cosmic.'[21]

A 2002 album review on the BBC Music website cites a recent 'glut of records ... that document the sound of the world doing its own thing in a variety of ways.'[22] In many cases, these recordings piggyback on the tools or 'data' of well-established fields of scientific research, 'so it's by no means obscure', says producer Joe Banks, 'it's just obscure to the general public. Quite often people involved in sciences have no idea that there could be any creative interpretation [of what they discover], by which you could gain any different perspective on the world.'[23] Irdial Disc's *Electric Enigma: The VLF Recordings of Stephen P. McGreevy* is one example of this type of work. It collects recording of 'natural radio' emissions, or energy in the extremely-low-frequency and very-low-frequency (ELF/VLF) radio spectrum that emanate from distant 'lightning storms, aurora (The Northern and Southern Lights), and earth's magnetic field (the magnetosphere).' These waves are not generally considered to be humanly audible, but they become so when picked up by a simple radio receiver.[24] McGreevy's recordings reveal a chaotic ecology of electromagnetic eruptions: 'sferics, chorus, hiss, tweeks', as well as the plunging tones of 'whistlers', the side effects of lightning strikes occurring around the globe. The combined effect is very peculiar – imagine scrolling the shortwave dial and stumbling on the crosstalk between a meteor shower and a synthetic jungle scene (alive with chirps and chatter, sounds like wind and water in the distance).[25]

The same basic principles are behind a series of recordings captured in the 1970s and 1980s by Voyager and other spacecraft, then released some years later by NASA and the Brain/Mind Research label under the titles *Jupiter, Saturn, Saturn's Rings, The Voice of Earth* and so on.[26] According to the liner notes, 'Although space is a virtual vacuum, this does not mean there is no sound in space. Sound does exist as electromagnetic vibrations. The specially designed instruments on board the various space probes used Plasma Wave antenna to record the vibrations used here, all within the range of human hearing.' The droning of the spheres thus collected was first discovered by accident, in the late 1960s, by researchers who 'often played back the microturbulent-wave electric fields recorded by the ISEE and Voyager spacecraft through an ordinary loudspeaker.' What they discovered was that each planet had a different audible character. The gas giants, Jupiter and Saturn, give off dense, reverberent drones – the latter sounds especially coarse, the former like a time-stretched metallic shimmer – while Saturn's rings are lower and quieter, like the sound of massive winds heard from inside a deeply resonant tunnel.[27]

The Voice of Earth presents something altogether more varied. Natural radio effects, recognizable from McGreevy, are here *en masse*, as hundreds of whistlers race through what sounds like a thick, slow-whirling storm, sometimes augmented by vast wind-like washes. These are the transduced sounds of 'interactions of the solar ionic wind ... plasma wave phenomena and ... the Earth's ionosphere and magnetosphere.'[28] Distinct from all of this, though, is a second layer of sound, a very low and ever-present drone. At some points, in the thirty-minute recording, it takes the shape of a steady, sine-like tone which, at high volume, weighs on the body even as it hovers near the edge of audition. Other times, it lilts in pitch, swells in volume and begins to move, as very slow beat patterns emerge. These low cycles are produced by what are known as Schumann resonances, or the resonant frequencies of the earth's magnetic field, with a fundamental near 8 Hz and peaks near 15, 20, 27 and 32 Hz (which, in musical terms, loosely corresponds to an octave series of C_{-1}, C_0 and C_1, supplemented by tones of E_0 and A_0). Like cymatics, Schumann resonances have been widely mythologized in New Age circles, taken as evidence of a transcendent cosmic order, or touted as a source of healing energy. Even the liner notes to the NASA recordings, written by long-time sound therapy advocate Dr Jeffrey Thompson, stray into this territory.[29]

What is important here, however, is how the NASA recording manages to involve the sonic body in a cymatic logic, rendering the otherwise inaccessible sensible. By transducing affects (motion and force events) from one vibratory axis (electromagnetic) onto another (acoustic), at the same frequencies, it affords an inkling of the periodic systems that surround and suffuse us. That is, by turning electromagnetic resonances into acoustic hums and throbs, solar winds into recognizably airy gusts and so on, *The Voice of Earth* gives a glimpse of an intense vibratory world that we inhabit, but which exists largely beyond the senses.

Processes of transduction are also at the core of a number of more recent projects – some more successful than others – that aim to reveal hidden worlds of low-frequency vibration. This includes 'StartEndTime' (2003) Mark Bain's 9/11 seismic data sonification project.[30] Said to capture 'the screamingness of the Earth'[31] during the 2001 terrorist attacks, the audio piece is derived from data streams 'acquired from Columbia University's Geological survey lab

> which run a network of earth monitoring stations in the area; with the closest being 34 km away from the epicenter of the event. A process of data conversion and signal translation was used to make the normally inaudible seismic waveforms both audible and to play back in real-time as the event unfolded. No other processing or effects were added to the tracks. The registration includes four events, two impacts and the two collapses along with the inbetween sounds of the drone of the earth. The heaviest impact of the collapse registered 2.4 on the Richter scale, a signal which travelled throughout the earth.[32]

Bain says the 'work stands not as a memorial per se but as an action of affect, where the global terrain becomes a sounding board, a bell-like alarm denoting histories in the making.' Conceptually similar, but somewhat more arcane, is a 2003 recording called *Infrasound-Tidal*, a peculiar collaboration between American artist John Duncan and Australian acoustic scientist/sound artist Densil Cabrera.[33] The project began in 1998, with Cabrera offering tidal measurement data to members of an online audio discussion list. Duncan 'responded that same day, intrigued to hear how tidal measurements would sound, more than with their value as scientific research.' The end result compresses five years of data into a collection of short audio pieces (low throbs, resonant ringing, airy textures) although Duncan's vague comments about modifying the material and destroying its linearity perhaps suggests its limitations as a properly cymatic investigation.

Closer to that documentary ethic, however, is Felix Hess' *Air Pressure Fluctuations* (2001), which captures airborne vibrations occurring in the range of 0.03 Hz and 56 Hz. 'Almost everything to be heard on this CD was inaudible, literally unheard of, in real time, because it was too low for our ears.' But by speeding up the recordings – compressing 120 hours of material down to just 20 minutes – Hess is able to transpose the subaudible into the sensible range, revealing a busy world of low-frequency wave activity in which the rumblings of urban industry and transportation vibrate together with neighbourhood-level events and global-scale air masses:

> One hears high-pitched whistles, beeps and insect like buzzes, which come from the deep rumblings of factories, trains and trucks and other motor cars, or even nearby washing machines. The opening and closing of doors gives rise to countless tiny clicks, which may add up to form a sound like soft rain on autumn leaves. The dawn of a new day, every four minutes on the CD, is marked by an upsurge of whistles and clicks: the world wakes up! Sonic booms of supersonic airplanes sound like thick paper being crumpled. The wind's turbulence causes localized pressure fluctuations, sometimes of overwhelming power; it seems fractal-like, and hardly sounds like stereo, left and right are nearly unrelated [as microphones were place 64 metres apart]. Finally, depending on the weather situation at large, an extraordinary presence may appear: a humming sound or a rich, deep drone, audible like a multi-engined heavy airplane in the distance. This deep droning sound, at times all but inaudible, is formed by oscillations in the atmosphere – microbaroms – caused by standing water waves on the Atlantic Ocean, far away.[34]

A largely unheard ecology of everyday vibration is thus brought within the range of the ear, and the sonic body more broadly. As a macro-level rendering of unsound events, it reveals rhythms of regularity and difference that would otherwise evade perception. 'The sensation of hearing the CD is deeply strange', writes David Toop, 'like being buffeted by a high wind and at the same time hearing the extreme high frequency activity of neural processing.'[35]

A speculative turn

At *BLDGBLOG,* architect and theorist Geoff Manaugh imagines prowling around London 'armed with contact microphones'. 'You could listen through headphones to the foundational moaning of old buildings, plugged directly in, the whole city an instrument of arches and railway viaducts, Tube tunnels and old churches, gravitational pressures.' One would hear '[t]he unsettling groan of wet masonry. Like the creaking timbers of an old ship – or like an iceberg: a landscape under strain, singing all but inaudible music.'[36] Later, he suggests:

> You could drill contact microphones into the surface of Greenland and listen to that terrestrial baritone, the ice a reverberatory – such a strange and haunting sound, like bells shattering, of pure ice hearing beneath your feet, caves and tunnels realigning along audio slip-faults. Someday perhaps we'll eavesdrop on breaking glaciers from within.[37]

In fact, a 2005 article in *National Geographic* describes nearly that in recordings that capture the 'singing' of an iceberg, discovered when researchers in the Antarctic found unexpected 'acoustic noise' in their seismic measurements.[38] What they heard was the sound of an iceberg scraping across an underwater escarpment for sixteen hours, causing tremors in the monolith, as high-pressure water was forced through the cracks and tunnels that traversed its interior. The original recording contains a fundamental frequency well below audition – near 0.5 Hz with a large amount of harmonic content – but a sped-up version (available on the *Science Magazine* website) reveals something described by the researchers as 'partly melodic, but not really melodic like singing, more like the screeching of a horror film in parts.'[39] The speed (and, therefore, the relatively high pitch) of this version seems to have been arbitrarily chosen by the researchers, but a curious coincidence emerges when the .Wav file is brought closer to the pace of the original in an audio editor. Slowed by eighty per cent, it bears a striking resemblance to the speculative drone work of German artist Thomas Köner, whose triptych of polar-themed releases (*Nunatak Gongamur* 1990; *Teimo* 1992; *Permafrost* 1993) takes Robert Scott's failed Antarctic expedition as a conceptual start point in an effort to imagine sub-zero relations between the biological and the mineral, human temporality and the long rhythms of geologic time.

Köner is easily grouped with other contemporary sound artists and musicians working largely with low frequencies in the overlapping areas of drone composition, environmental audio and what has come to be known as dark ambient (often bass-heavy, often linked with industrial music). Prominent in the field is Sweden's BJ Nilsen whose 'environmental' work under the name Hazard might be compared to Köner's in a number of ways: both explore relations between sound, terrain and natural forces; both foreground the role of bodily-felt vibration; and both are constructed from fragments of studio-processed source material. But on this last question, there is an important point of divergence. Hazard's *Wind*, for example, is built largely from recordings of turbulent air captured by collaborator Chris Watson (BBC sound recordist and former member of the industrial band Cabaret Voltaire); *Wood* 'is the sound of trees rustling in the wind, sticks and branches crackling and snapping apart', etc.[40] However, Hazard's work ultimately keeps nature at a something of a remove, sticking to what can be called an *extensive* ethic, that makes nature an object of human organization, and foregrounds, arguably above all, the mediating functions of digital recording and manipulation (i.e. a recognizably 'natural' original being unmade according to an aesthetic familiar from much glitch music of the last decade and a half). By contrast, Köner's 'Polar' works makes no use of field recordings in any form, but is instead assembled almost entirely from recordings of gongs, captured on tape using contact microphones, then substantially slowed, filtered and layered. In this sense, then, Köner's work is entirely synthetic. Unlike the Hazard material, there is no documentary component. And yet, it is arguably Köner who comes closer to a cymatic orientation, that is, to an *intensive* ethic concerned with fostering a mode of perception *in* the sonic body by putting it in an unfamiliar vibratory-conceptual relation.

The theme of Köner's triptych is ostensibly 'The North' but not in a metaphorical sense, nor as mimicry.[41] His work is more *of* the ice than about it, not representing landscape but attempting a pathic grasp of corporeal dissolution into it: the body prone, its cycles slowing towards freezing, its faculties reducing to nil, becoming buried, becoming crystalline, being absorbed into the longer rhythms of geologic time.[42] In this way, it attempts what Deleuze and Guattari call an 'inhuman becoming, experienced in the body as such'.[43] It is an experiment in producing a logic of sensation and a conceptual event. This strategy is developed along two, mutually resonant lines, one vibratory, the other sonic fictional.

Sonically, the triptych is characterized by its combination of austerity and low-end force. At its most amusical and impersonal, it seems entirely intent on engineering an unhoming. *Nunatak* is the most animated, sometimes even fitful. There are breath-like textures, but they are uncomfortably deep, prolonged and resonant. Briefly, we hear what could be a panicked voice, but it is too low, slow and muffled to make out. A sickening screech follows, after which, anything remotely evocative of the human quickly fades. Early on, *Nunatak's* sonic elements are in constant, if slowing, motion. But, over the course of the album, the all-pervading drone sets in, remaining in place through the end of the series. *Teimo* takes this further. Of the three recordings, it moves closest to silence and stasis, reaching a nadir in 'Nieve Penitentes 2' – its polarity-inverted drone designed to produce a slowly throbbing fullness in the ears.[44] It doesn't depict anything, but it induces a physical sensation of encasement and vestibular weight. After *Teimo's* quiet force, *Permafrost* is coarse and perhaps more unrelentingly barren. The drone hovers closer to the edges of audition, its modulations still slower, sometimes rougher. There are higher, wind-like textures again, but now they are more immanent than ambient. This is not a sound from aboveground, but from *within*, as if transduced and transmitted downwards by an all-enveloping materiality.

Working to intensify this sensory logic is a sonic fictional layer that is less narrative or construction of feeling than a priming of felt thought and listening flesh. (Massumi's 'back-forming' of affect is worth recalling here, as a means of identifying nature–culture modulation in place of the unidirectional dynamic of cultural mediation.) Describing the sonic fictional circuits that develop between audio objects and sentient flesh, Eshun has argued that 'as soon as you have music with no words, then everything else becomes more crucial: the label, the sleeve, the picture on the cover, the picture on the back, the titles.' They become catalysts 'for your route through the music, or for the way the music captures you and abducts you into its world'.[45] This begins with *Nunatak's* album art, which gives the only overt clues to the project's aims. The cover uses a photo from Robert Scott's fatal polar expedition (here Köner conflates north and south), while inside a handwritten note reads: 'We shall stick it out to the end, but we are getting weaker of course and the end cannot be far.' By the next release, the cover art consists only of a deeply textured field of blue, while the final album offers only a close-up of mineral grain in bedrock. However, there are sonic fictional links to be found in the titles: *nunatak* is an Inuk word describing rock formations that break through ice sheets; *nieve, nieval* and related are Spanish terms for snow; *penitentes* are tall, conical ice formations, often forming in vast fields and resembling the pointed hoods of Spanish Catholic nazarenos (penitent orders); a *serac* is a type of ice column, often dangerously unsteady for climbers; *ruska* is Finnish and refers to the russeting of leaves as seasons change; *firn* is granular snow left over from previous seasons; *permafrost* is soil that remains frozen for years on end; *schluss*, means end in German.

Then there is 'Ilira'. This is the first track on *Teimo*, but the term arguably describes the affective tone Köner sought to elicit throughout the series. *Ilira* is one of several Inuk words for fear, but one reserved for particularly paralysing and overpowering encounters. As explained by Hugh Brody, an ethnographer of the Inuit, *ilira* is the fear associated with 'people or things that have a power over you and can neither be controlled nor predicted. People or things that make you feel vulnerable, and to which you *are* vulnerable.'[46] *Ilira*, in Köner, works on several registers, and partially colludes with the triptych's cymatic dimension. First there is Köner's concerted effort to unhome through vibration. The drone, while always there, is also ever changing, and always (with adequate volume and bass) confronting the sonic body with differently-unsettling presences. Beyond this, though, the work of the sonic fictional component is to channel the bass-unhoming in a particular conceptual direction, drawing the imagination into the vibratory relation and pulling it towards a fearsome vista. The image that guides this strategy is that of Scott: lost, slowly freezing to death, freezing into the ground and eventually *becoming* the ground, as the world goes on. But if Köner's focus is 'a life', then it is a life of impersonal matter, not a biography.[47] The experiment, here, is to help us inhabit (however spectrally) processes and temporalities inherently beyond liveable experience – that is, rhythms of the human organism giving over to the orogenic rhythms of ice and rock. This goes beyond personal fears of death, towards chilling confrontations with orders of material existence that far outlast the human. In this sense, it veers closer to the cosmic and chthonic horrors that preoccupied H. P. Lovecraft. His own Antarctic epic, 'At The Mountains of Madness', begins with the unearthing of 'hellishly ancient' remains in the 'aeon-dead world of the ultimate south'. This leads to further discoveries that put the explorers in touch with orders of being and time that stretch the imagination into deeply unsettling territory. In the words of his narrator: 'we felt that we had established an unprecedented and almost blasphemous link with forgotten aeons normally closed to our species.'[48] Graham Harman calls Lovecraft's project a 'horror of phenomenology' in which 'humans cease to be master in their own house'. The glimpses it affords 'force us to confront "notions of the cosmos, and of [our] own place in the seething vortex of time, whose merest mention is paralysing".' This is *ilira* writ large.

If Köner's mode is cymatic, his tool is vibration and the affective tone is *ilira*, then *viscerality* is arguably his primary medium. In Massumi's theorization, viscera (literal gut feeling) has an essential relation to fear.[49] And Goodman crucially builds on this to link vibration to both visceral sensibility and strategies for inducing fear in the sonic body.[50] This is where Köner's exclusive use of contact microphones assumes crucial significance. Rather than capturing his gongs' airborne waves and their reflections in ambient space, Köner's sound is derived from the immanent acoustics of the metal. Recall the molten undulations observed in Fluke's cymbal, and consider the possibility that Köner is aiming to put the listener *in the shimmer*. That is, rather than making the sound emitted from matter the object of observation, he is attempting to put the sonic body, as best he can, inside sonified matter, to approximate a perception of body–ground continuity. If this is the case, then we can adapt a phrase from Steven Shaviro's work on horror film and sensation to say: *we have entered a new synaesthetic regime of the soundscape, one in which listening is visceral and intensive instead of representational and extensive.*[51] The logic of sensation thus produced constitutes an exteriorization of viscera. This new regime collapses the aural, the tactile and the proprioceptive into viscerality, which, itself, is drawn outwards from the encased body; innards are put in touch with the life of rock and ice via the shimmer of metal. As an inhuman becoming it could be called a *becoming-mineral* – an attempt to enter the sound world of the fossil and the ice mummy at no distance.[52] This is the mode of perception it seeks to fertilize. Its success is not based on getting it 'right' or exact. (By the same token, any similarity to iceberg recordings is ultimately inconsequential.) What matters is whether it works well enough to tilt bodily imagination towards processes and periodicities that are alien to it. As a cymatic investigation, it attempts to inhabit vibration, to grasp what it would be to sense it from within, rather than merely observing it at a remove.

Perceptual abstraction

'At certain crucial points this approach serves as a formula for opening a portal onto what David Toop has referred to as the dark void, that spectral realm magicked into being (or exposed by) the drone, in which audio apparitions and chimeras dance through smoke and mirrors, suggesting the existence of occult planes and dimensions, multiple other realities, worlds within worlds.'[53]

Recordings from the mysterious drone project called Eleh began appearing in 2006.[54] Released in small numbers, with almost no accompanying information, each vinyl side typically holds a ten- to twenty-minute investigation of simple waveforms (sine, square, saw) at frequencies rarely higher than 100 Hz and allegedly as low as 0.5 Hz. The sound is austere. There is no acoustic dimension, just signal – the 'dry', filtered and envelope-shaped outputs of basic oscillators (the sort found in electronic test equipment and analogue synthesizers) modulating together.[55] Using banks of these devices, Eleh can produce sustained tones, finely tune their frequencies, layer them and see how they interact. There are deep and steady tones, resembling electrical hum; elsewhere, the slow pulses of waves passing in and out-of-phase with one another. Some tracks throb and judder; in others, the rough harmonics of mixed frequencies and waveshapes take on a more industrial character, like the vibrations of heavy machinery transmitted through a building's foundation. Throughout the recordings, tones morph and slide as frequencies shift and wave cycles encounter each other in new ways; the consonances of octave ratios create moments of stasis and intensified sonic energy, while tonal and harmonic differences produce layers of rhythmic momentum and rupture.

Anonymous and secretive, Eleh is a myth-science unto itself, a bass-exploration project laced with sonic fictional clues to its methods and aims. Vinyl inscriptions read: 'Know Nothing' / 'Feel Everything'.[56] Titles suggest a mixture of the clinical and the mystical. Some have a quasi-scientific tone: 'Pulsing Study Of 7 Sine Waves' (Parts One and Two), 'Tone Phase 1 For 2 Guitars & 4 Oscillators',[57] 'Linear To Circular / Vertical Axis.' Others – 'Emerging Presence', 'That Which Is Heard' – suggest anomalies of extra-cochlear perception. Many more veer into a sonic mysticism rooted in the 'sensual mathematics' of just intonation (again, the principles of the Monochord) and the autopoietic strangeness of the subbass encounter.[58] *Intuitive synthesis* emerges as a descriptor of Eleh's project, describing the artist's tone-following empiricism, on the one hand, but also suggesting an interest in sonorous relationality more generally: the records operating as modulators of acoustic space and the bodies that occupy it.[59] To this end, some of the records come with very specific listening instructions – precise guidelines for positioning bodies and speakers, along with the more general dictum that 'volume reveals detail'. The overriding concern is not fidelity or 'audile technique', but the adequate staging of what could be called a *geometry of force*, one that presumably approximates a set of sonic-spatial conditions arrived at inductively by the artist in the process of perceptual experimentation and recording.[60] Rather than reflecting a stereophonic ideal, the instructions are better understood as the basic parameters of a vibratory experiment, in which the record is a participant. Elsewhere, the cover for *Fundamental Structure*, a cassette from side-project Deceh, features a hand-drawn diagram of Monochord divisions, while the liner notes describe the project as 'A close study of the harmonic composition of a Hammond organ and a Sruti Box with attention given to the organization of isolated frequencies and the effects of these vibrations on brain activity.'[61] The implication is not, of course, that the artist intends to supply 'results', but nor is the statement merely fanciful. Rather, it should be taken as a sincere invitation to explore particular qualities of vibration and an ensuing eventness of the sonic body. Intuitive synthesis therefore acquires several inflections, still meaning an inductive synthesis of tones, but also the synthesis of a vibratory milieu, and a re-synthesis of the sonic body in this 'atypical force environment'.

There are similarities to be found between Eleh other drone artists: the electrical hum of Eliane Radigue, Tony Conrad's experiments with sustained consonance, or the more synthetic and less textured moments in Pauline Oliveros. But a closer comparison would be to the Minimalism of La Monte Young, with its use of tone generators, and its focus on duration, drift and sound's physical presence. Sonically the two differ, with Eleh relying almost exclusively on electronic oscillators and very low tones, while Young also incorporates voice and acoustic instruments, working with a much broader frequency spectrum, and often focusing on complex mixtures of mid range harmonics.

In these respects, Young's work is still very much about the ear, while Eleh often aims to unhome it. To the extent that there are links between the two, they are often more conceptual and methodological, having more to do with shared interests in relations (tone, spatial, incorporeal) that can be conjured across the vibratory spectrum. Touch Records' Jon Wozencroft claims that Eleh has 'much to do with pre-modern ideas of resonance as a force field for the transformation of space and time. ... The disciplines that went into the building of cathedrals during the Middle Ages ... things lost to history.'[62] Young's work has been said to adhere to 'an essentially Pythagorean aesthetic,' its ultra-precise explorations of just intonation made possible by the electronic oscillator's ability to produce continuous, micro-tunable, tones. 'The move to just intonation', says Keith Potter, 'caused Young to become something of an expert in areas of acoustic theory which remain a closed book to many musicians.'[63] There was an empirical dimension to this education that involved close observation of the vibratory characteristics of intervallic relations, but it was primarily a mathematical–theoretical undertaking, resulting in Young's development of a notation system which expressed intervals as frequency ratios (i.e. in Hz, rather than standard musical notation). In comparison, Eleh's intuitive synthesis can perhaps be considered a less formalized and more ambulant (or sensual) plumbing of vibratory relations. This difference aside, both artists quite explicitly approach sound not so much as something created by the artist, but as a force, available in nature, that can be revealed, harnessed, channelled and shaped, yet which always retains the capacity to surprise. ('"We must let sounds be what they are," says Young, arguing that sounds have their existence, independent of human existence.'[64]) In Eleh's case, this leads to entire albums – *Homage To The Square Wave*, *Homage To The Sine Wave*, *Homage to the Pointed Waveforms* – devoted to exploring the singular relational capacities of specific, elemental waveshapes, at very low frequencies.

The affects of waves *in motion* arguably preoccupy both artists. This is evident in their shared focus on harmonic 'drift'. Wim Mertens describes drift as a 'deviation effect', the shifting phase relations that occur when, for example, two oscillators, set to the same frequency, slowly slide out of tune, or time, with one another. As the two tones pull out of consonance, the fractional echo between them creates a wispy, hollow-sounding, oscillation effect, sometimes called 'phasing'. As they drift further apart, the effect becomes more turbulent. Difference tones emerge, producing beating rhythms that shift in tempo along with the drifting of the interval. Drift effects can be subtle but disorienting, causing, as Young puts it, a 'sensational feeling that the body softly starts flowing off in space and time synchronously with these sine waves'.[65] It can induce a swimmingness of temporal perception, as time seems to expand and contract, simultaneously sliding forwards and backwards. Time's 'arrow' seems to speed up, slow down, fold back and accelerate again. In this way, it might be a version of the 'temporal smudging' described by Massumi: a small ontogenetic crisis in which confounded expectation (a breakdown in the linearity of experience) is countered by the mind's effort to race forwards in anticipation, and backwards in an effort to reconcile with experience.[66]

Artist and critic Henry Flynt has argued that such 'mis-leading' of perception, with the aim of problematizing objective reality and provoking imaginative adaption, has been a central concern for Young, particularly in his Dream House project. 'The installation', he says, 'offered a sustained experience of perceptual uncanniness', which, in its capacity to mystify through the body, contained the power to 'elevate' those who passed through it. It would be easy to read this as a claim to the drone's directly edifying effects, especially given the somewhat vague spiritualism that pervades much of Young's work. But both Young and Flynt seem to be identifying dynamics that are more affective than moral, closer to the pre-personal, modulatory dynamics that we have already seen at work in a variety of settings. Elevation is therefore better understood to describe a particular eventness of the sonic body: a spectral catalysis.

Eleh may in fact be a pun on Young's elevation (Deceh on 'descent'?), but certainly more in the latter, agnostic sense. And Eleh's singular interest in low-frequency modulation means that 'drift' takes on an added vestibular dimension (in which case, *Floating Frequencies* may be a reference to the felt-reality of being carried along by the drift). Moreover, while Young's Drift Studies often unfold at a nearly cosmic pace (years, in the case of the Dream House), Eleh's are often more abrupt, more varied and, owing to their low-frequency content, more jarringly physical. They don't just drift and beat, they swoop, sway, pummel and throb. This is the experience conjured by Eleh's 'In The Ear Of The Gods' (possibly punning on the 'Inner Ear of the Gods') in which layered sine waves eventually fall out of sync and into deep and throbbing oscillations. Writing in *The Wire*, Sam Davies calls it a 'forensic exploration of the limits of bass perception (and reproduction)' … ' "In The Ear Of The Gods" drops almost immediately into speaker-threatening sub-bass stasis ... When the unified tones finally shift fractionally, the resulting phasing has the kind of richly vertiginous wobble and warp that dubstep loves to play with.'[67]

Another track, called 'Phase One: Sleeps Golden Drones Again', is a similar but more elaborate experiment that builds slowly over twenty-three minutes. It opens with a pair of low tones – one constant, the other pulsed. The continuous sine wave hums the body steadily, but when the pulse hits, every six seconds, it sets off short strings of fading modulations (like a slow drip rippling through standing water). When a low, triangle wave joins the mix, the modulations become more varied and more forceful. A new harmonic in the drone begins to take over the head and fill the ears. Later, a subaudible element enters and sends the whole sonic field into faster, deeper oscillations.[68] At this point, at high volume, acoustic pressure cycles through the ears about once a second, modulating a lower hum that weighs in the oesophagus. A hollow drone beats incessantly behind the nose, pulsing with the insistence of a fresh burn, and the overall effect recalls something of the rough, drifting oscillations felt inside a dual turboprop plane. The final sonic element is another sine tone, which quickly rises to about 110 Hz, sustains for varying lengths of time on each repetition, then decays slowly. With each head-filling emergence, it produces a sense of tense stasis, before releasing into the lower drone and its steady pulse. By now, the room throbs and populations of disparate waves course across the body. When they change, you change: internal resonances charge and discharge; rhythms emerge between vibrating organs and bones. For twenty-three minutes, the body's image of itself rhythmically recomposes over and over.

Transversal strategies

We could perhaps borrow a phrase from the Op artist Bridget Riley to say that, for Eleh, 'perception is the medium'. In fact, Eleh may, in many respects, have at least as much in common with Op(tical) Art and related practices – occasionally grouped under the names Retinal Art or Perceptual Abstraction – as it does with the Minimalist music tradition. Eleh itself hints at this link. The *Homage* albums are an apparent nod to Josef Albers' vast series of colour-perception experiments under the title *Homage to the Square*, while Eleh's album art sometimes recalls the geometric experiments of artists like Riley, Victor Vasarely and Mon Levinson. There are certainly affinities to be found between Op's strategies for problematizing perception comparable tendencies in Eleh's work. And the language used by Op's artists and theorists often resonates much more strongly with Eleh's low-frequency investigations than does much of the literature on Minimalist music, which largely avoids sonic-sensory matters, in favour of the textual, music-theoretical and biographical.[69] Compare this to writings by and about Riley, which express an overriding interest in uncertainties of vision, the conditions of its breakdown and the provisional bodies engendered through perceptual unhomings.

Riley's works are entirely non-representational – often monochromatic, usually involving fields of repeated geometric forms – but this does not make them reducible to 'abstraction', in the usual sense (as in Abstract Expressionism).[70] If, as Deleuze argues, abstract painting works in much the same manner as figuration, passing through the brain and not working directly on the nervous system, then Op's strategies are opposite. It could be called a figural art, but in contrast to Francis Bacon's work, it stages its deformations (abstractions) largely in the viewing body, rather than on canvas.[71] Or more accurately, it 'charges a field' between body and canvas, exploiting light, colour and shape to elicit neuro-affective responses in the viewer. It unsettles and confuses. The pleasure in this art 'derives less from knowing what we are looking at than from the anxiety of *not-knowing*'. In his introduction to *The Optic Nerve*, Dave Hickey describes new theories of mind which paint consciousness as a 'fugitive epiphenomenon', something brought into being through its relations and encounters. If this is so, then the implications for art are profound, for 'if conscious awareness is not required to appreciate visual art then visual art is not an art of the mind, not a "liberal art". It is, more properly, an expression of what Riley calls "the eye's mind," or the body's thought'.[72] This suggests that at Op's core are assumptions of a parallelism between mind and body, and of that assemblage's inherent changeability – its exploitability. Eshun has made much the same claim about instrumental electronic musics designed to operate on the body's 'distributed brain', engineering unhomings in which 'Senses swap so that your skin hears and your ears feel. Dermal ears ... Ear tactility'.[73]

Eleh and Riley are both radical empiricists, one probing limit-fields of audition, the other vision. Each, in their way, begins with a simple shape (graphic or sonic). Each, through an investigation of its trajectories, intuits a relational potential immanent to that shape, and then pursues that relational line until it begins to insist weirdly in perception. For Riley, not unlike Eleh, this means pursuit of perceptual anomaly and strange spectra. There is a Spinozist tinge in the deceptively simple statement, 'I see, so to speak, what an oval will do', because this is really to ask: 'How far can an oval be pushed as an agent of deformation? How can shapes – through colouration, multiplication, and patterning – deterritorialize each other and produce unforeseen complexities on canvas?' Riley asks the same of circles, squares, triangles, straight lines and curved lines, much as Eleh asks: 'What can a square wave do? What can a sine wave do? What are the different affects of triangle and sawtooth waves?' Of course, in each case, this is equally to ask how perception might be drawn into that relation and unhomed, while the minimalist impulse wonders how intense a response can be elicited from a minimum of structural elements. When Riley speaks of 'charging' and 'modulating' space (concepts that are equally applicable to sonic practice), she is describing logics of sensation that operate directly on bodies, 'co-opting viewers' and working to conjure a 'consensual subjectivity ... a pact' (i.e. an operative reality). This requires a strategy, and hers easily falls under the heading of 'intuitive synthesis':

> initially you have a sort of 'hunch' about a configuration and the unit involved. Then you put the unit or structural elements that have occurred to you, through a whole series of different situational responses, provoking them, so to speak, to vibrate against each other in several ways, in a set of structural variations.[74]

The goal is 'an event rather than an appearance'. The role of the artist is to discover forces in nature, then prod them to the point of causing small ruptures in common sensibility.

Unhoming strategies are at the core of Op Art, with its many techniques for inducing perceptions of felt-motion and felt-presence, two broad categories of anomalous experience that we have encountered repeatedly in low-frequency milieus. Among these visual artists, there is a language of rhythm and vibration that is no more metaphorical than it is among the drone artists. It is, more accurately, a case of approaching the same affective registers from different directions. Riley, for example, has experimented widely with drift phenomena that may have more than a notional connection to those explored by Eleh and Young. Paintings like *Current* (1964), *Crest* (1964), and *Arrest 2* (1965), *Drift 2* (1966), and *Cataract 3* (1967) each comprise a field of undulant lines (shallow, sinusoidal shapes) – either black-and-white, or complimentary and contrasting colours that shade, barely perceptibly, through a gradation of hues.[75] In some cases, the lines are identical, but offset; in others, each iteration varies in slight ways from those adjacent to it. In either event, the lines can be said to be out-of-phase with one another. This produces a field of wave-like ripples, giving the canvas a liquid appearance. But resemblances like this are really only side effects of Op's effort to shift perception itself out-of-phase. As optical interventions, rather than images, the pieces are designed to induce a swimmingness of vision, caused by patterns that confuse the retina, depriving it of a focal point, and producing the impression of divergent kinetic tendencies in ostensibly still visual space. Pulled in different directions, the eyes dart, flutter and float. The canvas may appear to oscillate or pulse; the body may feel swayed and woozy, as reactions bordering on vertigo and motion sickness set in.

Such 'visually induced sickness' has been attributed to a dynamic called 'sensory conflict' or 'sensory rearrangement', and infrasound researchers have noted that it is not strictly an ocular effect. Rather, it is inherently intermodal, arising when the cooperation of senses involved in gauging motion and spatial relationships ('the eyes, the vestibular receptors, the non-vestibular proprioceptors') is disrupted. '[W]hen we expose ourselves to an atypical force environment ... this delicate harmony is artificially disrupted to produce a mismatch between signals communicated by the normally synergistic receptors.'[76] If low-frequency sound can produce discordant feelings of motion that pit vestibular stimulation against conflicting information from the eyes, then Op would seem to target the same effect from the other direction.

In *Perception and Imaging*, Richard Zakia explains how this sort of unhoming via the retina can be brought about:

> Contours, boundaries, and edges are very important to the process of visual perception. The eyes continuously search them out for information. Under certain conditions, a shimmering movement can occur at the *boundary* of an area. With colour images, boundaries of colour areas having similar lightness and complimentary hues, such as red and cyan, tend to appear to vibrate or shimmer ... Vibrations can also be seen with certain repetitive black-and-white colour lines.[77]

This shimmering can be subtle or violent. Zakia notes that the causes of this sensed motion are complex but appear 'to be related to physiological factors such as inhibitory processes in the retina and the tremors of the eye called *nystagmus*, and to perceptual phenomena such as simultaneous contrast.'[78] Nystagmus – the rapid, involuntary movement of the eye – is an effect that can also be induced by mechanical vibration or, as suggested in Tandy and Tempest, by the disorienting part-perception of present–absent sound (the eye attempting to situate the body relative to phantom vibration). Nystagmus is the involuntary induction of rhythm into a body, and Op attempts to graphically modulate those rhythms. For her part, Riley speaks in terms of retinal 'tempo', 'oscillation' and 'optical bounce' – 'a whole field in cyclic movement'. In other pieces the effect is closer to thrust than buoyancy. While some pieces 'float' the eye, others pull it forcefully into perceived warps (*Movement in Squares*

1961) and vortices (*Blaze 1*, 1962) in the canvas. Other pieces use tessellated patterns to induce a crisis of discordant perception – shapes that twitch and bend, movement everywhere, three-dimensional spaces that drift open and closed. '[T]his brinkmanship', says Riley, 'creates an allover disturbance. The result is a highly, even alarmingly mobile visual field, charged in its entirety and containing individual blurring drifts and tremors according to the density of the packing in any area.'[79]

Steve Goodman proposed the term 'affective hacking' to describe materialist strategies in electronic musics, but it could equally be applied to Op's interventions.[80] Riley draws on George Bataille's image of the obliterated eye to describe her work as 'a destructive operation done on quotidian reality ... a destruction that results in an animation and is, for that reason, "uncanny" – disconcerting, because what is thought to be inanimate appears to be alive.' Like low-frequency experimentalists, Op artists have intuited sets of techniques for producing various sorts of 'presences' – things that insist on perception and reveal its essentially synthetic operation. Mon Levinson, for example, pioneered the use of moiré patterns (identical geometric line patterns, overlaid at an angle) to trick the eye into perceiving spectral bands of colour where only black-and-white lines exist on the canvas (an effect that can be compared to the psychoacoustic effect of the missing fundamental).[81] Others exploited the ghostly effect that Goethe labelled 'afterimage', whereby impressions of light and colour persist in the retina after the original impingement has passed. Riley's *White Disks* (1964), for example, is a uniform white plane, geometrically dotted with black disks. View it under bright light and then close your eyes: the backs of the eyelids become the inverted canvas across which the disks faintly float. Open your eyes and, for a time, that lingering trace of past vision overlays and combines with present vision.

Eleh achieves something analogous with a rare resort to high frequency in a piece called 'Rotational Change for Windmill' (2010). 'Windmill' opens with an excruciating, high-pitched chirp that rings, like a bad case of tinnitus, over the insistent throb of a very low hum. The piercing sound cycles for four minutes before slowing and fading away, leaving only the drone. At this point, the ear relaxes, relieved but still pained. For a time, the experience leaves it slightly incapacitated. A paradox emerges as aural perception is muted, while at the same time, a phantom ringing, resembling the one on the recording, persists in audition. Is it really over?[82] Throughout these developments, though, perception of the low drone remains unaltered. The temporary damage caused by the very high-frequency component does not extend to those cilia in the ear canal that are tuned only to the lowest tones. And all the while, the various vibrations felt elsewhere proceed as before. The only difference is that now this low humming of the body begins to feel like a balm for the distressed ear.

If after-images, drift, induced rhythms and similar effects preoccupy both Eleh and the Op artists, then clearly there are more than superficial linkages between the two. Acoustic or ocular, all of the practices detailed above stage encounters with atypical forces that put bodies at variance with themselves, forcing sensory rearrangements and conceptual adaptations. Without denying the links of one to tendencies in Minimal and electronic musics, nor the other to post-war American painting, we can nevertheless theorize an alternative lineage of art practices that address different sensory modalities but share an ethico-aesthetic orientation. The disused term for Op – Perceptual Abstraction – can thus emerge as a conceptual tool for identifying those arts that take perception as their medium, and proceed by an intuitive synthesis to unhome it. At their most kindred, these practices don't merely elicit analogous effects, but actually meet, arriving by different routes, in the same intermodal space of sensory rearrangement.

Incipient dance

When a set of material-energetic conditions invites people to experiment with their bodies, in space, then we have the makings of dance. The ancient mound structures discussed in the previous chapter are examples of richly varied acoustic spaces built with the apparent intention of drawing bodies into patterns of exploration-through-movement: discovering different tonal niches and sound effects, discovering bodily and structural responses, turning felt-motion into actual movement, finding rhythms, investigating collectively. This can be called *incipient dance* (or, more specifically, the *audiogenesis of dance*), having nothing to do with questions of form, tradition or performativity – or even music, for that matter – but referring instead to the ways that unusual vibratory conditions can exert a figural pull and catalyse a spontaneous, and immanent, choreography. Erin Manning's concepts of 'preacceleration' and 'incipient action' are especially relevant here, as we examine sound installations of various sorts that have worked with similar principles.[83] Some use tremendous amounts of low-frequency energy in order to shake participants out of themselves and force physical adaptations. Others have proceeded by subtler, more teasing means, aiming to induce bodily-felt curiosity and spark an investigative 'dance.' In each case, however, the emphasis is on charging fields in ways that are meant to put bodies and subjectivities in motion.

Sonic architectures

Both La Monte Young and Maryanne Amacher have turned entire buildings into throbbing engines of perceptual abstraction. Neither has restricted their experiments to the low-frequency domain, but their mutual interest in sound's physical power means that the bottom end still looms large in their installations. This sets them apart from many of their contemporaries; Paul Miller notes, for example, that Amacher was 'one of the first people of the [John Cage/David Tudor] set to really deal with heavy bass, electronic bass, crazy bass.'[84] For his part, Young has often used 60 Hz electrical mains hum, or nearby frequencies, as a droning fundamental pitch for his projects and pieces. His work has also become notorious for its tremendous volume, deployed not just for its own sake, but also in an effort to rattle subjectivities loose and push them into a new place. This is the ethico-acoustic dimension of these works, which Young frames in cosmogenic terms when he calls them experiments in 'creat[ing] worlds of feeling which can't be achieved in any other way'.[85] The project becomes one of charging a field, overfilling sonic experience and seeing where it leads.

Monstrous sonics are crucial to this task, but they are also partly why recordings of Young and Amacher's sound spaces often only give part-impressions of a given installation. This has nothing to do with the relative 'authenticity' of the experience, but basic material hindrances – factors of force, frequency, scale and geometry. As critic Alan Licht realized, on first hearing Amacher's *Sound Characters* CD, 'this music [is] too massive to really be experienced in a living room. It's like having King Kong for a pet, it resists captivity at every level.'[86] The enormity of these works poses a challenge, but when it comes to recording, the terminally insurmountable factor is their essentially topological nature. They aren't premised on the ideal listening position of stereo or even multichannel sound; in a richly sonified building there are simply more acoustic dimensions, and more combinational potentials, than microphones could ever capture. The 'work' is not the building or even the 'composition' itself, but an eventness, in the form of each participant's affective route through a very complex geometry of forces: sensually navigating from room-to-room, across and around open spaces, investigating niches. Recalling the odd acoustics inside megalithic mounds, movement through this virtual architecture presents a morphing stream of encounters with standing waves, very localized tones, regional modulations and illusory combination tones. The ambulant testing of these vibratory relations becomes a form of intuitive synthesis.

This is the idea behind Young's *Dream House,* a series of semi-permanent audio-visual installations produced in collaboration with his partner, the visual artist Marian Zazeela. The *Dream House* is a synaesthetic environment, composed of tones from analogue oscillators and tinted, mobile lighting that 'create[s] seemingly three-dimensional colored shadows in a luminous field.'[87] The autonomous cycles of each element slowly drift in and out of time with one another, producing drifting phase relationships that are perceived across sensory modes. Visitors report that emergent properties of light and shape seem to become linked with tendencies in vibration. Similarly, sound is felt to pulsate with slow shifts in colour. 'High volume was also an attribute', writes Brandon Labelle, 'to the extent the sound took on physical mass – or better, the actual physical movement of sound waves became apparent in a way that was exhilarating for some, painful for others, but in any case inescapable.'[88] For those who remain still, in the space, the experience may be one of tremendous, undulant weight, shifting almost imperceptibly over time, except when the movements of others in the room introduce small turbulences in the sound. This is a clue that movement is key to the event, an invitation to explore. What one finds is that the space is structured by different qualities and quantities of vibration. At high volume, noticeable changes in air pressure can be felt when moving from room-to-room, and each of these internal regions becomes a distinct and navigable space – an acoustic 'niche'. In such a setting, the only semblance of a 'composition' is the succession of acoustic events engendered in the ambulant sonic body – passages from zone-to-zone, rhythms of stillness and motion. In some spots, a simple turn of the head can open onto a new sonorous space. Brandon Labelle writes that to enter this 'sonic field' was to be 'immersed as in a fluid, sounds oscillate across a range of frequencies through the movements of the body, enfolding the self in a sonic architecture that cannot be said to wither exist of not.'[89]

Comparable effects were explored by Amacher in the meticulously engineered *Sound House* and *Music for Sound Joined Rooms*. She often worked at crushing volume and, in contrast to Young, made extensive use of 'structure borne sound (sound transmitted through walls, floors, rooms, corridors) which acousticians distinguish from the "airborne" sound experienced with conventional loudspeaker placements.' The result was that 'the rooms themselves become speakers', producing sound that was not only transmitted at the body, in open acoustic space, but also induced directly, as mechanical vibration.[90] These sensory engineering projects also had myth-scientific element, being partly inspired by the technologies and becomings depicted in J. G. Ballard's collection of short stories *Vermillion Sands*. The book is full of singing plants, sound sculptures, extra-cochlear musics and houses that respond the emotions of their biological occupants.[91] For Amacher, Ballard's near-future fiction foresaw technologies 'which begin to match the range and subtlety of our perceptual modes.'[92] This meant the possibility of precisely engineering a misleading of senses into alternative realities, through what she termed 'Third Ear Music'. For Amacher, this meant pushing sonic perception beyond its recognized limits and making it do the unexpected, exploiting psychoacoustic effects (sound localization, combination tones), physiological capacities (resonances, pain) and limit-fields of perception. Her ambition was to conjure powerful and highly localized 'presences' – what she described as 'sound shapes' – that would be encountered by moving about the installation space, and perceived synaesthetically, as masses to move through or around; 'Staged at specific locations and heights, these sonic areas became tactile in presence, existing as "things in themselves".' In attempting to engender operative realities via the sonic body, she would ask: 'Does it make such a clear shape in the air we seem to "see it" in front of our eyes? Is there no sound in the room at all, but we continue to hear "after-sound" as our mind is processing sonic events perceived minutes ago?' Preparing spaces like the *Sound House* would typically take up to a month of residency, spent probing the building's sonorous character and testing potentially rich relations, before she could begin sculpting her 'perceptual geographies'. This process she compared to 'scripting a sonic choreography', with curious visitors as the dancers.

Dance with the Speaker

Sound you can feel and cannot hear, mirrors that refuse to show your reflection and chase you away with piercing tones the harder you try to locate yourself, sounds built upon sounds built upon shadows of other sounds ... these constitute a few ways I have built uncanny sound-mind spaces. And the persona, well yes, she too has appeared as well in my gestures. Another being defying time by reflecting a distorted history. This apparition weaves in and out like a long deep wave, a primal sound, a sonic anomaly. This projected presence, this noise-like interruption, has announced itself as an oscillating dream space in the collective memory of African-American history, both repressed and embraced. It bears the uneasiness of a haunting presence; a presence unverified, but whose existence cannot be refuted.[93]

Choreographies of niche-navigation also emerge in the (infra)sonic milieus engineered by Camille Norment. With *Groove* (2001), she invited visitors to enter an unassuming recessed area of a gallery space that was empty, to all appearances, and silent too. But in that nook, bodies encountered 'an unexpected sensory groove, an enveloping sonic space' produced by two subaudible frequencies, so low and so localized that they could only be perceived by passing through them. 'The effect', she writes, 'is unexpected and momentarily disorienting with its invasive patterns of "sound". A lingering visitor will experience subtle changes in pattern over time. Subjects may question their own perceptual experience as the persistence of paranoia strikes the mind through [the] body.'[94] In another installation, called *Dead Room*, the inaudible at least becomes visible. Viewed from the outside, the black, foam, cone-studded structure has the appearance of a 'science fiction fortress'. Inside, it is a clinically gleaming padded cell. The *Dead Room* comes alive, for three minutes and thirty-three seconds at a time, as eight subwoofers fill the space with infrasonic waves and its walls 'gently pulse in a bio-mechanical rhythm' with its occupants. 'The space is silent, but the sound can be seen, as the woofers throb, [and] felt, as the sound waves move through the body creating a subtle intangible disturbance. ... Visitors experience a [subtle], yet ever present, re-perception of the body.' Norment has carefully organized the pod's sonic geometry, noting that 'The placement of the speakers is important, as it governs where the sound hits the body. You can direct them to the head, the feet, the genitals.'[95] Occupants of the *Dead Room* will also notice a disconcerting effect on their ability to speak, as infrasound-modulated voices acquire a 'helium' inflection. Observing the installation at work, Norment also notices a tendency among participants to walk slowly around the room, often dragging a hand against its tactile surface, and becoming lost in these sensual revolutions. This becoming-dance was the (perhaps retrospective) inspiration for the couched reference to turntable rotations (33 1/3 RPM) in the playing time of the infrasound bursts.[96]

Lastly, though not specifically a low-frequency sound project, Norment's *Driftglass* bears mentioning because of the way it melds a vibration-induced perceptual unhoming (an obliteration of ocular expectation) with the affective politics of subjectivation (a becoming-invisible):

> In this work, the mirror is subverted as a place of self-reflection and creates a teasing act of disappearance. When approaching the mirror from an angle, a visitor simply notices a mirror, a surface reflecting people and the environment. It is only when viewing the mirror *en face* (and being caught in the sonic space of the mirror) that they uncannily see themselves as only a vague blur. Side by side, two or more persons will see clear reflections of each other while unable to see themselves clearly.[97]

Driftglass recalls Deleuze's comment that the mirrors populating Francis Bacon's paintings 'can be anything you like – except a reflecting surface.'[98]

And it would seem to draw from Ralph Ellison's novel *Invisible Man* in its investigation of race, gender and *faciality*. Faciality is Guattari's term for the relationality of the face, at the interface between 'subjectivation and significance'. The former belongs 'to the language of psychogenesis (how a living being grows into and negotiates the ambient world) and the latter to semiotics', the language of discourse, representation and construction.[99] Cultural geographer Arun Saldanha has called faciality the structure 'underlying all interactions, which pushes actual bodies into behaving in certain ways, whether they want to or not.'[100] It can be understood as an organizer of the social that operates on affective, rather than discursive, registers. And it has been called a 'virtual attractor' because it pertains to the relational tendencies and potentials of bodies.

Saldanha not only notes that, since Deleuze and Guattari, discussions of faciality have rarely moved beyond questions of visual representation, but he also points to theorists who find in it 'a more corporeal, even biological twist', looking beyond the functions of vision alone to treat it as 'an embodied and ethical process', that is, a self-organization of bodies outside of signifying regimes.[101] This has led Saldanha to a materialist re-theorization of race relations that begins by acknowledging the inescapability of the body, but avoids essentializing that body by recognizing it as an always-emergent contingency, one that not only overlaps with discourse, but also escapes it in any number of ways. His work on the racial segregation among dancers in Goa, India, reveals a self-organization of bodies in space – the pre-dawn dancefloor takeover by white dancers – that is unspoken, and even counter to the subculture's purported ideals, but which reproduces itself over and again (being carried out, in part, through modulations of sonic force that exploit the differing drug habits of the groups involved).

There is a related dynamic at work in *Driftglass*, as the arrival of a body in its space opens a network of affective circuits. The installation consists of a vanity mirror linked to proximity sensors which trigger both the sounding of a high-pitched ringing, and the vibration of the mirror, which causes it to produce a blurred reflection. 'From a distance, it would grant the person looking into it a reflection, but the closer they came, the louder and harsher the oscillating computerised feedback became. And, in a very unhomely touch, the reflection itself disappeared.'[102] In the end, the high-frequency feedback painfully affirms bodily existence on one level, but this is accompanied by a nystagmic denial of representation. It echoes the Prologue to *Invisible Man*, in which the narrator compares his situation to being 'surrounded by mirrors of hard, distorting glass'. The problem is not him, but 'a peculiar disposition of the eyes of those with whom I come in contact.' 'When they approach', he says, 'they see only my surroundings, themselves, or figments of their imagination – indeed, everything and anything except me.'[103] Using vibration to deny confirmation of self, *Driftglass* is less a metaphor for social invisibility than an effort to register in the viewer, affectively, the felt-reality of being invisible within the immediate social field. The mirror, in its vexing changeability – the teasing, almost cruel way it encourages the viewer to shift and twist, trying to insert himself into the picture, trying to gauge what it 'wants' – draws the implicated body into a 'dance' with an existential riddle. It seems likely, then, that the installation is built with the majoritarian visitor (white, male) in mind – the subject who is historically most secure in his own existence and visibility. Vibration thus becomes a tool for shaking that privilege loose, and, hopefully, instilling some visceral glimpse of what it would mean to become-*Other*.

'A people of oscillators'

Mark Bain's experiments in unhoming and collective modulation can be said to proceed by more seismic means. The 'vibration artist' comes as close as anyone to Vladimir Gavreau's vision of structures made to hum the tune of their own destruction. His strategies against architecture take inspiration from the myth-scientific figure Nikola Tesla, who, so the story goes, once brought his New York laboratory close to collapse using a steam-driven mechanical oscillator (essentially a small, unbalanced motor), that was tuned to one of the building's resonant frequencies, and coupled directly to the structure, allowing vibration to enter its frame by induction.[104]

> I was experimenting with vibrations. I had one of my machines going and I wanted to see if I could get it in tune with the vibration of the building. I put it up notch after notch. There was a peculiar cracking sound. I asked my assistants where did the sound come from. They did not know. I put

the machine up a few more notches. There was a louder cracking sound. I knew I was approaching the vibration of the steel building. I pushed the machine a little higher. Suddenly all the heavy machinery in the place was flying around. I grabbed a hammer and broke the machine. The building would have been down about our ears in another few minutes. Outside in the street there was pandemonium. The police and ambulances arrived. I told my assistants to say nothing. We told the police it must have been an earthquake. That's all they ever knew about it.[105]

Bain's experiments have led him to build his own 'portable earthquake machines', one comprising 'three six-ton earth compacting machines connected together and tuned to earth frequencies', the other consisting of 'a 6-meter long steel plate buried in the ground with three large vibronic activators mounted to it.' Invisible at surface level, the latter system produced 'severe tremors that spread outward to a half-kilometer radius in the surrounding area.'[106] In Boston and Pescara, Italy, he has 'activated' steel trestle-bridges, raising parallels with the Tacoma Narrows suspension bridge, which, in 1940, was set in a wave-like motion by moderate winds and began oscillating evermore violently until it collapsed. In Bain's case, the bridges are made to produce a 'low-frequency ringing tone that could be tuned to different harmonics including a frequency that would make rust flake off.'[107] Meanwhile, a 'whole building activation' in the Netherlands used very small, mechanical oscillators to drive wave energy into a structure causing 'severe damage on some of the thicker walls', while his 'ArchiSound' project in Oldenberg, Germany, used modified seismic sensors to amplify otherwise unnoticeable seismic energies and transmit them into the gallery space.

Like Riley, Bain rejects the notion that his art depends on learnt interpretation. His projects are non-representational and built to operate on affective registers; their conceptual dimension is meant to arise in the material encounter, without intrinsic reliance on theoretical foreknowledge. The 'work' is the relationality that emerges within the activated space and among its temporary occupants. In fact, Bain argues that his art projects are, at the very least, 'a relative of cinematic entertainment, amusement parks and thrill ride attractions.'[108] This echoes Tom Gunning's argument that the fairground is the common ancestor of both those avant-garde arts that foreground the role of sensation, and what he labels the 'cinema of attractions'. The latter is meant to describe tendencies in early cinema, before the ascendance of narrative film, that aimed for 'direct stimulation of shock or surprise at the expense of unfolding a story or creating a diegetic universe.'[109] The effect is exteriorizing:

> The cinema of attractions expends little energy creating characters with psychological motivations or individual personality. Making use of both fictional and non-fictional attractions, its energy moves outward towards an acknowledged spectator rather than inward towards the character-based situations essential to classical narrative.[110]

At the visual level, at least, such tendencies have been largely subsumed by modern narrative conventions, and a 'cinema of effects' (in the blockbuster mould of Coppola, Spielberg and Lucas). Yet it might be argued that the cinema of attractions has actually persisted in sonic design, even expanded by moving beyond the cochlea, into infrasound, felt vibration and vestibular techniques. The cinematic body is, in large part, a sonic body, and the technologies and concepts Bain employs belong to a long history of vibratory affect engineering in the cinema space. This includes the lingering influence of the Doctrine of the Affections in the manuals of both silent-era organists and contemporary sound designers; the low-end bombast and sound effects of Wurlitzer organs of the silent era; and the various room-shaking technologies explored since the advent of electrical amplification, including massive subwoofers, mechanical oscillators and subbass synthesizers.[111]

Bain feels a special affinity towards two of the more gimmicky technologies to emerge in the post-war period: the Percepto system of the late 1950s, and Sensurround, in the 1970s. Sensurround was initially developed for the action/disaster film *Earthquake*. It employed a series of amplifiers, up to 1,000 watts each, to drive a large subwoofer at frequencies as low as 15 Hz, and sound pressure levels as high as 120dBC (made possible by a 'folded' horn design that could, in a much smaller space, approximate the range and force of a standard horn with an area of 300 square feet).[112] Rather than requiring the soundtrack itself to contain infrasonic content (which would have been extremely difficult to record), the system used a 'low-frequency noise generator' triggered by cues encoded on the film, which could 'regulate the timing and intensity of the low frequency rumble' from the generator. The system was designed, says the Sensurround manual:

> to generate special audible and sub audible effects not yet possible to reproduce on presently available systems. *The audience will actually be participating in the film.* The torso will vibrate. So will the diaphragm. Flesh and auditory nerves will receive the sensations one might feel while experiencing the event depicted on the screen.[113]

Even closer to Bain's seismic art, however, was a technology devised for the 1959 B-horror *The Tingler*. The Percepto system used a network of mechanical oscillators attached to the bottoms of movie theatre seats. It 'sought to simulate the monster [of the film] loose on the floor under the seats [using] small motors from radar cooling units fitted with lopsided cams, bolted under the chairs and activated on cue by the projectionist.'[114] Percepto's deployment was clever in that it only went off under *some* seats, giving the impression to the audience as a whole, via the collective observation of individual reactions (screams, laughs, spasmodic movements), that the creature was snaking its way around the room, 'attacking' the crowd one by one. If Sensurround aimed for a total effect, Percepto was more spectral in its operation; it could haunt a room, texturing it with anticipation and suspense, even creating a social differentiation between the afflicted and those (so far) spared. Similar technology is actually still in use, in the form of the Butt Kicker, an oscillator device which converts a portion of a soundtrack's low-frequency sound energy content into mechanical vibration for direct induction into a seat. Consumer versions are available for home theatres (with an optional mounting kit for La-Z-Boy-style recliners), video gaming and car audio, while the Butt Kicker websites claims eighty movie theatre installations around the world.[115] Nightclub versions from various companies have been installed underneath dancefloors in order to 'transmit bass frequencies directly into the skeleton via the feet'.[116]

What interests Bain about these vibratory entertainments is not just the sensory thrill, but also their sociality, and how they can catalyse becomings among a collective sonic body. People put in strange situations, he notes, tend to adaptively self-organize. They watch other bodies reacting to a shared material reality, they communicate by various means, they band together and adjust.

This is true, for example, of the 'coming together' that often follows natural disasters. But it also happens, in similar and different ways, in the context of the thrill ride and the cinema of attractions, and Bain aims to induce something comparable with his vibration installations. The best example of these is his *Live Room* (1998), which repurposed a Cold War missile silo as laboratory for experimenting with relationality in vibration. In its original construction, the silo's floating floor was meant to dampen vibration, but Bain saw in it the potential to do the opposite, transforming it into a transducer or, in a sense, a giant speaker. He used six rotary-type mechanical oscillators introducing vibration into the structure, turning it into 'a tuneable musical instrument'. The result, he says, was 'a kind of tectonic sound machine which spectators [*sic*] could walk on and feel through their bodies.'[117] Peak frequencies were between 20 and 30 Hz with infrasonic beat patterns, giving it a rhythmic texture. There were shifting harmonic pulses produced by the interactions of the oscillators, and further modulated by the movement of people walking on the floor.[118] 'The subtle strangeness of this project', says Bain, 'revolves around the production and injection of these types of low frequencies.'[119] Participants described a wide range of neurophysiological responses but vestibular motion and balance effects were the most commonly reported: 'When positioned on the active floor panels, a feeling of shifting horizon can be felt due to the resonant stimulation of the inner ear. While standing in place, balance was altered, causing a sudden perception of "surfing" the architectural plane.'[120] At the highest amplitudes, he says, standing was no longer possible.

Bain is especially interested in the exteriorizing pull of such experiences, how they work to draw people out of themselves. He describes the effect as the emergence of a 'bridge' between the 'occupier and that which was occupied'.[121] This relational awareness occurs not only at the level of the silo and its occupants, but also within the collective sonic body, and across individual vibrating bodies, as they perceive their own internal rhythms and resonances relative to the larger acoustic event, and the sense experiences of others. Given this, and the emptiness of the space, he says:

> The *Live Room*, a space devoid of physical objects, was therefore composed of virtual objects, which haptically interface with the audience. By interacting with the cycling waveforms, the occupant was again occupied, infested

with frequencies, modulated by vibrational energy and imparted with the volumetric sensibilities inherent within the body. The audience therefore was the activated object, the sculptural form, traversing the site and feeling the liveliness of themselves, others and the space within.[122]

'Sympathetic vibration' thus emerges as an apt description of the 'relational connections' catalysed not only by the *Live Room* – the various networks of vibration and induction, but also in modulations of thought and collective experience.

In this, Bain shares something with those dancefloor and soundsystem cultures that engineer temporary, synthetic environments in order to explore unfamiliar qualities of being and 'mutant coordinates' of subjectivity. In both, there is an emphasis on strange horizons of the collective sonic body – a 'becoming-body'.[123] 'With my work,' says Bain, 'I envision an art of the future where the body along with the mind is driven through intensifying experiences and provoked into new territories in reference to location, to the self, to others and towards our machines.'[124] The *Live Room* is, therefore, a collective experiment. Bain's role is to engender the field, and tweak its parameters in ways that modulate the responsivity, but the investigations of participants on the floor are equally crucial to the event.

> This process usually involved traversing at a slow pace along the platforms as they investigated the sensations cascading through their bodies. If you imagine forty or more people doing this movement at the same time, what developed were simultaneous patterns of integration, separation and group dynamics. Seemingly chaotic actions began to turn into self-organising systems which followed the shifting frequencies that were continually changed by the operator. As the audience moved, it mimicked the patterns of sand found in Chladni figures. Individuals acted in a similar way to the separate grains of sand, shifting in relation to others and locating the nodal points along with the active areas.[125]

Bain's descriptions recall the earlier image of shimmering cymatic figures – rising and falling, synchronously contorting – in a speaker cone full of taut goop. The *Live Room* is, indeed, another form of cymatic investigation, one designed to explore the provisionality of the sonic body, the figural pull of weird modulations, and dynamics (social as much as material) of vibratory self-organization in sentient matter. Bain charges the field in various ways and watches the patterns unfold – rhythms, responses, mass effects, and individual variations. In these patternings, there are glimpses of something resembling dance – an *incipient dance* in which bodies alone and together are literally induced to move. They are forced to adjust, they become curious, they begin to test out their new (in)capabilities, they elaborate new responses, and they try them out together.

Eventually, Bain began to notice the installation's popularity with musicians and dancers who 'returned because they could use it as a tool to formulate body actions which were outside their normal performance routines. They seemed very concentrated and playful, lost in the physicality of it.'[126] He also compares the *Live Room* to the sonic space of the nightclub, and his own role to that of the DJ, the organizer of rhythms and frequencies, with the technological means to 'modulate the actions of many'. There is certainly something to the comparison: the technician spinning out logics of sensation, spurring figural mutations; dance examined outside the routine language of technique and 'performativity' to consider how experiments in movement arise from the immanent materiality of a milieu. In these ways, Bain's extreme experiment – turning a missile silo into a body-swallowing subwoofer – can actually help to guide investigations of other 'live rooms', that is, other spaces engineered with the specific intention of shaking bodies out of themselves and putting a sonic collectivity in motion.

5

Tone Scientists II: Bass Cults

Bass, The Bass, Bassline, Bass Kick, Touching Bass, Taste the Bass, Can U Feel It, When U Feel It, Feel It (Bass), Heavy Bass, Bass Shake, Bassquake, Body Shake, Bass Will Shake, Bass Vibration, Bass Power, Bass Trip, Bass Rush, Bass Reaction, Bass Reflex, Bass Induced, Bass Concussion, Bass Penetrates, Bass Breaks the Bones, Bass Overdose, Dred Bass, Bass Nightmare, Bass Terror, Ding Dong Bass, Tickatok Bass, Spectral Bass, Hard Bass, Maximum Bass, Big Bad Bass, Incredible Bass, Psycho Bass, Ridiculous Bass, Bass Bins, Bass Speaker, Dance With the Speaker, Bassline Kickin, Bass Pump, Bass Go Boom, Mash Up The Speaker, B-Line Fi Blow, Destroy Your Speaker, Woofer Wrecker, Popcone, Check Out the Bass, Come With the Bass, Tune Your Bass, Pump the Bass, Let the Bass Kick, Drop the Bass, Bomb the Bass, Survive the Bass, Bass Fanatic, Bass Constructor, Bass Generator, Bass Transmitter, Bass Finder, Lost in Bass, Da Bass II Dark, Bass Oddity, Wait for the Bass, Weight for the Bass, 100 Tons of Bass, Rocks the Bass, Bass Material, Bass Logic, Believe the Bass, In Bass We Trust, Beyond Bass, Sub Bass, Subsonic, Sub Dub, Deep Sub, Subsonic Sub, Sub Groove, Sub Hurts, Scottie's Sub, Illegal Subs, Sub Committee, Sub-Urban, Sub Audible, Sub-Bass Experience, Subsonic Shadow, Thunder, Thunderclap, Bassline Rumble, Hits Me Like Thunder, Feel the Thunder, Boom Bashin, Drumstruck, Low Frequency Overload, Back to the Scene of the Bass, (808) Bass Boom, The Incredible Bass Machine, Tales from the Bass Side ...[1]

99 machines. Titles on 10- and 12-inch vinyl hint at the fictions and affective strategies animating twenty-first-century bass cults.[2] In the decades since disco and the diffusion of Jamaican sound system culture, it is the dancefloors and studios of the Black Atlantic (and its musical satellites) that have become the busiest sites of low-frequency experimentation. This is where bass moves

beyond the familiar supporting role it holds in so much Western music (as rhythmic guide, melodic shadow, etc.) and begins to carve out its autonomy, taking over the mix, driving tracks, and sometimes pulling them right apart. These musics are spectrally distinct from those in the rock-pop mould that typically foreground the mid range, prioritize the communicative functions of voice, and, as a result, translate well to the small speaker systems of radio and television. In contrast, it can be reasonably argued that sound system–derived musics like dub, hip-hop, house, Miami bass, techno, jungle, and all their variants do not meaningfully exist without the low end.

These bass-centric musics rely on felt vibration. They have a more explicitly material aim, being designed to modulate flesh and space. More than communications media, they are technologies of affect engineering – ones backed by now vast collections of vernacular techniques and strategies, accumulated over decades of experimental practice. In some ways, they work with principles that have formed the basis of audiogenetic strategies for centuries – bass as an agent of unhoming and a catalyst of collective becomings – but with less moral prescription and greater interest in the open-endedness of the acoustic event. In this latter respect, then, they may share more in common with those varieties of audio art that make a project of charging spaces, abstracting perception, putting subjectivities in motion, and investigating unforeseen potentials in low-frequency encounters. Yet, their approach is typically less curatorial, their pace of invention much more intense, as multiple artists, operating in finely differentiated micro-scenes, compete with one another to devise new qualities of sonic experience, and new musical systems, conceived as technologies of the sonic body. In this environment, wholesale shifts in sonic practice may happen several times over in the time it might take a gallery work to move from conception to opening. The ethic can be called a populist vanguardism – one that hinges on feedbacks between the studio, the DJ booth, and the dancefloor.[3] At their most vital, such scenes repeatedly ask and elaborate the questions: 'How far can dancerly habits and potentials be pushed? How weird can it get, yet still move the crowd? How low can you go?'

'Bass culture', the term made famous by dub poet Linton Kwesi Johnson, has lately found itself applied broadly to a whole spectrum of musical activity that, notionally at least, traces some lineage to the Jamaican sound system. More recently, 'Bass Music' has become the indiscriminate catch-all term, and marketing shorthand, for vast portions of electronic dance music, whatever their actual spectral makeup.[4] In fact, in their current popular usage, both terms have become too vague to tell us much that we did not already know – that is, that some amount of low end is essential to most electronically constructed dancefloor musics. But this misses certain more elusive tendencies that cut across styles and scenes. The term *bass cult*, proposed here, aims to identify something more specific, but also more esoteric: an occulture of the low end; obsessive sects of technician-conjurers; elements of a myth-science in which sound and audio technology are mined for weird potentials, being endlessly broken down, reconfigured, tested on bodies, theorized and mythologized.[5] The following is an investigation of these bass cults – their sonic-spatial practices, conceptual language, and musical machines.

The Lab

The sonic practices of bass cults comprise a minor science of low-frequency sound and experience that is comparable in its basic orientations (and fixations) to those we have already encountered. Its primary concern is the vibratory relationality of the sonic body – what it can do, how it can be put at variance with itself in productive ways. As elsewhere, this involves following material tendencies in sound and sonorous space, testing possibilities, extracting concepts. Among bass cults, these experiments now span generations and continents, with some practices remaining localized, or secretly held by individual producers, while others have become commonplace in commercial studios.

Jamaica is a privileged site on this map – its modern obsession with low-frequency force being largely traceable to the arrival of the first electric bass guitars on the island circa 1960.[6] The new instrument, combined with increasingly powerful, makeshift sound systems, allowed the bassline to move to the foreground, becoming dominant in rhythm, melody, and the mix.[7] From the outset, the impetus was to go lower (the lowest note on a standardly tuned electric bass is E_1 or 41 Hz), and an emergent bass science set about testing the parameters of sound technologies and sensation. Producer Sylvan Morris reveals one pivotal moment in this process in an interview with dub theorist Michael Veal. In about 1963, he says:

> I noticed that the sound that I get from the back of the speakers in them days had a bassier sound than coming from the front. The front was stronger but there's a very low bass sound that you get out of the back. So I designed a box, and made my two apertures at the back, right? And put a mic there. That's where I pick up my sound from actually, from the back of the speaker. It's very deep, so this is how I got a lot of those deep sounds. Plus, Coxsonne had a Pultec equalizer which sort of enhanced that sound 'cause it sorta boost the very low 40 Hz region. That's how you get the Downbeat sound.[8]

This is an early example of a producer-engineer glimpsing an uncommon variety of vibration, pursuing it and devising techniques for its intensification. In bass cults, the same inductive ethic pervades every area of sonic practice. For music makers and sound system operators, in earlier years especially, the process often extended into the guts of machines – building their own equipment, modifying commercial gear, and tinkering constantly to make sound do more, and different, things.

At other times, this science quite literally becomes ambulant when it involves scavenging for discarded technologies and plunging into their sometimes obscure logics to see what they can do. Roland Corporation's TR-808 drum machine is among the most famous examples, and the story of its commercial failure and subsequent centrality to hip-hop, electro and house has been widely repeated. The synthetic timbres and metric rigidity that led more traditional musicians to reject it as an accompaniment tool were exactly the qualities that appealed to aspiring electronic producers enthralled by the cybernetic possibilities of Kraftwerk-styled robot funk. 'Everything sounded ultra-mechanical', says Tommy Boy Records' Tom Silverman of the machine logic imposed on music making and musical experience by 808's inbuilt 16-step sequencer: 'That's partly how the hiphop sound originated.'[9] Through the 1980s, the 808's deep, long-decaying kick drum proliferated across dancefloors: in hip-hop, it added a humming weight under rhymes and sparse, mechanical rhythmscapes; in-house and techno, alongside its successor the TR-909, it became the entraining pulse. In the mid-1980s, Miami bass producers made the extra innovation of liberating the kick from the 808's sequencer by recording it into more versatile Emu SP12 and SP1200 drum machine/samplers.[10] Now, in a sampled form, it could be triggered more rapidly, and syncopated, at sliding pitches, creating a shifting bed of intermodulating bass tones, harmonizing and beating together, like layers of short, pulsing sine-drones.

Diving further into their machines, artists begin to intuit even more arcane low-end potentials that hadn't been foreseen by their makers. Steve Beckett, one of the founders of Sheffield's WARP Records, describes how the label's early sound (sometimes called Bleep techno) was shaped in part by artists experimenting with the sine wave oscillator in their Akai samplers. 'It's not supposed to be for making music, just testing the equipment. You've got a treble tone, a mid tone and a bass tone, which people used to get the biggest bass possible. Then they'd overlay different bass sounds, so there might be three or four bass lines in one track.'[11] For the dub-influenced techno outfit Sweet Exorcist (which included Richard H. Kirk of the industrial band Cabaret Voltaire), this resulted in a series of tracks called 'Testone', 'Testtwo', 'Testthree', and so on, up to version six, featuring what was, to that point in time, an uncommonly powerful low end made possible by layering synth outputs with the sampler's harmonically clean subbass tone. This sort of spectral layering has become standard in bass-centric musics, with the primary bassline often being divided into separately treated high and low components, and supplemented by a subbass element (sine, triangle or filtered square wave) extending as low as 30 Hz.[12]

It has been common to treat this sort of repurposing as a 'misuse' of commercial technologies, which indeed it is, but Eshun sees another agency involved – what he calls a 'MachinicAutocatalysis' that 'opens up new vectors of technology.' In effect, he argues, the curious engineer is sensually lured into the logic of the machine, which is always latent with more connectibility than schematics, user manuals, or social constructions could ever predict. There is a private life of the machine – a man-made unknown – waiting to be engaged. One classic example is the other famously 'failed' Roland accompaniment device – the TB-303 Bass Line synth, which became the single most essential component of acid house music in the late 1980s. 'Acid House's druggy, darkly psychedelic but intensely physical sound, characterised by the 303's heavily distorted, corrosive squelches, was not a sound intended by the 303's designer, Tadao Kikumoto', writes *The Wire*'s Peter Shapiro, 'but was instead the result of some kids in Chicago randomly playing around with the 303's' pitch and filter controls.[13] In acid house, the 303's single oscillator gurgles and squeaks, its square and saw wave cycles prickle the skin and itch the brain. But with a slow sweep of the filter knob the edges gradually give way to a quietly roiling sub that bubbles up and around the body. 'Restricted by its one-octave range, the 303 could barely accomplish its appointed task but within this restriction', says Shapiro, 'an entire universe of sound could be created.'

Universes, and the prospect more to be found or synthesized: there is indeed a world-making dimension to these sorts of discoveries.[14] Whole musical cultures develop around them. Guattari writes that 'Musical machines establish themselves against a background of sonorous Universes which have been constantly modified since the great polyphonic mutation.' These 'technical machines', he says, 'install themselves at intersections of the most complex and heterogeneous enunciative components.' That is, they do more than make musical sounds; they vibrate at the interfaces of things, having the capacity to modulate matter, thought, language, figments of lived reality, and the ways we move, vary and band together. They can help catalyse and organize a collectivity – 'a people of oscillators'.[15] If there is a man-made unknown of the machine, and if new qualities of being are at stake, then there is, in a literal sense, an occult of audio technology – a layer of mysterious materiality and a dark agency. There is something shrouded, something to be deciphered and, by a mix of intuition and uncommon skill, channelled into something humanly useful. It is not surprising, then, that many dancefloor technicians see themselves as alchemists of sorts, revealing and mastering hidden forces of nature and the machine, concocting what Eshun calls 'impossible musics'.[16] For the most creative among them, at least, there is truth to it. This is the sense in which we hear talk of 'the lab' – the studio and the dancefloor understood, quite un-metaphorically, as the laboratory where experiments between machine, sound, and body are repeatedly staged, observed, reworked and tried again. The most potent discoveries are retained and developed further becoming part of an arcanum, of sorts – a secretly held knowledge of the sonic body and musical machines. This is the beginning of what we sometimes call *bass science*.

The Science

> Traditional science still means a depletion, cold scientists, extreme logic and all these corny cliches. But in musical terms, science is the opposite, science is intensification, more sensation. Science is rhythm intensified, rhythm estranged. And that's how a whole generation understands science. Then what they mean by abstract is sensations so new there isn't yet a language for them. So the shorthand is to just call it abstract. There's a whole generation who've grown used to thinking of sensory emotions without having a language for them yet.[17]

'Science' carries an extra inflection in Black Atlantic music cultures. It permeates sonic-cultural language and guides sonic practices, but with more suggestion of sorcery than positivism. When Mark Dery asked hip-hop theorist Tricia Rose to explain what rappers mean by 'droppin' science', she was partly right in saying it describes a certain lyrical hermeticism, but what is revealed is not necessarily, as she suggests, an 'incontrovertible' truth.[18] Here, Eshun is more convincing: 'To drop science is to mystify, rather than to educate. In HipHop, science breaks it down in order to complexify not to clarify.'[19] The aim is not *knowing* so much as sparking an *un-knowing*, an undoing of self-certainty. For the rapper in battle, it's not about enlightening opponents or reaching a consensus, but lyrically pulling the rug out from under them, leaving them vexed and speechless. The Science, therefore, speaks more to strategies of unhoming, esoteric techniques and a level of secrecy. We find the same ethic applied in other areas too: the construction of unsteadying rhythms, the unmaking of technologies and sonorous spaces, 'sampledelia', and experiments in bodily-felt vibration. In their various ways, these techniques work to produce an unusual eventness of the body by putting technologies to uncommon uses. As such, they end up having to invent their own bio-technical language – a minor language of the sonic body and the musical machine. They also need to find words and concepts to describe things not commonly felt (tales of becoming), and to imagine possibilities for the future.

If there is a dialect native to The Science, then it is sonic fiction. As Eshun has shown in *More Brilliant Than The Sun*, its traces are everywhere – in titles, album art, interviews, liner notes, vocal samples. But we miss this entire conceptual field if we reduce its utterances to the status of metaphor and hyperbole. If the tales seem grandiose, it is worth remembering that the experiences they describe are often, themselves, over the top; their audio practices truly are esoteric. That's the point. In the end, it is far better to take a stab at inventing suitable language than to not try at all. From this perspective, we can understand sonic fiction as the front end of an arcanum situated at the interface between sound, the sonic body and musical machines. It encodes techniques, theorizes uncommon varieties of sonic experience, and speculates on becomings, sometimes goading artists into trying improbable new things. This Science is, therefore, one of unhoming and strange invention.

This conception of science comes to bass cults by more than one diasporic route. Michael Veal has noted that in Jamaica:

> The term *science* has a double resonance ... often used colloquially to refer to the island's neo-African tradition of black magic, Obeah. Derived from the Akan term *obia* (ghost), the symbol of Obeah has sometimes provided a symbolic medium for the local grounding of global sound technology. [Musician] Kevin Martin has even observed that the terms *Dub* (noun) and *Dubby* (adjective) resonate etymologically with '*duppy*,' the Jamaican patwa term for ghosts or malevolent spirits.[20]

Similarly, in his book on Rastafarianism, Barry Chevannes writes that 'The obeahman is frequently referred to as a "science man"', a keeper of occult wisdom with the ability to reshape lived reality.'[21] Making the link too is Erik Davis, author of *Techgnosis: Myth, Magic and Mysticism in the Age of Information*. He notes an earlier study by Robert Pelton that 'points out the similarities between modern scientists and traditional trickster figures like Anansi, Eshu, and Ellegua.' Both, says Pelton, 'seek to befriend the strange, not so much striving to "reduce" anomaly as to use it as a passage into a larger order.' To which Davis adds that 'we could ask for no better description of the technological tricks pulled by the great Dubmasters'.[22] It is in this vein that reggae historian Lloyd Bradley describes dub as musical obeah, sonically organized to disorient, unsettle, unhome. Dub grounds its defamiliarizing sound design in massive low-frequency force: 'the crushing bass'n'drum remixes keep getting us on our toes with such seemingly arbitrary SFX as explosions, crashes, windows breaking and big dogs barking, while through the judiciously employed echo, some frighteningly large spaces open up quite suddenly under our feet.'[23] Producer Lee Perry is only the most obvious example of a Jamaican technician-conjurer (famously 'known to blow ganja smoke onto his tapes while recording, ... to bury unprotected tapes in the soil outside of his studio, and to spray them with a variety of fluids, including whisky, blood, and urine, ostensibly to enhance their spiritual properties'[24]), but the low-end psychedelia of King Tubby, Scientist, Mad Professor, and others is no less alchemical.

In Veal's description, Western sound technology, in Jamaican musical culture, has effectively occupied a position akin to what Deleuze and Guattari have called Royal Science – cold, rule-bound, and institutional.[25] The Science, on the other hand, pertains to the occult of the music machine, and the unfamiliar or intensified experiences that can be conjured by allying with it. Trained technicians like Tubby, Scientist, and others that followed, have therefore occupied an itinerant role, drawing on formal education in electronics, but diverting it to serve the peculiar needs of the dancehall, building and customizing their own amplifiers, pre-amps, speaker boxes, equalizers, and also applying it to the processes of recording, mixing and cutting (a 'myth-science of the mixing desk', in Eshun's description).[26] In the 1990s, the science fiction author Samuel R. Delaney described these unofficial, or mutant, technologies as 'black boxes', in order to distinguish them, and their social lives, from mass-market consumer electronics. Shortly thereafter, the British house/jungle producer A Guy Called Gerald coined the term Black Secret Technology, which we can understand to cover a whole spectrum of devices, concepts, musics and activities collected under the rubric of The Science.

The other most crucial reference point, however, is Sun Ra. It is difficult to overestimate just how much Ra's Myth-Science – developed over decades scouring libraries and rare book shops, synthesized over thousands of insomniac nights – has permeated the musical culture of the Black Atlantic, and even popular culture more generally. Among many other subjects, it drew on ancient hermetic writings, religious texts, the history of black American music, Theosophy, contemporary science fiction, developments in new technologies.[27] It helped revive modern African American interest in the history and influence of ancient Egypt, while also setting the course of what came to be called Afrofuturism.[28] It directly influenced musicians like Coltrane and Parliament-Funkadelic, but also, it would seem, the cosmologies of the Nation of Islam and The Nation of Gods and Earths (or '5% Nation of Islam'), the teachings of which, with their science fictional leanings and cryptic numerological systems, have since have become utterly engrained in hip-hop.[29]

As John Szwed explains: 'For Sonny "science" was somewhere between or beyond science fiction and science:

> More than a method of reasoning and a set of laboratory practices, it was also a mystical process, and (as the rappers imply by 'dropping science') a kind of secret or suppressed knowledge which had the power to create new myths, erase old ones, altering our ratio to each other and the rest of the universe. His thinking stemmed from an age when science, Hermetic philosophy, and magic were not so distinct, as well as from an earlier African-American understanding of 'science' which meant a magic based on writing, and where science might include 'conjure' or even 'blackness' itself.[30]

For Ra, music was an audiogenetic project. His Science aimed to defamiliarize this world and synthesize something new in its place (an Alter Destiny). Although his Neo-Platonist beliefs often led him to renounce the body in theory, in musical practice, there was very often an emphasis on sound's materiality and its neuroaffective uses. There was the roar of his 'Space Chords', sometimes there were pummelling Lightning Drums. He was among the first musicians to incorporate synthesizers into his work – including a Clavioline and his custom-built Astro Space Organ; later, a pre-production model from Bob Moog. For his 1983 recording 'Hiroshima' he drew apocalyptic rumbles from a pipe organ. From the late 1970s, he toured several times with a massive, hexagon-shaped light instrument – a relative of the vocoder, called the Outerspace

Visual Communicator (OVC), that was custom-designed for him by a fan, Bill Sebastien.[31]

His band went by dozens of names including the Myth-Science Arketsra, the Solar-Science Arkestra, the Transmolecular Arkestra, the Outergalactic Discipline Arkestra and the All-Star Inventions. Szwed writes, 'There was an element of secret knowledge about the unpredictability of the name of the band, as there was about the names Sonny gave to some of the instruments they used. ... Sonny was creating an instrumental mythos.'

> There was the flying saucer, lightning drum, space gong, space harp, space-dimension mellophone, space drum, space bells, space flute, space master piano, intergalactic space organ, solar bells, solar drum, sunhorn, sun harp, Egyptian sun bells, ancient Egyptian infinity drum, boom-bam, mistro clarinet, morrow, spiral percussion gong, cosmic tone organ, dragon drum, cosmic side drum, and tiger organ.[32]

Every record and performance was, therefore, conceived as a unique coming together of esoteric technologies, named less for their form or tonal essence, than for the uses they were put to in the singular relational assemblages they were meant to help engender. Fittingly, Ra called his musicians 'tone scientists'.

Bass science

The conceptual language of tone science cuts across twenty-first-century dancefloors. In the 1990s, the rhythmic contortions of UK jungle were sometimes described as *breakbeat science*. Jungle took the sampled funk loops upon which hip-hop had been built, sped them up and sliced them into their component pieces, thereby allowing individual percussive instances to be repeated, deleted, pitched up and down and flown around the stereo field. With the destruction of the loop in favour of an always varying rhythmic terrain, the break lost its regularity and took on a character closer to Bop drumming – with its manic irregularities and multiple, simultaneous tangents. Only now, via the sampler and the sequencer, the percussion became inhumanly fast and complex. The incorporeal effect is one of kinaesthetic bewilderment: 'How do I follow this? How do I move?' We find something kindred in sets of techniques, sometimes called *vocal science*, which first appeared in the productions of American garage producer Todd Edwards.[33] Edwards' vocals are sampled, sliced and into bits, and mapped across a MIDI controller keyboard, allowing them to be retriggered in kaleidoscope patterns of fractured speech. There are shards of words, inhales and exhales, all shimmering together at shifting pitches. Stray phonemes combine to make new phrases. Slices become spectral bits of melody-percussion, morphing together with organ stabs and hi-hats. The truncated gasps can even play confusingly on the breathing of the listener, and the overall result can be dizzying, almost hallucinatory. Later musics, notably UK 2-step garage, have adapted jungle-style rhythm science to drum machine sequencing, and melded it with Edwards-style vocal science.[34]

Bass science is another term in circulation. In the studio, it can mean any number of things, from the more alchemical aspects of recording, synthesis, and processing, to the arcane techniques of mastering technicians. Bass science begins to coalesce when producer-engineers start demanding more of the bassline – pushing it to the front of the mix and envisioning bodily vibration as their medium. In its earliest forms, it meant probing the deepest recordable tones, reinforcing the low end, and finding new orders of bass weight. (Jamaican 'drums-and-bass' mixes of the late 1960s were an early testing ground, while disco's own 'dub' mixes were behind the advent of the 12" single, with its capacity to capture very low tones at high loudness levels.) But soon, it also meant efforts to defamiliarize the bassline – to make it do impossible things.

In the 1970s, dub and synthfunk basslines started to move and modulate in strange ways. They became more elastic and spasmodic. Eshun points to the body-bending tones conjured by Bootsy Collins for Parliament-Funkadelic, using the aptly named Mutron filter unit from Musitronics corporation. This, he argues, is the beginning of properly mutant bass – synthetic bass designed to give the sonic body something new to ponder. 'Mutronic bass', he says, 'charms your stomach in a duet, tugs at your hips, humps your ass in a seismic bump. It heaves in a peristaltic motion like the amplified insides of a stomach.'[35] Later, Zapp added an uncanny twist to the formula by layering in a Talk Box device, like the one made famous by Peter Frampton, to modulate the Moog. On tracks like 'More Bounce to the Ounce' and 'I Can Make You Dance', Roger Troutman's basslines don't just hum the body, they almost seem to speak through it in a low, robotic drawl.[36] Elsewhere, around the same time, Jamaican and British digidub producers were among the first to explore the possibilities of subbass deployed on its own, either as verge-of-the-ear melody, or as something altogether more formless lurking heavily below.[37] In the latter case, the sub neither helped the beat, nor shadowed the tune, but seemed to come and go as it pleased, sometimes going silent before sneaking up in unsuspecting bodies. In some of these recordings, the captured sounds of distorting woofer cones and resultant room vibrations are actually more audible than the bassline itself.

Since the late 1980s, bass exploration has proliferated, in conjunction with the simultaneous spread of synthetic musics and affordable studio tools. Such an enormous variety of low-end vibrations have been committed to vinyl that it would be impossible to map them in any meaningful way. However, some of these sounds prove to be especially lasting and fertile, and they end up acquiring a life of their own: plumbed by producers for every possible affective nuance, some becoming the focal point of entire musical assemblages (e.g. acid house and the 303), others remaining more mobile, cutting across otherwise disparate sites at various moments in time. In these instances, we have more than just a 'sound', we have the emergence of a machinic lineage – call it a *bass phylum* – that comprises entire networks of circuitry, connections, sonorities, affects, sensations, strategies, technocultural practices, tales, fictions and a history (which, itself, is variously technical, commercial, experiential). Some of these begin with an especially resonant preset, native to a given musical machine (the Roland Alpha Juno's 'What the' patch is a non-bass example).[38] Others emerge through combinations of trial and error, accident, and studio experimentation. We can identify an 808 phylum that now stretches well beyond Miami, into Rio's funk carioca, Chicago's ghetto house and footwork (and far further in more subtle ways). The deep punch of the Yamaha TX81Z's 'Lately Bass' preset was endemic to dancefloors of several sorts through the early 1990s (as familiar in r&b and new jack swing as it was in electro-industrial and Belgian hardcore techno).[39] There are endless bass-reinforced variations of the Korg M1's 'Organ 2' present circulating in versions of house and garage (and even a subset of bassline house called organ house). There are also whole families of LFO-modulated 'wobble' bass that cut across jungle, bassline house, and dubstep.

Other phyla have more obscure origins, however, being the result of studio tangents that begin with a glimpse of sonic anomaly, then pursue and shape it until it does the most strikingly unfamiliar things. This is bass science at its most inscrutable, its practices at their most elaborate. These minor audio technologies often derive their names from the tracks or artists that launched them. For example, so-called Reese Bass was first heard in the 1988 tune 'Just Want Another Chance' by Detroit techno producer Kevin Saunderson, working under his Reese Project alias. Early on, it was widely sampled, which meant that it could be sequenced in new patterns and pitches, but also that it could be processed in ways that drew out latent sonic qualities. Eventually, it was also reverse engineered, meaning that it could be endlessly reinvented from the ground up. A Reese is a curious thing – a deep and hollow drone that might seem monotonous on first audition, but which reveals a dense and busy core at higher volumes. The sound is built from multiple saw waves (e.g. at minimum, an octave pair and a fourth, usually with a root between 40 and 60 Hz), detuned to produce a harmonic beating, filtered to remove most of high-frequency content, and sometimes further processed to elicit extra dimensions of movement and texture.[40] These out-of-phase waves produce drift effects not unlike those investigated by drone artists, so the perceptual effect of a Reese is one of simultaneous stasis (the monolithic weight of the drone) and divergent motion (via the drifting cycles). It smudges temporality, sounding as though it's hurtling through a tunnel, while seeming at the same time to flow back through itself. In highly linear rhythmic assemblages, like techno and speed garage, a Reese can produce a sensation of driving, yet liquid, momentum. Melded with the more fractured rhythms of jungle or 2-step garage, however, it can lend an extra swimmingness to already unsteadied bodies.

In jungle, we can also locate the origins of another phylum: Dred Bass, named for the 1994 Dead Dred track by the same name. Dred Bass is comparable to the wah-wah (envelope filter) effect used on electric guitars, but at far lower frequencies. On higher bass notes, the filter opens and closes more quickly, giving it a 'wallop' quality, but the lowest tones are slow and cavernous. In the mid-1990s, Dred Bass became a staple in jungle, often played in ragga-style patterns.[41] It then moved into the repertoire of UK speed garage artists, where it was used largest mainly for its long, enveloping qualities. By the mid-2000s, however, it had become dramatically more complex. In bassline house, one often encounters multiple, different Dred-like basses, at different pitches and speeds, often interspersed with wobbles, subs and filtered square waves, and interchanging as frequently as every one to two bars. When shards of vocal science are added to the mix, the total effect can be deeply unsteadying, despite the 4×4 beat.[42]

If some scenes like bassline house, acid, and Miami bass have organized largely around the possibilities of a single phylum, other bass-led musics leave more room for idiosyncratic investigation. The overlapped fields of UK garage and grime are good examples of the latter. In these settings, it's not unusual to find individual artists or crews, pursuing low-end anomalies and carving out their own special techniques. These inventions may be one-offs – tried in a single tune and then dropped – or they might be pushed further, explored over multiple tracks and closely guarded. For a given artist or crew, this can become a sonic signature that sets their tracks apart. As a secretly held technology, it can also attract remix work.[43] There are examples of producers spending the larger part of a career, even an entire discography, working on variations of a single sound. Consider the elastic square waves that pervade early Wiley/Roll Deep records (especially their bassline-only 'Devil's Mixes'), or the metallic throbs that run through Black Ops' 'Sublow' sound, as well as the bass-layered string samples unique to each. There is the hollowed-out, yet improbably weighty subbass of early Plasticman and Mark One recordings. DJs Wire and Narrows are known mainly for small discographies in which they reinvented Dred Bass to make it churn and bristle in long, floor-swallowing sweeps. We hear something similar in Alias, only more clipped and irregular, sounding somewhere between a sludgy punch and resonant growl. KMA Productions' small but influential catalogue is full of roiling, low-passed square waves that lurch around under a taught surface, periodically breaking through in thick, acidic gurgles.

Similar effects were explored more fully by UK garage producer Wookie. At points, the rubbery bassline in 'Duppy' seems almost impervious to the beat, playing strangely on the body's felt sense of time. It stretches and slows down, sometimes seeming to hover for a moment before sliding back into itself or snapping forward at the last moment. Elsewhere, the intermodulating bass tones in tracks like 'Storm', 'Down On Me' and 'Weird Science' erupt in bubbling slurps and voice-like formant effects. Wookie explains: 'I might make a tune called "Talking Bass" cos that's what it sounds like, my bass does speak, in a way. I make my melodies out of bass. ... I have a couple of Moog basses layered together, modulating the tone "til it's dark enough to play light on it, to play melodies on it." '[44]

Dubplates and mastering

Before these musics can be committed to disc and tested on sound systems, however, they have to pass through a final stage of studio processing. Mastering, and the related practice of lacquer cutting, are an arcanum unto themselves, and it is common to hear even the most technically skilled artists describing the work of a trusted engineer as something approaching a dark art.[45] There is indeed an air of mystery about this field, which performs an itinerant function between music and acoustic science, production and performance. Reinforcing this is the fact that, as a group, they are a notoriously secretive bunch, their personal sonic repertoires having been amassed through apprenticeships and years of practice, and refined in their own custom-built studios. Their job is to prepare a recording for pressing to vinyl or CD, or in some scenes, cutting one-off acetate discs, or dubplates, used in DJ sets. This involves treating the original material to basic adjustments like phase correction and taming excess bass, but the craft emerges in the engineer's ability to reshape the music's spectral character in subtle or drastic ways, drawing out qualities of sound that remained obscure during the production and mixdown stages. It is always an intuitive process: the engineer following contours in sound, altering their dynamics via banks of compressors; making phase and equalizer adjustments (even carefully infusing distortion) to elicit new qualities of space and harmonic colour. When bass is the central component of a track, the engineer's job becomes one of finding nuances of the low end (shapes, textures, motion) and delivering extra orders of weight, while still maintaining a workable spectral balance. Moreover, it demands an understanding of how low frequencies operate in sonorous space, specifically in the atypical force environment generated by a powerful sound system (skills entirely distinct from those of radio-oriented mastering).

Given this, bass cults have tended to rely on just a small few engineers and mastering houses around the world that are known for their skill with the low end. (Exceptions being dub and dancehall, which sometimes keep this work in-house, as in the case of London's Ariwa Studios).[46] Among the most prolific and influential in the field is Herb Powers Jr (or Herbie Jr). His technical discography stretches from funk to contemporary r&b, but in the early 1980s, Powers was crucial in shaping (literally) the sounds of electro and hip-hop. His credits include Afrika Bambaataa's 'Planet Rock' (an 808-enforced reworking of Kraftwerk's 'Trance Europe Express') and T La Rock's 'It's Yours' – the pair of which was foundational to Miami bass. He also mastered much of the thunderous, drum machine-driven hip-hop that dominated the decade (including foundational tracks by Run DMC, LL Cool J, Just-Ice). Other figures whose work helped define particular musics include Mike 'Full-O-Bottom' Fuller (Miami bass), Brian 'Big Bass' Gardner (West Coast rap) and Ron Murphy (Detroit techno). In the last two decades, the aquatic subbass of dub techno has been inseparable from Berlin's Dubplates and Mastering, which has, more recently, left a spectral stamp on the sounds of Continental digidub and dubstep.

In London, Transition Studios has become virtually synonymous with expertly tailored bass, in part through their work for jungle and dub artists, but above all for their association with the subbass-centric dubstep scene.[47] In fact, it could be argued that Transition's owner, Jason Goz (who has since mastered Eleh and organ recordings for Touch Records), did as much as any single producer to fashion the bottom-and-tops minimalist sound of dubstep in its middle period, circa 2004–6.[48] Not only did Transition master the majority of dubstep releases during this time, they also cut most of the pre-release dubplates played by DJs during a period when the music was still primarily experienced via the massive sound systems at London's Plastic People and Mass nightclubs (both of which have, incidentally, been host to a series of 'Deaf Raves' at which music is supposed to be felt, if not heard).[49] If the music was tailored for these atypical sonorous spaces, then there is a sense in which the engineer's experience of a given sound system's capabilities, combined with felt memory of those rooms, has been fed back into the mastering console and made to speculatively shape sound. Put another way, the system and room, via the sonic body, begin to exert a reciprocal influence on the sonic character of the music.

Engineering the vibratorium

Of course, bass science has always extended beyond the studio too, with dancefloors being the other major site of sonic body exploration. Here we can borrow and adapt Nicolas Ridout's concept of the vibratorium to describe the dancefloor as a space shaped by bodily events and modulatory potentials more than sign systems, a space 'where the vibrations get right into you, before you start making sense of them.'[50] Sarah Thornton writes, 'In the 1950s, record playback technology was not able to fill a large ballroom with high fidelity sound. Even in the early-1960s, few discotheques could provide all-around sound, highs or lows, or thumping bass'.[51] Yet, by this time, the Jamaican dancehall was already dramatically expanding its audio capabilities, driven by competition between sound system owners. The most powerful of the early sound systems might be capable of a hundred watts, but these were quickly supplanted by custom-built systems capable of many hundreds (later, thousands) of watts, and incorporating 15- and 18-inch speakers that had never before been used for music.[52] Early on, this often meant finding engineers willing and able to break with common-sense precepts of electronic engineering in order to devise black boxes with capabilities far beyond those of any commercially available musical equipment.[53] It also meant scavenging for suitable components in unlikely places, as in

> [the] well-worn story of an unnamed sound man going into a marine equipment dealership in Miami and trying to buy the type of loudspeaker that ocean-going liners would used to herald their approach in foggy conditions. When the astounded salesman had come to terms with the idea that this decidedly un-nautical customer wanted to use it to play records, the nonplussed Jamaican had but one question: '*It tek two t'ousand watts?*'[54]

The object of these elaborate efforts, says Lloyd Bradley, was ever-deeper and more powerful bass: 'the bass ... to *make* you move up your waist'.[55]

This is vibration as a material catalyst of dance. That some sound systems added 'Hi-Fi' to their names (Hometown Hi-Fi, Jack Ruby Hi-Fi, Fat Man Hi-Fi, for example), should not be mistaken for evidence of an overarching audiophilic sensibility in the usual sense. Fidelity (we can ask 'to what?') was never the real concern when systems were judged by the weight of their bass, and records were played through echoes and phasers. Rather, the sound system, with its arrays of bass bins and amps, its sound effects and custom pre-amplifiers, has always been less about *re*-production of texts than the production of singular intensities. In this assemblage, the record is still raw sonic material, something to be repeatedly staged anew. There is also an element of sound design that extends beyond production and into sonic-spatial techniques of 'stringing up' the equipment. For his part, Tubby was known to surround the floor with bass bins and place his tweeters up in the trees.[56] The effect – with voices and cymbals flying overhead, and deep undulations invading from below – was a bewildering sense of 'sound from everywhere'. The sound system thus becomes an engine of bodily mystification. By the mid-1970s, similar ethico-acoustic strategies had begun to appear in the New York disco scene too. Extensive experiments with different speaker systems and sound reinforcement techniques were carried out in clubs like The Loft and, later, the Paradise Garage (the namesake of garage music).[57] One major innovation was the discovery that a rear-ported bass speaker, correctly positioned in a corner, could use the entire room as its cabinet, effectively putting the dancefloor *inside* the speaker, and turning the space into a singular, throbbing mass.[58]

Together, by the mid-1980s, the combination of The Garage and the Jamaican sound system had effectively become the model for virtually everything that followed. They established the basic technologies and principles, but the experimental ethic persisted too. So when German visual artist Elsa For Toys reflects on the early days of German Rave, she still calls it a period of 'intensive space research', concerned with devising techniques of sonic-spatial organization and audio-visual synaesthesia. In one case, she describes mounting a full array of bass bins from the ceiling just 'to see what happens when the bass comes from above'. In an interview intercut with old video of light and sound experiments she says, 'It had something very scientific about it. People thought about things like: "This time we did this. And if we could do that now, and couldn't we do this?"' One of her contemporaries describes what it was like to be there: 'This strange feeling of being fogged in one of these joints and not knowing where you are exactly, and with these strobe lights and these sounds blasted in your ears. This hadn't been experienced physically before.'[59]

In these ways, then, bass science operates as part of a larger project of affect engineering – a bio-aesthetic project that encompasses a wide range of technological and spatial practices. It aims to catalyse dance, to tilt bodies towards collective motion. Its focus is always a potential dancefloor, a becoming-body and the singular eventness of uncommon vibratory experience.[60] In these situations, saying 'you had to be there' is far less a claim to exclusivity or authenticity than a statement of material fact.[61] As UK dub producer Mikey Dred says, 'I can tell you about sound system from now until tomorrow morning, but you have to feel sound system to know what sound system is about.'[62]

Affects and affectations

These are examples of dancefloors defined more by their *affects* than their *affectations*. We can work through the distinction via Tim Lawrence's ethnography of New York's heterogeneous disco scene, and his identification of divergent sensory strategies operating in its two most famous venues, Studio 54 and David Mancuso's Loft. DJ Nicky Siano describes Studio 54 as a carefully curated visual economy, constructed from the outside-in, as a sea of representations and fixed subject roles – a spectacle of wealth, celebrity, beauty and exclusivity, all reinforced by an iconic velvet rope and the crush of paparazzi. 'It was all Fellini and no funk', says Siano, 'a million other things beside the audio experience.'[63] The club had a large and powerful sound system, but one described as 'not very musical'. It served mainly to provide the pageant with an upbeat din, the DJ's role being reduced, in large part, to a form of sign-play. Whereas the DJ-as-affect-engineer attempts to work on the autopoietic capacities of the sonic body, the DJ-of-signs stays in the realm of the known (familiar rhythms, sounds and forms – 'the hits'), playing what amounts to a game of text-recognition with the pose-striking crowd. This is the dancefloor-of-affectations, a sonic space, but one organized largely around appearances, meanings and performative gestures. The important point here is not its superficiality (the accusation often, and unfairly, levelled at disco as a whole) but that its strategies are more semiotic than material, and secondly, that it reinforces interiorized subjectivities rather than modulating them in ways that might force them open.[64]

It is arguably the dancefloor-of-affectations that has almost singularly preoccupied popular music scholars. This should be taken less as a reflection of sonic-cultural reality than as a projection of existing dispositions – the dancefloor organized around signifying regimes being a ready fit for analyses rooted in notions representation, performativity and the postmodern.[65] But the dancefloor defined by its affects is a very different proposition. To borrow from Guattari, the question there is 'How are sounds and forms going to be arranged so that the subjectivity adjacent to them remains in movement, and really alive?'[66] Compare the experience of Studio 54 to that of The Loft, characterized as the latter was by the hot proximity of jostling flesh in a throbbing, often unlit room. Turning off the lights was part of Mancuso's strategy for undoing social difference, drawing people out of themselves and into the pack.[67] Touch played a role as well: 'Unable to avoid body contact on all sides', says Lawrence, 'individual dancers had little choice but to dissolve into the amorphous whole.'[68] Clocks were banished in order to suspend quotidian time (a technique also used in casinos), allowing dancers to 'forget their socialized selves ... and experiment with a different cycle.'[69] 'There were no mirrors', either, 'because if you were dancing wild and caught a glimpse of yourself and saw how ridiculous you looked you would maintain yourself.' Working in conjunction with the club's powerful sound system, these are some of the ways in which The Loft, as a project, sought to shake its occupants out of themselves and catalyse a new, if temporary, collective body. As a sort of social cymatics, it was very much a dancefloor-of-affects.

Entering this conceptual space, for the popular music scholar, requires a suspension of habit and an effort at new, sonorous modes of thought. It forces theory into the immanent workings of the vibratorium: geometries of force, the spectral, rhythmachines and the modulatory eventness of bodies. That said, it is important not to understand this shift as a simple pitting of the sonic against hegemonic ocularity. The real interest here is the a-signifying work of affect, by whatever route; the inherent co-functioning of the senses means that affect engineering is always a synaesthetic project. So while we have turned to darkened rooms for examples of dancefloors that deprivilege looking, and perhaps allow greater attention to sound, the point is not that they abolish the visual dimension. The underfilling of vision in darkness is no less a perceptual event than the overfilling of vision with lasers and strobe lights. Both are cases of vision pushed into a limit-field – a breakdown that draws in the imagination as it opens up to intermodal resonances. Both can collude, in their own ways, in a sonically-led unhoming. Properly assembled, the vibratorium becomes a staging ground where people are pulled out of themselves and dropped in an uncommon logic of sensation. Here, bass-centric music is best understood as a bio-aesthetic technology, working to rhythmically reorganize bodies and pre-accelerate them in different directions. This is its role in the audiogenesis of dance.

Entering the rhythmachine

I was instantly entrained in a new kind of dancing – tics and spasms, twitches and jerks, the agitation of bodies broken down into separate components, then reintegrated at the level of the dance floor as a whole. Each individual part ... was a cog in a collective 'desiring machine,' interlocking with the sound system's bass throbs and sequencer riffs.[70]

This was Simon Reynolds describing his own abduction by audio at a rave in the early 1990s. Reynolds's writing of this period was an important influence on Eshun and others who have since gone looking for language native to machine musics and the incorporeal strategies of the vibratorium. In his work, we find electronic musics treated as technologies of the body, the dancefloor treated as a space of affects and machinic relations. He tries to inhabit sound and sensation, asking how sonic experience might inform thought, and not just the other way around. 'For the critic', he says, 'this requires a shift of emphasis, so that you no longer ask what music "means" but how it *works*. What is the affective charge of a certain kind of bass sound, of a particular rhythm?'[71]

It makes sense for the theorist to begin from these questions because they are the same ones motivating the people making, playing and enjoying the music. Lawrence, for example, describes disco's 'peculiar functionality' and the way 'DJs and dancers would home in on a record', again, not because of who or what it represented, but 'because it worked'.[72] For DJs and producers, the job has always been one of *diagramming* the vibratorium: observing bodies in motion, injecting rhythms, testing responses, gauging tendencies, devising ways of plugging into and varying its affects.[73] Parallels can be drawn with Mark Bain investigating the self-organization of bodies in his *Live Room*, or the way theorists of the Affections intuited compositional strategies by watching the effects of sound and song on parishioners. 'I watched and felt the tension of people's bodies waiting for the next record and saw how their bodies reacted to changes and breaks on the records', says disco remixer Tom Moulton, describing how the dancefloor became the object, but also the source, of his studio strategies.[74]

This is an early moment in what Eshun calls the *rhythmachine* – a term meant to describe the operative logics of sequencer-based musics, built for the DJ mix, and conceived as technologies for animating the sonic body. In practice, we can think of the rhythmachine operating on three levels. In the largest sense, it identifies the great meta-machines of the last three decades – house & garage, hip-hop/breakbeat, electro & techno, dancehall, perhaps followed by jungle and UK garage.[75] At this level, it is comparable to genre, but, again, with the emphasis placed on how the music functions. There is little point in trying to make this taxonomy too rigid, because meta-machines are always encroaching on one another and rapidly sub-dividing. But what this dimension of the rhythmachine manages to convey are the broad consistencies that extend beyond individual scenes and underlie those rapid mutations.[76]

If this is the rhythmachine at its most general, then its most specific form is the individual unit of the *track*. The track replaces the song when pieces of music are no longer conceived as complete wholes but as connection machines, designed to be linked together in a desirous assemblage. Tracks are made to be mixed – structured to synchronize and resonate together. They are also unmade in the mix, in the ways they play off each other, retexturing and redirecting one another. In this latter sense, the track is also where deterritorializing ruptures can emerge; a single anomalous tune can spark a reinvention of the dancefloor (and studio practice), and even form the nucleus of a new scene.[77]

The space between the meta-machine and the track is the second level of the rhythmachine. Here again, the concept invites us to investigate the material workings of things, but now in relation to what we would typically call a style or sub-genre, as well as an associated musical scene. This includes many dozens of permutations that internally differentiate, and also cut across, the various meta-machines. Consider, for example, that house, alone, sub-divides into multiple versions of Chicago house, as well as acid, deep house, hard house, Italo, funky house, UK funky, jazz house, ghetto house, French house, microhouse, tribal house, electro house, tech house, breakbeat house and so on. Cycles of invention and obsolescence have become so intense that machinic lineages can be hard to trace. Moreover, many of those machines undergo wholesale changes every few years, with links to previous iterations becoming almost unrecognizable. Scholarship in popular music and subcultural studies has commonly treated splintering dancefloor scenes in any of several ways: as patterns in identity formation, marketing and consumption, or gatekeeping and the exchange of (sub)cultural capital.[78] However, this work tends to miss the obvious fact that these splits are most often premised on the reordering of functional logics and affective strategies: how things move, how they connect with one another, how they sound and feel.

With this in mind, the rhythmachine is best understood as something akin to an operating system, installed at the nexus of the studio, the DJ booth and the sonic body. It sets a working tempo range (often as narrow 2–4 BPM); it selects a set of basic rhythmic dynamics and components (e.g. regular or broken, straight or swung, to what degrees?); and it identifies a spectral character (e.g. what sources and qualities of lows, mids and hi?). With these limitations imposed, the rhythmachine becomes a challenge to the producer to see how far it can be pushed in various directions without collapsing. These are formal concerns in a sense, but more to the point, they determine how tracks will work together in the mix (their compatibility), as well as how they might modulate the vibratorium.[79] This is where the workings of the low end become especially important. If the rhythmachine is an operating system, then its kernel is its *drums-and-bass*. Repeatedly, we see what could be called drums-and-bass moments, in which an established machine is stripped to its most elemental components and rebuilt to move and vibrate differently, whether in subtle or drastic ways.

The notion of drums-and-bass as rhythmachinic kernel is traceable to two developments in Jamaican recording studios of the 1960s and 1970s. The first is the advent of the 'riddim', or the concept of the generic rhythm pattern that could be reused in multiple recordings (there are, for example, many single-riddim records, featuring performances by different artists over the same beat). This is when rhythms begin to be treated in a manner similar to software – like sets of algorithms that can be run on an assemblage, but also hacked into doing new things. The second development was the appearance, in the early 1970s, of 7-inch reggae singles featuring an instrumental b-side – often called the 'drums-and-bass version' – which would strip away vocals and other instrumentation, to foreground the low-end activity of the riddim. 'A typical drum & bass mix', says Michael Veal, 'would focus on the propulsive motion of those two instruments throughout.'[80] Soon after, New York disco and hip-hop DJs simultaneously began working with the 'break' – that portion of a tune where all but drums and/or bassline are stripped away. DJs Kool Herc (himself a Jamaican ex-pat and sound system operator) and Grandmaster Flash have described this as the moment of maximum intensity, when crowd energy would peak. [81] Tom Moulton's tape-based disco edits, or 'dubs', proceeded in much the same way, dramatically extending drum breaks and pumping up the bass.[82]

If later developments were much more rapid, they very often followed the same pattern of paring the machine down to its most basic elements and tinkering with the kernel. 'With techno there was only one law at first: the bass drum straight, everything else is allowed', explains producer Mike Ink. 'This means that every year from the early- to mid-90s, techno provided the opportunity to reinvent itself three times. And always develop back to the basic structure, and to work up to then unknown sound dimensions.'[83] We see the same in jungle – also known as drum-and-bass – which passed through multiple iterations (darkside, ragga, jump up, hardstep, techstep) in only its first four years. Likewise in UK garage, beginning with mid-1990s experiments in melding quickened US garage beats with jungle basslines, and continuing through the stark rhythmic investigations of the early 2000s, that led to grime and contemporary dubstep. Writing on dubstep's reinvention as languid bass-and-drum minimalism, critic Mark Fisher called it 'a new degree-zero' in the 'continuum' of rhythmachines that had been busily mutating since the early-rave period. Of the irregular subbass throbs in kode9's 'Sine of the Dub' (2004), Fisher says, 'Its ruthless reductionism was almost a clinical operation, as if the track were designed to answer the question: how stripped-down can a track be and still belong to the continuum?'[84]

Of course, there is also a second aspect of the rhythmachine at this level – one that extends beyond the internal relations of the music itself. As a connection machine – rooted in a diagramming of the floor, built to move the sonic body – the rhythmachine is also a logic of sensation. For Eshun, it's an 'operating system for the redesign of sonic reality'. We can call it a *physio-logic* of the dancefloor. From this perspective, drums-and-bass moments are more than just formal investigations, they are experiments with the tension-limits of bodies and beats. In the simplest terms, they ask: 'What will work and what won't?' Their focus is as much a collective sonic body as an individual one; there is necessarily a sociality to these physio-logics, not only because they are oriented towards dance, but because any given one will attract some people and repel others (who may, themselves, engineer an alternative).

This sort of collective grouping around very specific affects (rhythmic and spectral) has been taken up by Goodman, who proposes the concept of 'speed tribes',

> Where 'speed' refers not so much to the drug of choice, as a precise operating logic distributing and segmenting youth culture. ... The lines which differentiate these speed tribes are almost imperceptible, sometimes boiling down to minute nuances of rhythmic composition, timbre or an allegiance to synthetic over organic 'musical' values. Or these nuances can relate to divergent compositions of the collective body, seemingly along traditional sociological lines (race, class, gender). But what is of interest here is the affective trajectories of these networked collective bodies, understood as

ecologies of speed; those molecular seepages and rhythmic infections which deviate from molar social segmentations.[85]

Speed, in this Deleuzian usage, refers to the intensive motion of bodies and beats – their internal rhythms and bubbling potentials. This is contrasted with outward movement, which is understood to be extensive.[86] So, in Erin Manning's theorization of dance, intensive motion refers to the pre-accelerations and incipience of becoming-bodies, while extensive movement describes the actual 'displacement of a limb or the whole body across space'.[87] Brought back to the rhythmachine, this collection of concepts can help us grasp, with some intimacy, how the audiogenesis of dance might operate in a given assemblage, at a particular moment in time (dates are important, here, because these scenes/machines change so quickly). Bass cults can therefore be understood as those speed tribes that gravitate towards the low end, building bass-led physio-logics in order to find and develop specific intensive and extensive capacities of the sonic body.

Three physio-logics

We can end by examining what it might mean, in practice, to investigate the rhythmachinic workings of several bass cults, attempting to discern their strategies and to theoretically inhabit their physio-logics. The following presents three drums-and-bass moments – in jungle, dubstep and footwork – that are notable for the ways in which bass works undermine the beat. Escaping from metric regularity and upending the 'well-balanced' mix, low-end undulations now move to the foreground, sometimes taking tracks over altogether. Again, this is not entirely new. Erik Davis makes a link between dub and jungle, noting those moments when bass begins to deterritorialize the beat ('Good dub sounds as if the recording studio itself has begun to hallucinate.'). Similarly, Eshun draws a line between Moog-funk and post-rave experiments in which mutant bass starts wandering around on its own. 'Instead of anchoring the track to the heartbeat, bass mutation kneads dispersing tremors across the body surface, so that the skin turns into a giant palpitating, convulsing heart.

This induces a queasy motion sickness, as if the carpet's undulating beneath you.'[88] When bass begins to escape the beat, we enter a new regime of the rhythmachine.

Jungle (1994)

Jungle is, of course, inseparable from its breakbeat science. Eshun calls the sample work underlying its 'Escherized' rhythms an audio version of *motion capture* – the break's live drummer, digitally indexed and re-animated to do physically impossible things.[89] Deployed on the dancefloor it becomes a sort of loose cybernetics – a playing of the sonic body designed to draw it into improbably complex patterns of movement. In Davis' terms, jungle challenges the dancer to navigate a 'polymetric' terrain, composed of multiple, changing, separately cycling and stereo-panned, percussive elements.[90] There, the body is continually remade as it locks into different rhythmic niches and strings them together in a virtual rhythm (which will inevitably break down again and again in the mix).[91] Reynolds describes these felt conundrums as they shape the jungle dancefloor:

> Triggering different muscular reflexes, jungle's multi-tiered polyrhythms are body-baffling and discombobulating unless you fixate on and follow one strand of the groove. Lagging behind technology, the human body simply can't do justice to the complex of rhythms. The ideal jungle dancer would be a cross between a virtuoso drummer (someone able to keep separate rhythms with different limbs), a body-popping breakdancer, and a contortionist.[92]

The aim of jungle's breakbeat science is a body in flight, or maybe more accurately, a molecular body pulled out of itself along multiple, fractal trajectories by the heterogeneous momentums of its broken breaks. There is, therefore, an element of transduction involved, as the intensive rhythms of the track are actualized in the extensive movements of flailing limbs.

This is only half of the equation, however, as jungle's physio-logics ultimately hinge on tensions that emerge between its volatile percussion (tempos of 160 BPM, but with niches cycling at 240, 320, etc.) and its half-time basslines. If its drums take flight, the bass applies weight – causing vestibular chaos as it floods and wallops the body. Typically moving at a much more languid 80 BPM (closer to dub or the slowest hip-hop) it is more 'undulant carpet' than anchor, working to inject the body with intensive rhythms that can play against the outward pull of the percussion. Take, for example, Remarc's 'Thunderclap', one of the many tracks from this period to set a Reese bassline against its clattering breaks. The tune's kick drums knock around, almost at random, barely maintaining the semblance of a beat; snares, at sliding pitches, ricochet through the stereo field, often slurping backwards or erupting in machine gun rushes; clipped cymbals crash, while hi-hats, ticking at various speeds, are always popping up and disappearing. Below this, though, is the low growl of the drone, steadily cycling through the same three or four tones, eight bars at a time. Lingering around 60 Hz, it energizes the chest cavity. Its slow regularity gives the body a second layer of rhythm to occupy ('one can skank to the slow bass pulse or attempt to articulate the frenetic, unpredictable multiplicities exploding up top'[93]). The droning Reese also adds an entirely incongruous element of drift to the experience, because as much as the body feels the outward pull of the percussion, it is also possessed by the heavy swimmingness of the beating saw waves. In Thunderclap's physio-logic, the dancer is pummelled, pulled upward and out, dragged down, floated forward and back, filled with energy and hummed all over.

Dubstep (2005)

Dubstep began as something quite slinky and spry – a more sub-centric offshoot of 2-step garage, with its syncopated and heavily swung beats. Like jungle, its basslines would typically run at half the track's nominal tempo, allowing dancers to slip between its slow grooves and twitchy drum machine patterns. At 140/70 BPM, however, its ecology of speeds was very different. Internal rhythms and bodily movements that would be too rushed, or just not possible, at 160 BPM, now had time to unfold and develop nuances. Strictly at the level of tempo, it was still at pace with some of rave's speedier techno, but without the sense of headlong linearity. Instead, it was full of fits and gaps, leaving plenty of wiggle room between its halting beats. Through the early 2000s, however, most of the music's up-tempo elements were steadily stripped away, allowing the basslines to come forward. Increasingly, the garage component was dubbed out of the mix, becoming barely audible in the percussion even as its rhythms continued to animate the machine. By 2005, minimalist 'halfstep' tracks like Wonder's 'What', Digital Mystikz' 'Horror Show' and Loefah's 'Midnight' had effectively flipped the music's two-tiered tempo by spacing out the kicks and snares, and carving out the middle frequencies to let the (sub) bass take the lead. 'Midnight', for example, marches slowly – a kick on the one, a snare on the three. There is still a 2-step swing to it – the spectral shuffle of the hi-hats adding a teasing lilt – but the rest is bass. Toothy, envelope-filtered pulses play a slow back and forth with a cleaner, heavier sub. One rises roughly out of the chest and smacks against the walls, the other is more barometric, weighing on the room as a whole. Other tracks, like Skream and Loefah's '28g' and 'Monsoon Remix', were dominated by deep, body-oscillating wobbles; the basslines in D1's 'Crack Bong' and 'Higher State' sound – but also *feel* – like violently flexing woofer cones; the gliding sinewave subs of Digital Mystikz tunes like 'Ancient Memories' and 'Mood Dub' could warmly hum a room, while 'Walking With Jah' made it feel as though a battery of pummelling drums was threatening to come through the floor. In this new rhythmachine, it was the undulations of multilayered basslines, rather than the beat, in any familiar sense, that gave the physio-logic its rhythmic texture.

At the time, the joke was that nobody danced at dubstep parties, but this misses point. If the swaying bodies on the floor seemed self-absorbed, it wasn't that they lacked energy. If anything, energy was in excess, it just hadn't yet found a mode of outward expression. Mark Fisher compared it to a state of catatonia, in the sense suggested by Deleuze and Guattari that implies neither disability nor isolation.[94] For them, 'Catatonia is: "This affect is too strong for me".[95] If that affect is low-frequency sound, then we are dealing with something similar to what Julian Henriques called sonic dominance, or overwhelming vibrational force as a catalyst of collective becoming. Understood this way, catatonia is the opposite of incapacitation, being instead a matter of *capacitance*: of bodies charging, filling (perhaps overfilling) with energy and waiting for an outlet.[96] By Deleuze and Guattari's account, catatonia is pure, immanent potential – its outward stillness belying its intensive speeds and its brimming potential to spring forward along any number of trajectories.[97] By this definition, the 'catasonic' body doesn't lack dance.[98] It is full of potential dance. But more to the point, it has its own unique mode of intensive dance that takes place at the level of viscera – internal modulations, rhythmic cascades of hums and resonance, bodily-felt anticipations, pains and pleasures and so on. The collective dimension emerges in sonorous space when the room throbs as a singular mass, putting everyone on the same wavelength. When the Digital Mystikz invite us to 'Meditate on Bass Weight', it's a call to get catasonic, find its rhythms, be mystified together and see where it leads.

Footwork (2009)

If dubstep demotes the beat, footwork obliterates it. A distant, but direct descendent of the Chicago house scene of the 1980s (via intervening generations of ghetto house, and the influence of Miami), footwork has stripped away nearly everything recognizably danceable about house music. The steady kick of the early Chicago sound is often compared to a heartbeat, pulsing comfortably at 120 BPM. In footwork, it's closer to a cardiac arrhythmia, unfolding at 160 BPM, but often in half-/double-time, and with only the most virtual sense of a groove.[99] It's still house music, only sped up and abstracted. As fast as it is, it can feel practically still, yet also erratic, and liable to explode. In RP Boo's 'Eraser', the only semblance of a beat comes from sparse, unevenly placed snares, hats, ticks and seemingly random bursts of synthetic toms. A pair of voices spits out menacing mantras ('Burn burn, Let 'em, Live and let die') that recombine over and over throughout the track. The only other constants are the sound of phasing electrical hum and the irregular twitches of a massive, muffled subbass. DJ Rashad's 'Ghost' starts out even more barren, with similar subbass pulses, but now more insistent, along with flutters of un-quantized hats and another voice: 'i-i-i-i-i-i-i-i-i-i-th-GHOST GHOST-GHOST GHOST GHOST-GHOST'. The beat switches up when 808s join the mix, giving it something like a galloping 4×4 rhythm, but made fluid and wobbly by all the layers of intermodulating bass tones. Over top it's the names of dancers ('some mighty fine ghosters' from Legends Clique): 'Poo AG-Que LightBulb Poo AG-Que LightBulb Poo AG-Que LightBulb Poo AG-Que LightBulb i-i-i-GHOST GHOST GHOST'.[100] The 808s (traces of Miami) are everywhere in DJ Emloe's 'Whea Yo Ghost At, Whea Yo Dead Man', lurching around at multiple pitches. A 'chipmunked' voice sings sweet, indecipherable things next to a hypnotically overlapping 'Wh-Whea Yo Ghost Wh-Wh-Whea Yo Ghost Whea Yo Dead Wh-Wh Dead Man'.[101] DJ Roc's 'Make Em Panic' is just slow sine wave sub-tones, scattershot drum machine bursts and: 'Get em in the circle Get em in the circle, Make em panic Make em panic Make em panic Make em panic, L-l-l-l-l-l-l-l-l-ook at his face, He scared, You don't wanna a battle, Panic panic panic panic'.

Footwork is a competitive dance culture. Whereas other iterations of Chicago house have been party oriented (a club crowd moving together on the floor), footwork's focus is *the circle*, where dancers from rival crews battle each other one at a time.[102] The circle is all about capacitance. It's a doubly charged space, where thronging spectators and subbass vibration work to catalyse dancers into mystifying contortions. Here, sonic body and rhythmachine become difficult to separate, as blurring feet under strangely still torsos *become* the rhythm that seems to be missing-but-implied in the stripped-back tracks. The circle's becoming-body weaves a virtual groove between low-end pulses and arrhythmic drum machine bursts, which become jump-off points for the dancer's flourishes. Now the role of the incessant vocal samples becomes evident, working to intimidate ('get that fool up out the circle'), demand specific moves ('whea yo ghost at') and generally ratchet up the pressure. The tracks themselves are built in close collaboration with dancers. Sometimes, custom machines are built for specific bodies, and producers often work with dancers in the studio, asking at every stage whether it moves the right way: 'Is this working? Are you feeling that?'[103]

Movement thus becomes essential to understanding sound in footwork, and vice versa. Strictly at the sonic level, it is easy to compare footwork to dubstep. Both are minimalisms organized around an unusual focus on subbass in lieu of beats. And in practice, both work to build capacitance, charging a space and a collective sonic body, filling them with speeds and potentials. The difference, however, is that the circle finds a mode of outward expression. In this sense, it's practically the opposite of dubstep's catatonia, being much closer to the 160 BPM kinetics of jungle.[104] Only now, the rhythmic work is handled, in very large part, by the dancing body rather than the track.[105] The track (as machine) becomes less a thing to be shadowed in movement, than an affect generator and virtual sequencer. It charges bodies, but also, in its clipped, rhythmic blasts, it gives them a spark, something to latch onto and to work with. It opens a channel through which the intensive speeds of the sonic body are transduced into mystifying bursts of extensive movement. The challenge is to do with *style*.

Conclusion: Where next?

A trip to the ear doctor:

A patient exits, unseen voices drift into the waiting room: 'Oh it's just marginal, it's nothing. He wouldn't even notice if he wasn't a musician.' That caught my attention. I was there because I'd discovered an auditory anomaly of my own. Running test tones and sweeps through a new pair of reference headphones, I found that frequencies between 100 and 125 Hz were fading almost entirely from my left ear, even as the right one became uncomfortably full. Either side of that range, it would all come flooding back, but within that narrow band, the tones produced a disorienting imbalance. 'Those frequencies don't matter,' said the audiologist. 'We don't test for them. We only care about speech frequencies.' He wondered why I should care, so I told him about my work. Visibly unimpressed, he responded with a short lecture on the phonetic acoustics of churches and train stations. 'You need to learn about that,' he said, before moving me on to the ENT. There the question was the same, but the response was more inquisitive: 'Really? Tell me more ...' For a few moments we talked about organs, bodily vibration, and synaesthesia. Then, a cursory look up my nose and he showed me the door. Smiling, he said: 'Wow, that's kind of fascinating, even if it has no utility.' An inadvertently apt summary of a strange visit. I never learned what was wrong with my ear.

This episode collects, in microcosm, some of the concerns that spurred this project, and various themes that emerged in the process. Here, it seemed, were the 'Two Cultures' watching each other with suspicion through the smudged window of a soundproof booth. Differently trained people with overlapping interests found themselves nearly unable to converse. In fact, there was a tangible resistance from one side, conveyed in the none-too-subtle suggestion that audiology has nothing to learn from the study of sonic culture. In that tiny room, the human perception of sound was reduced to the mechanism of audition as a medium of verbal communication. There was an unequivocal disinterest in anything outside a specifically valued frequency range. And, of course, any vibratory activity beyond the ear, nose and throat was moot. Here, again, was science missing nature by design. In this setting, myself and 'the musician' were turned into 'sensitives' – statistical outliers troubled by things too spectral to take seriously.

It can be easy for those of us in the humanities to be critical of science when its representatives so avidly perform its most reductive and unimaginative traits. But we should also avoid the temptation to caricature. In the first place, we've seen how culturalist approaches routinely make similar errors and elisions, in their own ways. Nature is just as readily missed by the overextended language of mediation. The technician's singular interest in 'speech frequencies' is, therefore, mirrored in the equally narrow and too-habitual emphasis on texts, culture as communication and sonic experience as a technique of the listener. Similarly, we can find epistemological parallels between the cochlearcentrism that still prevails in sound studies and the tendency to atomize the sensorium in so much empirical research. Both, therefore, work to write out movement and unforeseen becomings, meaning that the incorporeal rarely even enters the discussion.

At the same time, however, the sciences are indispensable to a materially-minded cultural theory for the simple fact that they can reveal dynamics in the world that would otherwise remain obscure, even as they constitute experience. Disengagement is not an option if we hope to make convincing claims about bodies' participation in culture, and not just those notional 'bodies' construed in discourse. Here, it is worth recalling Massumi's argument that neither science nor philosophy has a greater claim to reality; they (along with art) simply have different claims to it: 'Science and philosophy are symbiotic activities. ... There are not "two cultures." There are two (actually many) process lines playing the same nature–culture continuum. Both sides should accustom themselves to the idea of sharing their reality.'[1]

At the most fundamental level, the preceding has been an effort to open a conceptual field in that region where scientific activity trails off and the interests of the humanities are not yet operational. Low-frequency vibration is especially suited to this task because it cuts back and forth across the nature–culture continuum in so many ways. As we've seen, turning attention to these modulatory agencies reveals blind spots in dominant modes of analysis, but it also points to innumerable new routes of enquiry. Adopting this approach means loosening habits and asking unfamiliar questions. It means accounting for spectral agencies, getting to know physio-logics and vibratory topologies, before making claims about the subjects of sonic experience. This is its empirical dimension, but there is also a speculative one that forms through glimpses of strange alliances and transversal strategies (e.g. the way vestibular sensibilities would seem to collude with liturgy, composition, stone-cutting, glass-making and the organ builder's arcanum, in a project of numinous audiogenesis). This is one sense in which the working concept of myth-science has been crucial here – proceeding additively, fostering intuitive leaps and opening thought to operative (or machinic) logics.

This project has, therefore, been an experiment. Rather than taking a familiar route that begins from presumptions of cultural specificity (asking how bass acquires different meanings within this or that cultural formation) we have taken a more inductive path, following qualities of vibration across vastly different sites – seeing how it mingles, how it unhomes, watching it acquire catalytic functions, however spectral. The concept of the sonic body has been deployed as a corrective to approaches that would reduce sonic experience to either neurophysiology or mediation, each of which reinforces dualistic thought in its own way. Instead, the effort has been to grasp the implications of a parallel mind-body, and the incorporeal spheres of its sonorous flesh. The focus has been the body as a process, a vibratory eventness that is also always conceptual, and a site of creation. In general, the discussion has avoided definitive statements about the nature of this sonic body, which is always, potentially, becoming something other. The aim has instead been, in Hans Jenny's words, to fertilize a mode of perception – to find ways of conceptually inhabiting the vibratory encounter, finding means to render it sensible in language, and letting theory be informed by it. Tales of becoming attempt to do just this, which is why they have assumed such an important role here. As movements-in-thought that arise in the immanent relations of the modulatory encounter, they tell us more about materiality than the transcendent language of culturalism ever could.

Pursuing these lines of thought has meant pushing sound studies beyond the ear, and music into questions of a-signifying vibration. This has any

number of implications for future work in these areas, which I will begin to broach in a moment. However, I also hope that certain broader implications for cultural theory in general have emerged over the course of these varied ethico-acoustic investigations. Conceived in part as a challenge to the predominance of culturalist models in the humanities, one of this project's larger aims was to devise and test new ways of doing cultural studies (broadly conceived). This has meant a radical expansion of scope, on the one hand, but it also means becoming more attuned to the singular and attempting to get intimate with materiality-in-process (with all of the attendant implications for rethinking experience, trajectories of subjectivation and the ways nature and culture can become one another). In this respect, the preceding has taken up Brian Massumi's challenge to cultural studies to unsettle itself, unsettle its neighbours and embrace its creativity.[2] The field, he argues, is uniquely positioned to lodge itself between philosophy, science and art, where it could play the role of the 'intercessor', critically unhoming each and synthesizing productive new relations. The itinerant figure of the sonic body has been conceived here with such deterritorializing moves in mind.

At present, some of the most exciting moves in this general direction are happening under the sometimes overlapping banners of 'speculative realism' and 'new materialism'.[3] The former is more or less unified by a shared effort to undermine 'correlationism', or the tacit belief that 'we can aim our thoughts at being, exist as beings-in-the-world, or have phenomenal experience of the world, yet we can never consistently speak about a realm independent of thought or language.'[4] 'From this correlationist stance', it is argued, 'there results a subtle form of idealism that is nonetheless almost ubiquitous' in Western thought, from Kant through to the textual and constructionist fixations of recent decades. The alternative, an effort to think through the workings of a non-anthropocentric ontology, is an inherently speculative project – one that requires equal parts of imagination and rigour, along with a renewed willingness to engage the natural sciences in creative ways. Though hardly synonymous, there are certainly resonances to be found between aspects of these speculative realisms and what I have called myth-science that would be worth further exploration.

Similarly, new materialist scholarship has often sought 'to counter the narcissistic reflex of human language and thought' while more adequately accounting for non-human agencies.[5] Extending this line of thought, portions of the present text have pointed towards the prospect of a nebulous 'man-made unknown' that emerges in the affective ecologies of things considered inanimate, inert or irrelevant, when out-of-mind or not at our disposal. In describing a becoming-autonomy of humanly-produced things, the man-made unknown is the flip side of a world 'constructed' in the social and mediated by shared ideas. In this respect, there is a connection to be explored between the man-made unknown and themes in Eugene Thacker's *In the Dust of This Planet*. Arguing that 'one of the greatest challenges that philosophy faces today lies in comprehending the world in which we live as both a human and a nonhuman world', Thacker offers three linked concepts: 'the-world-for-us' (the world within our domain), 'the-world-in-itself' (nature in its unknowable autonomy) and 'the-world-without-us'. He describes the latter as a 'horror of philosophy', an always-receding horizon of knowledge that nevertheless draws the imagination towards it.[6] To this, the man-made unknown adds a fourth dimension that could be termed (if awkwardly) *the-world-for-us-without-us*, because it confronts us with uncanny agencies – a self-activity of structures, substances and systems – that cast doubt on our ability to master even the things we invent, or to fully comprehend what they might become. It therefore represents something of a limit-field for the anthropocentric study of media, culture, science and technology. Learning to think this shadow ecology will be a growing challenge in an age of rapid and often bewildering complexification.

Returning to sonic themes, we can also imagine several further trajectories for future work. Among the most obvious would be an expansion into other frequency bands where different affective dynamics would prevail (hence Goodman's effort, in *Sonic Warfare*, to theorize a range of differently composed sites along a vibratory continuum). Certainly, the sonic body does not belong exclusively to bass. Low-frequency force was selected here because its effects can be so strong and varied, because it is already so rich as a myth-scientific field, and because it so often operates 'below the text'. But another investigation could just as well enquire into the unique relational capacities of mid-range frequencies and their mixtures (including, perhaps, questions of tactile perception, din, texture as a carrier of memory, masking and phantom sound, unhomely harmonics, vocal affects, deterritorialization of the voice and so on).

At the same time, perhaps we shouldn't rush back towards ears and audition, at least not as we usually think of them. The preceding was meant, in no small part, to make the case for an 'extra-cochlear' sound studies that recognizes the inherent co-functioning of the senses as well as the very blurry limits of what we call sound and what we consider sonic perception.[7] Adopting this approach would push sound studies in new epistemological directions and force a reconsideration of its material parameters. The question then becomes: does sound studies allow itself to broaden into 'vibration studies' (theorizing phenomena that have been largely ignored outside of a few science and engineering journals concerned mainly with health and safety)? If not, where is the arbitrary line drawn? If audition remains the near-exclusive focus, how fraught are the epistemological manoeuvres that keep it so?

Similar questions face music, and perhaps popular music studies especially. The argument here, in large part, is that the field might be rejuvenated through greater attention to sound's a-signifying materiality – how things sound and feel, even how they escape and confound perception, not just what they are purported to mean or how they're 'consumed'. In making this argument, I am not suggesting that either sound studies or music should effectively become subsets of sensory studies (nor, for that matter, that any foundational concerns of either should just be abandoned), but that both have the opportunity to bring the body, materiality and non-human actants more meaningfully, and more heterogeneously, into cultural theory, and that this might have a productively destabilizing effect. In other words, each could more enthusiastically play the role of the intercessor – catching affects from art, poaching from science, unhoming the humanities and so on. As I've argued (and sought to demonstrate in Chapters 1 and 5), electronic dance music studies is especially well positioned to take up this challenge, given its interest in those musics that most consistently make an explicit project of the sonic body. At present, however, work in the still-coalescing field has mostly concerned itself with repeating the moves of its predecessors in popular music studies, (sub)cultural studies and ethnomusicology. It has yet to really find its unique capacities and to devise novel conceptual tools that are as daringly synthetic as some of its subject matter. Notable exceptions include Arun Saldanha's 'Deleuzian musicology' of Goa trance and Julian Henriques' writings on the transductive capacities of sonic bodies. But nearly two decades after its publication, Eshun's *More Brilliant than the Sun* remains the most crucial, yet chronically overlooked, guide to how such a reinvention of the field could work and what is at stake.[8]

Lastly, we might consider what could be called cinema's sonic body and the affective strategies of sound designers. Scholarship on film sound has been expanding rapidly the last two decades, but still without a great deal of attention to sound's a-signifying intensities, while the low end has yet to be taken up in any substantial way, despite its now-essential role in the affective work of so much mainstream film. At the same time, the recent wave of Deleuze-inspired cinema scholarship might be conceptually well equipped to take up these questions, but its attention to sound has, so far, been quite limited. This leaves much to explore. Earlier chapters have sketched a line through the bombastic Wurlitzers of the silent era, the persistent influence of the Doctrine of the Affections, and various technologies of anomalous vibration, including early devices that preceded Dolby and THX, and later ones that take advantage of modern bass extension. Such investigations could easily expand into home theatres, where the subwoofer is a privileged component (being the '.1' in any Surround Sound setup), and where other forms of entertainment very clearly target the sonic body through the same apparatus. Video games are the most obvious example, with their bottom-heavy sound design typically taking cues from Hollywood's affect engineers. But we could also look at the spectral work of recent television advertising, or the subwoofer-oriented sound design of live sports (how, for example, the boards are mic'ed for hockey broadcasts, so that we viscerally feel some of the violence in every body check). Clearly, the sonic body is a going concern (so stated or not) in soundtrack and broadcast studios of all sorts, making this a rich field for future research.

* * *

In 2016, 'bass' is everywhere – the cultish aspect having largely diffused into popular enthusiasm. In recent years, 'bass music' has become the pervasive, if vague, marketing term for various electronic dance musics that are at least notionally bass-centric. But low-frequency fixations have been growing beyond the dancefloor too. The most immediate ripples have been felt in those experimental electronic musics that take their cues from the clubs, but aim their productions at headphones and home stereos. More than their predecessors in the decade or so after rave, many of these post-dubstep/post-techno and other projects are making a prerequisite of subbass weight.[9] Metal and pop are getting heavier too, the former via dubstep and southern rap (see productions for Britney Spears and Miley Cyrus, for example), the latter under the influence of bands like Earth and Sunn O))) whose low-register drones explore sensations of chthonic drag and malevolent stasis. At the same time, low-frequency drone projects and the heavier, or 'dark', side of ambient (Thomas Köner, Eleh, Nate Young and BJ Nilsen, among others) also seem to be finding new popularity and often hybridizing with various combinations of the above. Even the pipe organ (recently called 'hot' by Pitchfork.com) is making a minor comeback in experimental circles.[10] Touch Records' *Spire* series of concerts and recordings is one example, typically putting the old machines in the hands of contemporary laptop artists. Similar events have also featured at Krakow's Unsound Festival and Montreal's Mutek Festival. Recognizing the trend, the July 2012 issue of *The Wire* devoted itself almost entirely to bass in its various forms. Subtitled 'Low End Theories', it featured '75 monumental bass experiences' with David Toop and others supplying articles on aquatic sounds, burial mounds and 'the society of the subwoofer'.

Why the rising interest in lower registers? This is a question for a different project, but we can briefly sketch a collection of sonic-cultural tendencies that have combined and intensified in recent decades. The spread of 'blockbuster sound' into the home has already been noted, but the society of the subwoofer owes even more to the diasporization of sound system culture. The pitch-shifting of the pop spectrum begins with globalized reggae (which British studio engineers once feared would destroy their equipment), but it really gains speed when funk, disco and synth pop get filtered through relocated dancehall technologies. In the United States, of course, this leads to hip-hop, which, by the late 1990s had contributed substantially to the *phat*-ening of pop, and, arguably, technoculture more broadly. Consider, for example, the bass-heavy car stereos which were once linked almost exclusively to rap music in

American urban centres. By the mid-1990s, they were an evermore common feature of youth car culture, generally, while in the 2000s, they've become a standard audio upgrade package offered by most auto manufacturers. (Similarly, the combination of Mega-Bass®-equipped Walkman and studio-sized headphones once marked a hip-hop fan in a crowd. Now, bass-reinforced, over-ear headphones are the non-denominational norm.) The same period also saw the spread of affordable electronic tools for making new and deeper varieties of bass.[11] Still more recently, the advent of software synthesizers (many of which emulate older technologies like the MiniMoog, the 808, the 909, etc.) has meant that practically any computer can now produce more, and more deeply reinforced, varieties of sound than were ever conceivable before. At the same time, the internet has facilitated the rapid spread of these musics, sounds, tools and sonic practices. One effect is that bass-as-arcanum is now being supplanted by YouTube tutorials explaining how to make a Reese bass, how to layer your subs, how to scale an organ and so on.

If popular interest in bass-body encounters is becoming so pervasive, then it is worth ending on a cautious note. For the most part, the preceding chapters have focused on the molecularizing (or spectralizing) aspects low-frequency encounters – how they can put bodies at productive variance with themselves and their surroundings, how subjectivities can be opened to new connections under the influence of mystifying vibration. These claims should be taken only as efforts to grasp the workings of certain modulatory relations and not as a simplistic (or over-complicated) celebration of some virtue supposed to reside in this or that quality of sound. The emphasis has always been on the ethico-acoustic dimension, not morally loaded discourses of Good or Bad. On this point, we can again look to Deleuze and Guattari, who are sometimes portrayed as cheerleaders of the molecular, the nomadic, of smooth spaces and bodies-without-organs when, in fact, they leave us at every step with a caveat: Royal and nomad science are symbiotic; 'never believe that a smooth space will suffice to save us'[12]; beware the cancerous or fascist body without organs. The same cautions can be applied here. There are, equally, totalitarian sonic bodies and black holes of bass strategy.

Despite all the current enthusiasm for bass, and for vibration in itself, it should be remembered that there is nothing inherently good, pleasurable, progressive, transgressive or even interesting about low tones. They can be tedious and banal. They can be irritants that keep us awake, distract us, keep us half on edge.[13] When deployed aggressively, without imagination, or with misanthropic intent, they can be oppressive and even violent. Bass can be used to shut down becomings as much as it can work to catalyse them. It can empty the catasonic figure of its intensive speeds and leave it a shivering shell.[14] It can be so overcoded by the power relations in which it participates that it leaves no room for subjective movements (besides looking for an exit).[15] In the end, what it is, does and means, is always situational. This is not at all a recourse to construction. Quite the opposite: it is always a matter of immanence, and an acoustic ethics. How does a given vibratory milieu augment or diminish a body's capacity to act – alone or collectively? What might emerge in the encounter? What are the stakes? We'll never know just what a sonic body can do. All the more reason to keep asking the question.

Notes

Introduction

1 Description of a scene from the Bristol dubstep documentary *Living Inside the Speaker* (2009).

2 For a discussion of frequency (Hz), sound pressure levels (SPL) and the 'equal-loudness contours' of the human ear, see F. Alton Everest, *Master Handbook of Acoustics*, 4th edn (New York: McGraw-Hill, 2001), pp. 50–6.

3 As we will see, this fascination extends well beyond popular music, its influence being evident in religious cultures, military research, urban legends, science fiction, art practices, sound design, etc.

4 The sonic body has no exclusive relationship to bass, but low frequencies certainly are best equipped to elicit widest range of vibratory effects, whether powerful or liminal.

5 The term is used passingly in: Ronald Bogue, *Deleuze's Wake: Tributes and Tributaries* (Albany: State University of New York Press, 2004), p. 88; Steve Goodman, *Sonic Warfare: Sound, Affect, and the Ecology of Fear* (Cambridge, MA: MIT Press, 2010), p. xvi; and Brandon Labelle, *Acoustic Territories/Sound Culture* (New York: Continuum, 2010), pp. 105–7.

6 Julian Henriques, 'Sonic Dominance and the Reggae Sound System Session', in Michael Bull and Les Back (eds), *The Auditory Cultures Reader* (Oxford: Berg, 2003), pp. 471–2.

7 Moves in this direction have become more common in recent years. See, for example: Eshun (1998); Schloss (2004); Goodman (2004, 2010); Henriques (2003, 2010, 2011); Saldanha (2007); Veal (2007); Birdsall and Enns, eds (2008); and Labelle (2010).

8 For a critique specifically related to the theoretical orientation of this project, see: Brian Massumi, *Parables for the Virtual: Movement, Affect, Sensation* (Durham, NC: Duke University Press, 2002), pp. 1–4. For a broader critique of constructionist approaches in the humanities and social sciences, see: Ian Hacking, *The Social Construction of What?* (Cambridge, MA: Harvard University Press, 1999).

9   As far as our perceptual and intellectual capacities are concerned, there is
    always an 'excess of reality'. Massumi, *Parables*, p. 190.

10 See Jane Bennett, *Vibrant Matter: A Political Ecology of Things* (Durham, NC:
    Duke University Press, 2010).

11 For example: Theodore Gracyk, *Rhythm and Noise: An Aesthetics of Rock*
    (Durham, NC: Duke University Press, 1996); Matthew Bannister, *White
    Boys, White Noise: Masculinities and 1980s Indie Guitar Rock* (Farnman, UK:
    Ashgate Publishing, 2006); Tara Rodgers, *Pink Noises: Women on Electronic
    Music and Sound* (Durham, NC: Duke University Press, 2010). There is also a
    growing literature on noise music: Paul Hegarty, *NoiseMusic: A History* (New
    York: Continuum, 2007); Joanna Demers, *Listening Through the Noise: The
    Aesthetics of Experimental Electronic Music* (New York: Oxford University Press,
    2010); and Michael Goddard, Benjamin Halligan and Nicola Spelman (eds),
    Resonances: Noise and Contemporary Music (New York: Continuum, 2013).

12 Among the most prominent are Tricia Rose, *Black Noise: Rap Music and Black
    Culture in Contemporary America* (Middletown, CT: Wesleyan University
    Press, 1994); Tony Mitchell, *Global Noise: Rap and Hip-Hop Outside the USA*
    (Middletown, CT: Wesleyan University Press, 2001); Anthony B. Pinn (ed.),
    Noise and Spirit: The Religious and Spiritual Sensibilities of Rap Music (New
    York: New York University Press, 2003). See also Mitchell's ongoing 'Local
    Noise' project.

13 'Jeep Beats' was the term for bass-centric tracks in the American Northeast,
    heading into the 1990s, while Florida and California produced the ideal of the
    full-sized, domestic car stuffed with speakers and amplifiers. Chuck D covers
    both with the line: 'My [Oldsmobile] '98 was '[19]87 on the record yo, so now I
    go [Ford] Bronco.'

14 Ben Malbon, *Clubbing: Dancing, Ecstasy and Vitality* (London: Routledge,
    1999), pp. 86–7. This assessment of dance-related scholarship is from 1999, but
    it remains accurate. The uncritical overview continues:

> Dancing can be a form of sexualised ritual (McRobbie 1991), a form of
> expression (Storr 1992), a kind of exercise (McRobbie 1994a), a form of
> individuation yet also one of unity (Frith 1995), a language (Shepherd 1991),
> yet a language that is non-textual (Frith 1995). Dancing within clubbing
> can be about fun, pleasure and escape, about being together or being apart,
> about sexual interaction or display, about listening to the music, and even
> a form of embodied resistance and a source of personal and social vitality.

15 Massumi, *Parables*, p. 2.

16 Kafka wrote: 'Metaphors are one of the things that makes me despair of
   literature.' For Deleuze and Guattari, 'Kafka deliberately kills all metaphor, all
   symbolism, all signification, no less than all designation.' Against the fixation on
   representation in Kafka scholarship, and calling for more imaginative theory,
   they argue: 'Metamorphosis is the contrary of metaphor. There is no longer any
   proper sense or figurative sense ... It is no longer a question of a resemblance ...
   Instead, it is now a question of a becoming.' Gilles Deleuze and Felix Guattari,
   Kafka: Toward a Minor Literature, trans. Dana Polan (1975; Minneapolis:
   University of Minnesota Press, 1986), p. 22.

17 cf. Chapter 4.

18 Kodwo Eshun, *More Brilliant Than The Sun* (London: Quartet, 1999), p. 103.

19 Alexander Weheliye cites Eshun's influence when he asserts that

   it seems that much recent work in literary and cultural studies desires
   nothing so much as to affirm and perform its professionalism while at the
   same time mimicking the disciplinary maneuvers of history and sociology
   respectively. As a consequence, the various critical interventions of the last
   thirty years have been absorbed at an accelerating velocity, while daring and
   adventurous models that query the status quo remain few and far between.

   (*Phonographies: Grooves in Sonic Afro-Modernity* [Durham, NC: Duke
   University Press, 2005], p. 199)

20 Despite explicitly stating the terms and rationale of this experiment, Eshun
   has still been criticized for breaking with normative practice. Nabeel Zuberi,
   for example, cites him for technological determinism, commodity fetishism,
   heterosexism and inattention to economies of sub-cultural capital, as well as
   the 'hyperbole' of his descriptive language. 'Is This the Future? Black Music and
   Technology Discourse', in *Science Fiction Studies* 34 (July 2007), pp. 288–90.
   This misses two fundamental arguments of the book. First, if writing about
   sound is often artificially constrained, then we should work to deterritorialize
   it in ways that bring thought closer to the workings of sonic experience. In fact,
   sonic cultures often devise their own conceptual languages that can do this very
   work, but these are commonly neglected or treated only in figurative terms by
   music scholarship. The implication in Zuberi is that attending to them means
   ignoring matters of greater social relevance. But Eshun does not reject the
   social. He only proposes a different route to it, one that might force inherited
   wisdom to be rethought. Ultimately, Zuberi only works to reinforce Eshun's
   point that, when critical positions become normative and habitual, they can
   obscure aspects of the world they purport to describe. Worse, they can fail to

recognize their own privileged position and repress outside thought: 'Theory always comes to Music's rescue. … Like a headmaster, theory teaches today's music a thing or 2 about life. It subdues music's ambition, reins it in, restores it to its proper place'. Eshun, *More Brilliant Than the Sun*, -004.

21 Simon Reynolds and Kodwo Eshun, 'The Natural Laws of Music: Discussing the State of Music Criticism,' *Frieze* 46 (May 1999), http://www.frieze.com/issue/article/the_natural_laws_of_music/ (accessed 28 July 2010). As noted in Chapter 2, chills and piloerection (goosebumps) can both be elicited by low-frequency sound energy.

22 Note that the following categorizations are generally blurry and overlapping. For overviews of the field, see Pinch and Bijsterveld, eds (2011); Stern, ed. (2012). Social histories of technology: Altman (1992, 2004); Théberge (1997); Gitelman (1999); Pinch and Trocco (2004). On reproduction: Chion (1994); Kittler (1999); Lastra (2000); Anderson (2006); Devine (2012). On listening cultures, sound language, audile technique: Silvermann (1988); Natiez (1990); Sterne (2003); Bull and Back, eds (2003); Erlmann (2004, 2010); Porcello (2004); Ihde (2007); Chion (2009). On the sociality of sound and space: Schafer (1994); Keightley (1996); Feld (1997); Bull (2000, 2007); Thompson (2002); Bijsterveld (2008); Schwartz (2011); Blesser and Salter (2009); and Labelle (2010).

23 In his historiography of sound reproduction, Kyle Devine argues that, if there is a mainstream of sound studies, then its focus has been a sonic-cultural terrain that can be called 'acoustic modernity', while scholarly treatments of sound technologies, within this context, have centred on the general themes of reproduction, fidelity, objectivity and rationality. *Imperfect Sound Forever: Loudness, Listening Formations, and the Historiography of Sound Reproduction* (Carleton University: PhD dissertation, 2012). For a constructionist overview of sound studies from the perspective of science and technology studies, see: Trevor Pinch and Karin Bijsterveld, 'Sound Studies: New Technologies and Music', *Social Studies of Science* 34 (2004), p. 635.

24 Goodman, *Sonic Warfare*, p. 79.

25 Howes and Synnott founded the Concordia Sensory Research Team (CONSERT) in 1988. Important early publications include David Howes (ed.), *The Varieties of Sensory Experience* (Toronto: University of Toronto Press, 1991); and Anthony Synnott, *The Body Social: Symbolism, Self, and Society* (London: Routledge, 1993).

26 David Howes (ed.), *Empire of the Senses: The Sensual Culture Reader* (Oxford: Berg, 2005), pp. 4–5.

27 Ibid.

28 Massumi, following William James, Deleuze and Guattari, rightly observes that, in fact, nature 'changes at the slightest move'. Therefore, 'the concept of nature concerns modification not essence.' *Parables*, p. 7. Or, in Sun Ra's words: 'Nature never repeats itself. Why should I repeat myself?'

29 Howes, *Empire of the Senses*, p. 4.

30 The point is to borrow from science in order to make a difference in the humanities. But not only that. The point is not just to make the humanities differ, but also to make them differ from the sciences in ways they are unaccustomed to. In other words, part of the idea is to put the humanities in a position of having continually to renegotiate their relations with the sciences – and, in the process, to rearticulate what is unique to their own capacities. ... The fact of the matter is that the humanities need the sciences – entirely aside from questions of institutional power but rather for their own conceptual health – a lot more than the sciences need the humanities. It is in this connection that the issue of empiricism takes on added importance. Reopening the question of what constitutes empiricism is perhaps one way to get the attention of the sciences. (Massumi, *Parables*, pp. 20–1)

31 Brian Massumi, *A User's Guide to Capitalism and Schizophrenia: Deviations from Deleuze and Guattari* (Cambridge, MA: MIT Press, 1992), p. 47.

32 See: Massumi (1992, 2002, 2011).

33 Kenneth Surin, 'Spinoza, Baruch (1632-1677)', in Adrian Parr (ed.), *Deleuze Dictionary* (Edinburgh: Edinburgh University Press, 2005), pp. 260–2.

34 Gilles Deleuze, *Spinoza: Practical Philosophy*, trans. Robert Hurley (San Francisco: City Lights, 1988), pp. 85–91.

35 Ibid., pp. 17–29.

36 Gilles Deleuze and Felix Guattari, *A Thousand Plateaus: Capitalism and Schizophrenia,* trans. Brian Massumi (Minneapolis: University of Minnesota Press, 1987), pp. 256, 400; Melissa Gregg and Gregory J. Seigworth (eds), *The Affect Theory Reader* (Durham, NC: Duke University Press, 2010), p. 2; Manuel De Landa, *A New Philosophy of Society: Assemblage Theory and Social Complexity* (New York: Continuum, 2006), p. 10; William James and Ralph Barton Perry, *Essays in Radical Empiricism* (London: Longman, Green and Co, 1912), pp. 92–102; Massumi, *Parables,* pp. 14–15 and the chapter 'The Autonomy of Affect', pp. 23–45.

37 Massumi describes the emphasis on the 'situatedness' of things (e.g. subjectivities), rather than the movements and transitions between them, as a case of theoretical 'gridding'. Gridding reproduces rationalism's preoccupation with categorical division by making everything a matter of fixed difference,

rather than investigating processes of change and differentiation that emerge
when things interact and pass from one state to another.

38   Deleuze and Guattari, *A Thousand Plateaus,* pp. 429–31.

39   Massumi, *Parables,* p. 6; Gregg and Seigworth, *Affect Theory Reader,* p. 3.

40   See: 'November 28, 1947: How Do You Make Yourself A Body Without
Organs?', *A Thousand Plateaus*, pp. 149–66.

41   A concise genealogy of this 'turn to things' – whether under the banner of new
materialism, the non-human turn or speculative realism – can be found in
Richard Grusin's introduction to *The Nonhuman Turn* (Minneapolis: University
of Minnesota Press, 2015). Grusin notes a number of converging lineages. One
begins with Donna Harraway's 'Manifesto for Cyborgs' (1985) and becomes
particularly influential in feminist studies of media and technology. Another
is Bruno Latour's actor-network theory (ANT) which brings an understanding
of objects (especially technical ones) as social agents to science and technology
studies (STS) as well as new media theory. In affect theory – with Eve Sedgwick
and Sylvan Tomkins representing one direction, and Spinoza-Deleuze-Massumi
et al. another – Grusin sees a third route to the non-human because 'it
provides a model to think about the affectivity of both animate and inanimate
nonhumans.' (p. xvii) My investigation of the non-human is informed primarily
by this perspective and its extension in theories of assemblages (via Deleuze,
Guattari and De Landa).

42   Also see: Diana Coole and Samantha Frost (eds), *New Materialisms: Ontology,
Agency, and Politics* (Durham, NC: Duke University Press, 2010); Rick Dolphijn
and Iris van der Tuin, *New Materialism: Interviews and Cartographies* (Ann
Arbor: Open Humanities Press, 2012).

43   cf. Chapter 2, note 9.

44   Sun Ra's Myth-Science was foundational to what has since come to be known
as Afrofuturism. For Ra, it meant the application of imaginative force to the
alteration of lived reality, a strategy by which African Americans might invent
their own 'Alter Destiny'. As he put it: 'Myth permits man to situate himself with
the past and the future. What I'm looking for are the myths of the future, the
destiny of man. ... I believe that if one wants to act on the destiny of the world,
it's necessary to treat it like a myth.' Quoted in Graham Lock, *Blutopia: Visions
of the Future and Revisions of the Past in the Work of Sun Ra, Duke Ellington,
and Anthony Braxton* (Durham, NC: Duke University Press, 1999), p. 61. This
interventionist, world-making ethic is very different from the structuralist
conception of myth (as the product of a transcendent symbolic order) critiqued
by Deleuze and Guattari for its tendency to reinforce interiorized subjectivities.
A Thousand Plateaus, pp. 235–45.

45 Becoming-actual can be understood to mean livably true if not objectively 'real'. The concept of hyperstition is understood here to describe accumulations of circumstance that acquire an evidential force and begin exerting a reality-shaping influence (cf. the infrasonic 'hauntings' of Chapter 2). In contrast to superstition (the application of transcendent myths to elements of experience), hyperstition describes the immanent dynamics of myth's emergence: swarms of anomaly pushing themselves into thought, recasting perceived reality and catalysing conceptual shifts (becomings-in-thought). Hyperstitional becomings are sometimes the aim or product of a myth-science (cf. the numinous strategies described in Chapter 3). See: Goodman, *Sonic Warfare*, pp. 2, 201n. 6. See also http://www.ccru.net and the discussions at http://hyperstition. abstractdynamics.org/.

46 *More Brilliant than the Sun*. Eshun avoids a strict definition, instead letting examples accumulate towards a working concept. The following proceeds in the same way.

47 Deleuze and Guattari identify a category of stories about experience – 'tales, or narratives and statements of becoming' – that are fundamentally different from the transcendent 'myths' of structuralist analysis (as well as the 'constructions' of its descendants). These stories speak of affects and relationality, immanence and intensity: 'Must it not be admitted that myth as a frame of classification is quite incapable of registering these becomings, which are more like fragments of tales?' Deleuze and Guattari, *A Thousand Plateaus*, pp. 237–43.

48 Ibid., pp. 361–74.

49 James argues that traditional empiricism isolates objects and places emphasis on individual parts, treating the 'universal as an abstraction.' It is 'disjunctive' and divides the world, he says, while radical empiricism is conjunctive, attending to continuity and change. Rationalism, on the other hand, 'tends to emphasize universals and to make wholes prior to parts in the order of logic as well as that of being.' Rationalism's universals differ from radical empiricism, says James, because they use transcendent, *a priori* ideas to hold the parts together (an 'artificial correction'), whereas radical empiricism acknowledges the immanent relations of parts as something real and sensible in itself. James, *Radical Empiricism*, pp. 41–4. The concept of radical empiricism has been further developed by Massumi, via the influence of Deleuze, Guattari and Alfred North Whitehead. Writing in *Parables*, he notes that 'if [his own] incorporeal materialism is an empiricism it is a radical one.' Massumi, *Parables*, p. 16. Further discussion can be found in Brian Massumi, *Semblance and Event: Activist Philosophy and the Occurrent Arts* (Cambridge, MA: MIT Press, 2011).

50 'Affect engineering' – see Goodman, *Sonic Warfare*, p. 179.

51 'Machinic lineage' simply combines Deleuze and Guattari's interchangeable terms, 'machinic phylum' and 'technological lineage.' They write: We may speak of a *machinic phylum* or technological lineage, wherever we find *a constellation of singularities, prolongable by certain operations, which converge, and make operations converge, upon several assignable traits of expression.'* (*A Thousand Plateaus*, p. 406) 'The *machinic phylum* is materiality, natural or artificial, and both simultaneously; it is matter in movement, in flux, in variation, matter as a conveyor of singularities and traits of expression. This has obvious consequences: namely, this matter-flow can only be *followed*' (p. 409). Manuel De Landa distils the concept succinctly when he describes machinic phyla as: 'all processes in which a group of previously disconnected elements suddenly reaches a critical point at which they begin to "cooperate" to form a higher level entity.' Manuel De Landa, *War in the Age of Intelligent Machines* (New York: Zone Books, 1991), p. 6.

52 See Deleuze and Guattari, *A Thousand Plateaus*, p. 60; and *Kafka*, p. 22 for an expansion of this discussion.

53 The key is to avoid cliché. For Deleuze and Guattari, the task is 'To make the sequences vibrate, to open the word onto unexpected internal intensities – in short, an a-signifying intensive utilization of language.' *Kafka*, p. 22. For Eshun the strategy is 'to exaggerate … impossibility, until it's irritating, until it's annoying, and this annoyance is merely a threshold being crossed in the readers' heads, and once they unseize, unclench their sensorium, they'll have passed through a new threshold and they'll be in my world. I'll have got them. The key thing to do is to register this annoyance, because a lot of the moves I've described will provoke real annoyance, the lack of the literary, the lack of the modernist, the lack of the postmodern. All of these things should provoke a real irritation, and simultaneously a real relief, a relief that somebody has left all stuff behind, and started from the pleasure principle, started from the materials, started from what really gives people pleasure.' *More Brilliant Than the Sun*, p. 193.

54 Massumi, *Parables*, p. 5.

Chapter 1

1 Description of the author's experience at FWD, a dubstep and grime event held at Plastic People nightclub in Shoreditch, East London, from 2001 to 2013.

2 The sonic body is 'an affair of relations', as William James would have said. Investigating it means attending to circuits rather than poles, not just the parts

of a relation (a sound, a body, a subject, etc.) but relationality itself. James argued that both the rationalist and empiricist traditions had failed to grasp that relations are at least as significant and as real as their terms. In 'The Thing and its Relations' and other essays, he theorizes a monist continuity of experience, which he argues is only divided in reflection. This 'immediate flux of life', he argues, 'furnishes the material to our later reflection with its conceptual categories.' James, *Radical Empiricism*, pp. 92–122. Following Deleuze, Massumi writes: 'Call the openness of an interaction to being affected by something new in a way that qualitatively changes its dynamic nature *relationality*. Relationality is a global excess of belonging-together enabled by but not reducible to the bare fact of having objectively come together.' Elsewhere: 'Relationality is the potential for singular effects of qualitative change to occur in excess over or as a supplement to objective interactions. Relationality pertains to the openness of the interaction rather than to the interaction per se or to its discrete ingredients.' *Parables*, pp. 224–5.

3   Deleuze ('the body without organs') and Massumi ('body without an image') both write of the provisionality of the body, and how it operates as much in the incorporeal realm of its potentials as in its objective fleshiness. For a popularized explanation of kindred concepts from cognitive science, see Sandra and Matthew Blakeslee's *The Body Has a Mind of Its Own* (New York: Random House, 2008).

4   James used the term 'pure experience' (without implying 'authenticity' of experience) to describe monist smooth space in its totality. Patterns of differentiation therein he describes as 'concatenated unions' or relational groupings that achieve a certain 'hanging-together', which is comparable to Deleuze and Guattari's concept of consistency.

5   Fractals are commonly given as an example of rhythmic patterns 'emerging from chaos'. The important lesson to take from the discovery of the fractal is that chaos is not a zero-sum condition. As Guattari writes, 'it is not pure indifferentiation; it possesses a specific ontological texture. It is inhabited by virtual entities and modalities of alterity which have nothing universal about them.' Felix Guattari, *Chaosmosis: an ethico-acoustic paradigm* (Bloomington, IN: Indiana University Press, 1995), p. 81. So chaos is a heterogeneous space and the differences therein give rise to multiplicitous tendencies which may themselves 'swarm' in various directions. Hence, Massumi uses the term 'fractal attractor' to describe the heterogeneous pull of the virtual. *A User's Guide*, pp. 35–9.

6   James used the term 'conjunctive difference' to indicate change that links together rather than dividing. *Radical Empiricism*, pp. 107–8.

7   Gilles Deleuze, *Difference and Repetition* (New York, Columbia University Press, 1993), p. 139.

8   (Emphasis added) Massumi, *Parables*, p. 14. The depiction of nature-culture as a continuum (the dynamic space between two terms) and not a binary (i.e. nature/culture) is key here. All further uses of that contraction in the following pages are meant in this sense.

9   Guattari uses the term 'machinic heterogenesis' to describe the same dynamic of emergence in a field of multiplicitous relations.

10 On what a becoming-dog would mean, Deleuze and Guattari write, 'You do not become a barking, molar dog, but … you emit a molecular dog.' *A Thousand Plateaus,* p. 275.

11 On mediation/modulation, see the chapters titled 'The Political Economy of Belonging and the Logic of Relation' and 'Strange Horizon: Buildings, Biograms, and the Body Topologic' in Massumi, *Parables*, pp. 68–8, 177–207.

12 *A Thousand Plateaus,* p. 274.

13 See Chapter 2 for Guattari's non-anthropocentric theorization of enunciation and a-signifying semiotics.

14 This discussion and subsequent quotes drawn from Massumi, *Parables*, pp. 71–80.

15 Gilles Deleuze. *Francis Bacon: The Logic of Sensation* (1981), trans. Daniel W. Smith (Minneapolis: University of Minnesota Press, 2001), pp. 40–1.

16 In *Radical Empiricism,* James repeatedly stresses the realness of relations, which is to say the reality of the virtual as it operates on the actual.

17 Guattari, *Chaosmosis*, p. 115.

18 'Patently, art does not have a monopoly on creation, but it takes its capacity to invent mutant coordinates to extremes: it engenders unprecedented, unforeseen and unthinkable qualities of being. The decisive threshold constituting this new aesthetic paradigm lies in the aptitude of these processes of creation to auto-affirm themselves as existential nuclei, autopoietic machines.' Ibid., p. 106.

19 Massumi, *Parables*, p. 77.

20 Guattari's machinic philosophy poaches the concept of 'autopoiesis' (derived from the Greek *auto-* meaning 'self' and *poiesis* meaning 'creation') from the cybernetic theorists Humberto Maturana and Francisco Varela. For Guattari, the 'self-creation' of autopoiesis describes self-organizing systems (cutting across the biological, individual, social and technical) that are dynamically imbalanced and open to differentiating influence. Such processes of 'heterogenesis' (contrasted with the 'homogenesis' of a closed system) are crucial, he argues, to genuine becomings and the emergence of new thought,

subjectivities and social-material relations. See Gary Genosko, *Félix Guattari: An Aberrant Introduction* (New York: Continuum, 2002), pp. 195–6. The term is used here via Guattari (*Chaosmosis*), but also via Massumi, for whom it becomes more or less synonymous with the terms self-activity/self-variation/self-variation. Massumi, *Parables*, pp. 206, 280n. 13.

21 James, *Radical Empiricism,* p. 106.

22 Sun Ra on myth as a cosmogenetic arcanum: 'We hold this myth to be potential. They hold their truth to be self-evident. But our myth is not self-evident because it is a mystery.' *Sun Ra: A Joyful Noise*, dir. by Robert Mugge (1980; Paradox 2003 dvd).

23 This is why Deleuze and Guattari call the secret a *war machine*. Of secret societies, they note that there is always a secret hind society guarding it, but that the secret is always concerned with influence in wider society ('secrets secrete'), therefore putting them in a double motion. More worrisome are imperceptible secrets (hidden ones as opposed to those known to exist) which have a special relationship with paranoia. *A Thousand Plateaus*, p. 290.

24 What Massumi labels the back-formation of affect, when culture feeds back into, but not subsume affective circuits. *Parables*, p. 9.

25 Eshun uses the concept of the audio-social to move musical discussion away from textual interpretations and towards a ways of thinking through the cultural activity of sound and sensation. 'You can talk about the audio-social and immediately you've connected the sound to everything else; the literary just never really seems to appear, except as different kinds of Sonic Fiction.' *More Brilliant Than the Sun*, p. 183.

26 DJ/producer kode9 describes the sensory experience of a DMZ dubstep event held at Third Base nightclub in Brixton, South London. Interviewed in the BBC web documentary *The Sound of Dubstep* (2006), http://www.bbc.co.uk/dna/collective/A10695684 (accessed 5 April 2007).

27 Jon Ronson, *The Men Who Stare at Goats* (New York: Simon & Schuster, 2006).

28 This includes the myth of the 'brown note', an infrasonic frequency said to force defecation, as well as the belief, given momentum by an offhand report in *Playboy* magazine, and prevalent in some bass music and car stereo circles, that a tone at 33 Hz will bring a woman to involuntary orgasm. Infrasound experiments have provided no support for the former, while a quick online survey of sex toy specifications would seem to disprove the 'magic frequency' suggested in the latter.

29 See Vladimir Gavreau, 'Infrasound', *Science Journal* 4/1 (1968), pp. 33–7. Gavreau appears to have published at least three articles on the subject but,

adding to the mythos, two of the journals are very difficult to locate. Jürgen Altmann's 'Acoustic Weapons – A Prospective Assessment' in *Science & Global Security* 9 (2001) is a comprehensive survey of the field since Gavreau. Meanwhile, Geoff Leventhall singles Gavreau out in his recent survey of infrasound research, calling his work in the 1960s 'misleading', and blaming the ensuing media coverage for further 'sensationalizing' the field. The effect on popular belief, argues Leventhall, with an oddly psychoanalytic tinge, is that 'The aura of mystery and danger still persists today, deep in the minds of many people, where it waits for a trigger to bring it to the surface.' Geoff Leventhall, 'Low Frequency Noise. What We Know, What We Do Not Know, and What We Would Like to Know', *Journal of Low Frequency Noise and Active Control* 28 (2009), pp. 79–104.

30   Steven Shaviro, *The Cinematic Body* (Minneapolis: University of Minnesota Press, 1993), p. 143.

31   Ibid., p. 129.

32   Here, familiarity with the track is no guarantee against shock. In the mix, there are always surprises on the horizon – the next blend bringing new rhythmic tensions or the contrasting vibrations of another bassline.

33   Mid-2005: Plastic People in Shoreditch, East London, was home to FWD>>, the club night run by Ammunition Productions and typically credited with incubating the early dubstep scene. Its counterpart was DMZ, hosted by the record label of the same name at Third Base nightclub in the basement of a converted church in Brixton. Both of these rooms combined relative darkness and small size (compared to the city's more prominent venues like Fabric or Ministry Sound) with disproportionately powerful sounds systems that were tuned to project subbass-centric music with great clarity and spectral definition as well as acoustic force. See Chapter 5 for an expanded discussion of the darkened, high-wattage dancefloor as multisensory environment. For a discussion of the Plastic People sound system, with owner Ade Fakile see: http://www.theguardian.com/music/musicblog/2015/jan/07/london-club-plastic-people-remembered-ade-fakile-floating-points. On the subject of creating music specifically for that space, UK garage/proto-dubstep producer Zed Bias has said: ' "*Plastic People* had an incredible sound system, and we all grasped onto that as producers, because when you've got such a powerful system to play you can really fine-tune your mix downs. A lot of us ended up making tunes specifically for FWD>>. This totally shaped how the music was sounding, because we knew what was heavy and what would work on the dancefloor, but it was also a listening place as well ..." ' Quoted in Lloyd

Bradley, *Sounds Like London: 100 Years of Black Music in the Capital* (London: Serpent's Tail, 2013), p. 373.

34 cf. Chapter 5.

Chapter 2

1 See Johann Wolfgang von Goethe, *Theory of Colours* (1810), trans. Charles Lock Eastlake (Cambridge, MA: MIT Press, 1970); and Arthur Schopenhauer, *On Vision and Colours* (1816), trans. Georg Stahl (New York: Princeton Architectural Press, 2010).

2 Ludwig Lavater's *Of Ghostes and Spirites, Walking by Night* (1572), quoted in Owen Davies, *The Haunted: A Social History of Ghosts* (London: Palgrave Macmillan, 2007), pp. 2–3.

3 H. P. Lovecraft, 'The Colour Out of Space', in S. T. Joshi (ed.), *The Call of Cthulu and Other Weird Stories* (London: Penguin, 1999), pp. 179–99.

4 From 'The Whisperer in Darkness' in the same collection. In 'The Music of Eric Zahn' the narrator explains: 'I often heard sounds which filled me with an indefinable dread – the dread of vague wonder and brooding mystery. It was not that the sounds were hideous, for they were not; but that they held vibrations suggesting nothing on this globe of earth ...' While in 'The Transition of Juan Romero' it is a chthonic pulse: 'THAT SOUND ... THAT THROB DOWN IN THE GROUND!' H. P. Lovecraft, 'The Transition of Juan Romero', http://www. hplovecraft.com/writings/texts/fiction/tjr.aspx (accessed 5 June 2013).

5 'Colour Out of Space', p. 174.

6 This theme is most prominent in 'The Call of Chthulu'.

7 A speculative sub-genre existing between horror and science fiction. Often associated with the American pulp magazine *Weird Tales*.

8 'Against the model of philosophy as a rubber stamp for common sense and archival sobriety ...' Graham Harman, 'On the Horror of Phenomenology: Lovecraft and Husserl', *Collapse IV: Concept Horror* (2008), p. 334.

9 Ibid., p. 342. Harman's readings of Lovecraft (2008, 2012) share interests in common with the present discussion of spectral encounters and non-human agencies, but it is important to note a fundamental divergence. Espousing his own brand of speculative realist thought called object-oriented ontology, his work explicitly prioritizes 'the things in themselves' (or 'intentional objects') over their relations. He praises 'recent philosophies of "the virtual" ' for 'insisting on realism against any idealism or narrowly physical materialism,' but

says 'they are wrong to hold that objects are always utterly specific.' Ultimately, Harman says that 'true realism requires that things be considered apart from all relations' (2008). However, the argument in *Low End Theory* is that attention to sound makes this impossible. Vibration, as energetic tendency, is more relation than thing. It cannot be meaningfully described as an object and it undermines the discrete objectness of the things it modulates. Whether this poses a problem for object-oriented philosophy is a subject for another discussion. More recently, Harman (2011) has argued that realisms (like his own) and materialisms (like the ones that inform this book) are not in fact compatible, the latter being a 'disast[rous]' impediment to the urgent task of the former. That ontological debate is beyond the present scope, but it is taken up in Steven Shaviro's recent book *The Universe of Things: On Speculative Realism* (2014).

10 For Goodman, the term unsound

> describes the peripheries of human audition, of infrasound and ultrasound, both of which modulate the affective sensorium in ways we still do not fully comprehend. In its negative connotation, unsound aptly describes the colonization of inaudible frequencies by control. But most important, unsound also names that which is not yet audible within the normal bandwidth of hearing – new rhythms, resonances, textures, and syntheses. Most generally, then, unsound denotes sonic virtuality, the nexus of imperceptible vibration, masked due to limitations on not just the deficient physiology of the auditory system, but also the policing of the sensible enacted by groups defined by their affective affinities determined by taste, expertise, or other audiosocial predeterminations such as class, race, gender, and age. (Goodman, *Sonic Warfare*, p. 191)

11 'Enunciation becomes correlative not only to the emergence of a logic of non-discursive intensities, but equally to a pathic incorporation-agglomeration of the vectors of partial subjectivity.' Guattari, *Chaosmosis*, pp. 22, 36.

12 See the chapter 'Too-Blue: Color Patch for an Expanded Empiricism' in Massumi, *Parables*. The organizing parable of the chapter is a colour recognition experiment in which subjects were asked to match colours from memory with patches presented to them. Invariably, the subjects chose colours that 'exaggerated' the object of memory. They were always 'too-blue', etc. 'Too-blue' becomes a term for expressing the self-activity of a materiality as it enters a context (e.g. a tightly controlled scientific experiment) and begins to redirect it. This is the sense in which colour 'insists' – in perception, in memory, in imagination and the beginning of its ingress into the social and a becoming-cultural of nature.

13   Jeffrey Sconce, *Haunted Media: Electronic Presence from Telegraphy to Television* (Raleigh, NC: Duke University Press, 2000), p. 7.

14   Ibid., pp. 59–91.

15   Ibid., pp. 124–66.

16   Although the exact form that 'presence' is imagined to take may vary greatly from medium to medium over the last 150 years, a consistent representational strategy spans these popular perceptions of electronic media. Grounded in the larger and more long-standing metaphysics of electricity, fantastic conceptions of media presence ranging from the telegraph to virtual reality have often evoked a series of interrelated metaphors of 'flow', suggesting analogies between electricity, consciousness and information that enable fantastic forms of electronic transmutation, substitution and exchange. (Sconce, *Haunted Media*, p. 7)

17   This is often true even of work that foregrounds 'embodiment', as the bodies in question are too often only discursive ones. Sconce's stance on this point is confirmed when he uses a perfunctory critique of Marshall McLuhan to obviate attention to the nervous system in relation to electronic media. Ibid., pp. 4, 128–9.

18   The *man-made unknown* is the other side of a technological world supposed to be circumscribed by its social construction. The term describes a machinic agency which diverges from human control and intent. It can mean a confusion of nature/culture distinctions, referring to developments which are potentially, but not inherently, social. In the urban landscape, this includes vast sections of infrastructure (ancient, disused and abandoned sewers and subway tunnels) which have effectively 'gone native', falling off of maps, partially reverting to nature and put to new uses, whether by flora or fauna. Architecture has its equivalent in old buildings rebuilt, divided, joined, built over and around, within which epochs blur and spatial relationships became confused, even in the minds of their daily occupants. Other cases include the accidental development of psychedelic drugs in pharmaceutical laboratories, and the latent potentials of computers, code, synthesizers, etc. are still others.

19   'In the end', Sconce writes, 'we are always left with a material machine at the heart of such supernatural speculations, a device mechanically assembled, socially deployed, and culturally received within a specific historical moment.' The a-signifying semiotics of the machine, wave energy and body are, therefore, precluded. Ibid., pp. 4, 20.

20   The premise was plausible at the time. In 1937, Amateur American astronomer Grote Reber built one of the first radio telescopes in his own backyard.

'National Radio Astronomy Observatory, Rote Greber and his Radio Telescope', http://www.nrao.edu/whatisra/hist_reber.shtml (accessed 2 December 2011). The same basic technology has been used for decades by SETI and other projects aimed at locating extraterrestrial intelligence.

21 Sconce, *Haunted Media*, pp. 139–43.

22 Owen Davies, *The Haunted: A Social History of Ghosts* (New York: Palgrave Macmillan, 2007), p. 46.

23 Reports collected in large part by the Society for Psychical Research. Ibid., pp. 8–9, 13–44.

24 Deleuze, *Francis Bacon*, p. 32.

25 *Francis Bacon*, directed by David Hinton (1985; DVD Arthaus Musik GMBH, 2002).

26 Daniel W. Smith, Introduction to *Logic of Sensation*, p. xxii.

27 Deleuze, *Logic of Sensation*, p. 16. Smith adds:

> In Deleuze, in other words, the power of Nature in the unformed or the deformed appears in the form of the nonorganic life of things: 'The non-organic life of things, a frightful life, which is oblivious to the wisdom and limits of the organism. ... It is the vital as potent pre-organic germinality, common to the animate and the inanimate, to a matter which raises itself to the point of life, and to a life which spreads itself through matter.' (Introduction, p. xxii)

28 Ibid., p. 32.

29 To borrow a phrase from Massumi. *Parables*, p. 74. This, again, is effectively the definition of the body without organs and it recalls the soccer discussion in the first chapter. As Deleuze describes it: 'This rhythmic unity of the senses, can only be discovered by going beyond the organism,' towards the virtual, the body without organs.

> The body without organs is opposed less to organs than to that organization of organs we call an organism. It is an intense and intensive body. It is traversed by a wave that traces levels or thresholds in the body according to the variations of its amplitude. Thus the body does not have organs, but thresholds or levels. ... Sensation is vibration. (Ibid., p. 39)

30 In the previous chapter, we saw how bass-centred musics can be deployed to generate a logic of sensation on the dancefloor. Bodies were targeted with particular combinations of frequency and force with the aim of producing an uncommon eventness. The present discussion aims to reveal less obvious vibratory logics that emerge when largely unheard sounds twig a range of senses beyond the ear.

31 Deleuze distinguishes between two forms of analogy: (1) an indexical form that works through resemblance, and (2) a 'sensual' form that works by 'non-resembling means', an immediate connection without translation. He uses analogue and digital synthesizers as examples. The digital works through translation and reproduction whereas the voltages of analogue modules work directly on each other without translation. Their effects vary depending on what module they are feeding into, but those effects are direct analogues of the energy fed in. 'Painting is perhaps the analogical art par excellence.' *Logic of Sensation*, pp. 94–5.

32 Ibid., pp. 44–5.

33 The vestibular system is that portion of the inner ear that does not participate in audition but which is involved in perceptions of motion, balance and spatial orientation. Proprioception is the body's sense of its own movements and the relative positioning of its parts.

34 As James argues, different thought paths can reach the same conclusions, or *termini*, while travelling different routes. We are always 'virtual knowers' of experience before that knowledge is confirmed. *Radical Empiricism*, pp. 52–91.

35 Ultimately, the body without organs is the concept that underlies both the figural and spectral.

36 Massumi, *Parables*, p. 20.

37 Most notably, studies on electromagnetic radiation as a potential catalyst of haunt-like experiences. Michael Persinger's work is significant both for helping to found this field of research, and for making transversal links between certain types of hauntings, religious experience and other deterritorializing events, asking whether similar material conditions and neuroaffective responses may be found across varied cultural sites. See *The Weather Matrix and Human Behavior* (New York: Praeger, 1980), *Neurophysiology of God Beliefs* (New York: Praeger, 1987), and, with William G. Roll, 'Investigations of Poltergeists and Haunts: A Review and Interpretation', in James Houran and Rense Lange (eds), *Hauntings and Poltergeists: Multidisciplinary Perspectives* (Jefferson, NC: McFarland, 2001), pp. 123–63. Richard Wiseman has drawn on Persinger's research to undertake field experiments at purportedly haunted sites, and has noted apparent links between electromagnetic conditions and sensations of presence, which seem to be independent of belief and prior knowledge of the sites in question. See Wiseman, Caroline Watt, Paul Stevens, Emma Greening and Ciaran O'Keeffe, 'An Investigation Into Alleged "Hauntings"', *British Journal of Psychology* 94 (2003), pp. 195–211.

38 Vic Tandy and Tony R. Lawrence, 'The Ghost in the Machine', *The Journal for the Society for Psychical Research* 62/851 (1998), p. 361.

39 Ibid., pp. 361–2.

40 The relationship between ventilation-produced infrasound and cognitive effects is also well-documented, although mainly within the parameters of 'health and safety', in the literature of industrial noise and vibration. For example, Norm Broner and Sinclair Knight Merz note that

> Low-frequency ventilation noise has been shown to affect a mentally demanding verbal reasoning task and work efficiency, and quality was found to be impaired. Further, LFN has been found to impair performance on tasks with high and moderate demands on cognitive processing when performed under high workload. LFN has also impaired performance on some of the low-demand tasks and a moderately demanding verbal task under low workload.

In 'Effects of Infrasound, Low-Frequency Noise, and Ultrasound on People' in Malcolm J. Crocker (ed.) *Handbook of Vibration and Noise Control* (London: Wiley, 2007), pp. 320–6. For an extensive bibliography of related literature, see Christian Sejer Pedersen, Henrik Møller and Kerstin Persson Waye, 'A Detailed Study of Low-Frequency Noise Complaints', *Journal of Low-Frequency Noise and Vibration* 27/1 (2008), pp. 1–30.

41 Most notably in a brief discussion of film-making techniques aimed at inducing 'cinerama sickness'. J. T. Reason, 'Motion Sickness and Associated Phenomena', in W. Tempest (ed.), *Infrasound and Low Frequency Vibration* (London: Academic Press, 1976), pp. 308–9.

42 'In practice it is often difficult to measure, or even identify, some of the relevant variables.' M. J. Griffin, 'Vibration and Visual Acuity', Ibid., p. 264.

43 Massumi, *Parables*, p. 190.

44 More recently, Geoff Leventhall cites research which shows just how much individual sensitivities can vary across the average audible spectrum, noting that: 'The threshold of an individual may differ from the average. Investigations at higher frequencies have shown that an individual threshold exhibits a "microstructure" in which there are fluctuations in sensitivity of up to 12dB at specific tones. (Cohen, 1982)'. 'A Review of Published Research on Low Frequency Noise and it Effects' (UK: Department for Environment, Food and Rural Affairs, May 2003), p. 14.

45 N. S. Yeowart, 'Thresholds of Hearing and Loudness for Very Low Frequencies', in Tempest (ed.), *Infrasound*, pp. 37–62.

46 Jean-Francois Augoyard and Henry Torgue, *Sonic Experience: A Guide to Everyday Sounds* (Montreal: McGill-Queen's University Press, 2005), pp. 130–5.

47 B. K. N. Rao and C. Ashely, 'Subjective Effects of Vibration', in Tempest (ed.) *Infrasound*, pp. 211–12. See also Augoyard and Torgue, *Sonic Experience*, pp. 99–110.

48 D. E. Parker, '7. Effects of Sound on the Vestibular System', Ibid., pp. 151–86; and H. E. von Giercke and C. W. Nixon, '6. Effects of Intense Infrasound on Man', Ibid., pp. 142–4.

49 Reason, p. 299–348.

50 H. E. von Giercke and C. W. Nixon, p. 116.

51 *Logic of Sensation*, p. 44.

52 Vic Tandy, 'Something in the Cellar', *The Journal of the Society for Psychical Research* 64.3, no. 860 (2003), pp. 129–40.

53 In 2002, artist and sound engineer Sarah Angliss, along with psychologist Richard Wiseman, conducted a musical performance/'psychological experiment' called *Infrasonic* at London's Purcell Room. Audience members listened to a pre-recorded piece of music while being unknowingly subjected to periodic blasts of powerful infrasound. While admirable as an art intervention, where the project perhaps became too reductive was in its reliance on a follow-up questionnaire to determine the 'results', with respondents being asked to quantify their experience of the event on scales labelled 'Happy-Sad', 'Aroused-Sleepy', 'Excited-Bored' and so on. See http://www.sarahangliss.com/ infrasonic-the-experiment (accessed 5 June 2010); a 2008 article describes an experiment called 'The "Haunt" Project' which involved building a room within a laboratory and attempting to 'haunt' it with both infrasound and electromagnetic radiation. The results were inconclusive. While the authors express a preference for the electromagnetic hypothesis, they find nothing in their own experiment to support it. And here too, the project seems hindered by its reliance on questionnaires which seem to miss the vagaries of the spectral by design (e.g. 'Felt a presence Y/N'). Christopher C. French, Usman Haque, Rosie Bunton-Stasyshyn and Rob Davis, 'The "Haunt" Project: An Attempt to Build a "Haunted" Room By Manipulating Complex Electromagnetic Fields and Infrasound', *Cortex* doi:10.1016/j.cortex.2007.10.011 (2008), pp. 1–11; J. J. Braithwaite and M. Townsend set out to debunk the infrasound hypothesis. They question Tandy's character while their case against him relies largely on an overstatement of one possibility (that ocular vibration might cause visual anomalies) raised in his first article. They say he has failed to prove that infrasound *alone* can *cause* a perception of haunting (whereas Tandy himself seems to have understood infrasound as one factor in a set of relations). They propose that electromagnetic radiation is the real culprit but base this only on

the supposition that it would likely be present alongside infrasound in many places. It is worth noting that Braithwaite considers scepticism a methodology and a virtue, bragging about this stance elsewhere (UKSkeptics.org forum), and claiming it keeps the researcher rooted in 'the real world'. This position is utterly at odds with an effort to think the incorporeal and the machinic, and to imagine how 'operative' realities might emerge. 'Good Vibrations: The Case for a Specific Effect of Infrasound in Instances of Anomalous Experience Has Yet to be Empirically Demonstrated', *Journal for the Society of Psychical Research* 70/885 (2006), pp. 211–24.

54   Sigmund Freud, 'The Uncanny', *The Standard Edition of the Complete Psychoanalytic Works of Sigmund Freud Volume 17,* ed. and trans. James Staachey (London: Hogarth Press, 1957), p. 244.

55   Ibid., pp. 234–8.

56   Massumi has made a similar argument regarding the interiorizing tendencies of phenomenology:

> For phenomenology, the personal is prefigured or 'prereflected' in the world, in a closed loop of 'intentionality', the act of perception or cognition is a reflection of what is already 'pre'-embedded in the world. It repeats the same structures, expressing where you already were. *Every phenomenological event is like a returning home.* [emphasis added] This is like the deja vu without the potent of the new. (*Parables*, p. 191)

If the predominant conception of the subject in cultural theory is largely descended from the subjects of psychoanalysis and phenomenology, then an incorporeal materialism of the sonic body has to begin from a different position. To this end, Goodman proposes

> An ontology of vibrational force [which] delves below a philosophy of sound and the physics of acoustics toward the basic processes of entities. Sound is merely a thin slice, the vibrations audible to humans or animals. Such an orientation therefore should be differentiated from a phenomenology of sonic effects centred on the perceptions of a human subject, as a ready-made, interiorized human center of being and feeling. (*Sonic Warfare*, p. 81)

57   Ronald Simons, *Boo! Culture, Experience and the Startle Reflex* (Oxford University Press USA, 1996), p. 3.

58   Ibid., pp. 8–9.

59   Ibid., pp. 4, 235.

60   Ibid., pp. 6–7. Simons cites both the nature/culture debates within cultural anthropology and the broader critique of essentialisms in post-structuralist thought.

61 Ibid., pp. 19–38.

62 Ibid., pp. 39–46.

63 Ibid., pp. 10–15. These insights on repetition and singularity will become especially significant when the discussion moves beyond inadvertent sonic startles, and turns towards effects sought and elicited in religious, musical and other art/media contexts. As Sun Ra observed: 'Nature never repeats itself; why should I repeat myself?'

64 Again, speaking to each startle as a unique event and the autonomy of affect, rather than the return of the familiar, as in Freud's uncanny.

65 Curiously, Simons says that he sees no political implications in the discussion of startle. Ibid., p. 8. Goodman amply disproves this with his discussion of the use of sonic booms by Isreali Defence Forces as a sonic weapon in Gaza. *Sonic Warfare*, pp. xiii–xvi.

66 David J. Hufford, 'An Experience-Centred Approach to Hauntings', in James Houran and Rense Lange (eds), *Hauntings and Poltergeists: Multidisciplinary Perspectives* (Jefferson, NC: McFarland, 2001), p. 34. Here too, there is an affinity with Massumi: 'Experience, normal or clinical, is never fully intentional. No matter how practiced the act, the result remains at least as involuntary as it is elicited ... the personal is not intentionally prefigured. It is rhythmically re-fused, in a way that always brings something new and unexpected into the loop. The loop is always strangely open.' *Parables*, p. 191.

67 See: 'Why You Can't Tickle Yourself' in Blakeslee and Blakeslee, *The Body Has a Mind of Its Own*, p. 118.

68 Though typically used as a synonym for ghost- or alien-related phenomena, by its strictest definition supernatural simply refers to 'some force beyond scientific understanding or the laws of nature.' *OED*.

69 Hufford, 'An Experience-Centred Approach', p. 34.

70 To this end, Hufford proposes the term 'core experience' to describe the 'raw material' (not 'end product') of belief systems. This should not be interpreted as a crude recourse to 'raw experience'. Rather, it is meant to suggest, much as Simons does, the material relations that underlie experience, engendering but also, importantly, constraining it. In this way, Hufford manages to account for the ontogenetic function of difference while also limiting explanations that slide towards pure relativism. His 'core experience' might be loosely compared to the 'machinic relations' of Deleuze and Guattari, or James' 'pure experience'.

71 Hufford describes stories of belief as a social resource. 'Beliefs about the supernatural and the reasoning by which they are derived and applied are to be found in stories. They are not *hidden* in these stories, because the stories are constructed specifically to carry on a discussion, even a debate, about

the beliefs. They are therefore displayed quite prominently.' He compares the study of such tales to the study of informal speech in relation to Official English. Informal speech, he notes, carries its own logic. Ibid., p. 25. Deleuze and Guattari describe three essential features of a minor literature: (1) a deterritorialization of dominant language; (2) this as having a political immediacy; (3) and involving a collectivity. *Kafka*, pp. 16–27.

72   Hufford, 'An Experience-Centred Approach', p. 20.

73   Hufford notes that William James' concept of the *ineffable* is commonly used to say that 'nothing can be said about these experiences'. This is a misinterpretation, he says, arguing that there is a significant difference between 'nothing to say' and 'the struggle for words'. The latter points to something that exceeds, defies or deforms language and highlights its failure, forcing the speaker to invent ways to describe experience. James' ineffable is therefore closer to a concept like Massumi's escape of affect, or the 'excess of reality' that cannot be reconciled in language.

74   Adapted from: Caroline Franks Davis, *The Evidential Force of Religious Experience* (Oxford: Clarendon Press, 1999).

75   Massumi, *Parables*, pp. 111–12.

76   James, *Radical Empiricism*, p. 57.

77   Ibid., pp. 67–73, 88. Massumi sums up radical empiricism as 'the felt reality of a relation'. *Parables*, 16.

78   Hummer interview in *The Hum*, directed by Tom Feiling (Faction Films 1997 dvd).

79   David Deming, 'The Hum: An Anomalous Sound Heard Around the World', *Journal of Scientific Exploration* 18 (2004), pp. 571–5.

80   See *The Hum* for reports from sufferers. See Deming (above) and Leventhall ('A Review ...') for overviews of reported qualities and effects.

81   *The Hum* travels the UK, documenting a number of these searches, including both the highly-controlled efforts of scientists and the more makeshift efforts of Hummers.

82   'If a source is located, the problem moves into the category of engineering noise control and is no longer "the Hum".' Leventhall, 'A Review', p. 43.

83   Frits van den Berg, 'Low Frequency Noise and Phantom Sounds', *Journal of Low Frequency Noise and Active Control* 28/2 (2009), pp. 105–16.

84   He summarizes as follows:

> The laboratory production of the Ganzfeld is an experimental device dedicated to the mutual exclusion of the other senses. The Ganzfeld is the limit toward which vision separates out from the other senses. Remember

that the addition of a stimulus in another sense mode was incompatible with the maintenance of even those ambiguous characteristics that the limit-field could be agreed upon as having. Other-sense stimulation made the limit-field fall away (made vision most decisively take flight from its conditions)—precisely because it was no longer a 'pure' field of vision but a mixed or intermodal field. The disjunctive limit of vision thus precariously neighbors a hallucinatory, intermodal (conjunctive) limit. Pure and alone, it is emergent, populated by spontaneous appearances presenting potentials for object constancy. In mixed company it is hallucinatory, populated by paradox: objects without constancy. (Massumi, *Parables*, p. 154)

85   Ibid.
86   Van den Berg, 'Low Frequency Noise', p. 112.
87   R. N. Vasudevan and Colin G. Gordon, 'Experimental Study of Annoyance Due to Low Frequency Noise', *Applied Acoustics* 10 (1977), p. 66.
88   Deming, 'The Hum', p. 580.
89   Ibid., p. 579.
90   Of the audible spectrum, as an average and in practice, Leventhall says:

It is clear that the audiogram is not a smooth curve and that there are pronounced individual differences. Low frequency audiograms of complainants have shown that some hum complainants have low frequency hearing which is more sensitive than the average threshold, whilst others are less sensitive (Walford 1978, 1983), as would be expected in any population of subjects. Thus, complainants do not necessarily have enhanced hearing acuity at low frequencies. (Leventhall, 'A Review', p. 15)

91   A military or industrial source might also explain why The Hum often seems to go silent when efforts to tack it down have been publicly announced. As one researcher put it, The Hum 'avoids publicity'. Deming, p. 590. That HAARP should arouse such suspicion and paranoia among some is not surprising given its quasi-science fictional background:

Haarp is studying exactly the same phenomena which [Nikola] Tesla first considered nearly 100 years ago. [It] is based on the ideas of Bernard Eastlund, who holds three US patents (4,686,605 – 4,712,158 – 5,038,664) ... [entitled]: method and apparatus for altering a region in the earth's atmosphere, ionosphere and/or magnetosphere; method and apparatus for creating an artificial electron cyclotron heating region of plasma; and method for producing a shell of relativistic particles at an altitude above the earth's surface. This last patent, which describes an anti-missile shield which could destroy the electronics of hostile missiles or satellites, is the realization of Tesla's 'Death Ray'. It works by creating a plasma packet of high-energy particles – Tesla's Colorado lightning experiments on a large scale.

Robert Lomas, 'Essay: Spark of Genius', *The Independent* August 21, 1999, http://www.independent.co.uk/life-style/essay-spark-of-genius-1114136.html (accessed 9 November 2011).

92   First observed by A. H. Frey in 'Human auditory system response to modulated electromagnetic energy', *Journal of Applied Physiology* 17 (1962), pp. 689–92. Later, partially confirmed by J. A. Elder and C. K. Chou in 'Auditory Response to Pulsed Radiofrequency Energy', *Bioelectromagnetic Supplement* 6 (2003), pp. 162–73. Notably, though, Elder and Chou do not comment on the vestibular-like effects noted by Frey.

93   In Frey, we find a curious offhand remark with possible links to urban legends and wave-related paranoias. In lab tests, he says, sensitives found a method for eliminating the uncomfortable effects of audible radio frequencies: '[we] have found that the sensitive area for detecting RF sounds is a region over the temporal lobe of the brain. One can shield, with a 2-in. piece of fly screen, a portion of the stippled area shown in Fig. 6 and completely cut off the RF sound', p. 692. Put another way, a piece of metallic shielding is alleged to protect the brain from electromagnetic radiation, much as it would protect a cable or sensitive electronics from interference. If there is any truth to this, might it be the origin of the 'tin foil hat' – by now an image synonymous with conspiracy theorists and individuals suffering from paranoid delusions of mind control by invisible waves? If so, might a combination of anomalous sensitivity and electromagnetic circumstance be relevant factors in some cases of the latter?

94   Ibid., p. 689.

95   Broner, 'The Effects of Low Frequency Noise', pp. 483–500.

96   Massumi, *Parables*, p. 247.

97   An equal-loudness contour is a graphic depiction of average hearing ability as it varies across the frequency spectrum. Acuity is greatest in the range associated with human speech, but trails off steeply at lower frequencies. This means that sounds in this lower region require vastly more sound pressure in order for the ear to perceive them at the same level as those higher frequencies. An equal-loudness contour charts this relationship between sound pressure level (SPL) and hearing ability across the frequency spectrum.

98   Acoustic researcher quoted in *The Hum*.

99   Two conclusions from the WHO report: 'When prominent low frequency
      components are present, noise measures based on A-weighting are
      inappropriate.' 'Since A-weighting underestimates the sound pressure level of
      noise with low frequency components, a better assessment of health effects
      would be to use C-weighting.' Quoted in Leventhall, 'A Review', p. 5.

100   K. E. Haneke, B. L. Carson and E. A. Maull, 'Infrasound: Brief Review of
      Toxicological Literature. Infrasound Toxicological Summary' (National
      Institutes of Health, 2001), p. 5.

101   Leventhall, 'Low Frequency Noise', pp. 97–8.

102   'Hidden Sensory System Discovered in the Skin,' *Science Daily,* http://www.
      sciencedaily.com/releases/2009/12/091208083524.htm (accessed 13 December
      2009).

103   Robert Roy Britt, 'Controversial New Idea: Nerves Transmit Sound, Not
      Electricity', *Live Science,* http://www.livescience.com/humanbiology/070312_
      nerves_work.html (accessed 14 March 2007).

Chapter 3

1   By their standard definitions, 'strategy' refers to a methodology in the abstract –
     overall aims and management of resources – while 'tactics' are the plans and
     means adopted to carry out a specific action or achieve a particular end. Recent
     cultural theory, particularly in the wake of Michel de Certeau, has tended to
     depict strategy as belonging to the totalizing logic of Power, while tactics are
     often celebrated as bricolage means of resistance. That distinction would seem
     to find a close parallel in Deleuze and Guattari's depiction of Royal and nomad
     science (Logos and nomos, the molar and molecular, etc.). Yet the semantic
     distinction between strategy and tactics does not appear in their work, nor in
     Massumi, who, of becomings, writes that they rarely happen alone and can
     'can only ever proliferate with carefully formulated group strategies.' Strategies,
     he says, are 'less theories of becoming than pragmatic guidelines serving
     as landmarks for future re movement. They have no value unless they are
     immanent to their "object": they must be verified by the collectivity concerned,
     in other words submitted to experimental evaluation and remapped as
     needed.' This is the sense in which I will proceed to theorize *bass as a strategy,*
     effectively treating numinous uses of low-frequency sound as a radically
     empirical approach to the sonic body. It is concerned with spectralization and

its potential uses, but there is nothing about it that is inherently oppressive, nor transgressive either.

2   Goodman, *Sonic Warfare*, p. 18.

3   Gavreau, 'Infrasound', pp. 33–7.

4   Glenn D. White and Gary J. Louie, *The Audio Dictionary*, 3rd edn (Seattle: University of Washington Press, 2005), pp. 329–30.

5   Ibid., p. 182.

6   Hermann L. F. Helmholtz, *On the Sensations of Tone as a Physiological Basis for the Theory of Music*, 2nd English edn, trans. Alexander J. Ellis (New York: Dover Publications Inc., 1954), p. 36.

7   Ibid., pp. 41–2.

8   Chladni's work anticipates twentieth-century research in cymatics, or the study of visible wave phenomena. So-called Chladni figures are produced by resonating a plate covered with sand. Upon removal of the energy source, the sand remains 'frozen' in the shape of the plate's nodal patterns.

9   Ibid., pp. 41–2.

10 Helmholtz, *On the Sensation of Tone*, pp. 38–9.

11 Ibid., p. 129.

12 Jonathan Sterne, *The Audible Past: Cultural Origins of Sound Reproduction* (Raleigh, NC: Duke University Press, 2002), p. 66.

13 Helmholtz, *On the Sensation of Tone*, p. 18.

14 Ibid., pp. 175–6.

15 Donald Tuzin, 'Miraculous Voices: The Auditory Experience of Numinous Objects', *Current Anthropology* 25 (1984), pp. 587–8.

16 Joseph Conrad, *Heart of Darkness* (1902) (London: Penguin, 1980), pp. 28–9, 105. Conrad ultimately inverts the source of the 'darkness', linking it instead with the inhumanity of colonization, but the drum nevertheless remains its animal its pulse.

17 This is evident in a majority of texts cited in this chapter.

18 This may have reached its apotheosis in the 1976 article 'A Psychoanalytic Study of the Bullroarer', in which Alan Dundes writes: 'Previous scholarship has suggested the bullroarer is phallic, but this theory does not satisfactorily explain why women may not see it or why it is associated with making wind.' The bullroarer is, in fact, a *wind instrument* capable of very pronounced, airborne modulations. Dundes, however, 'draws attention to the possible anal component of male initiation arguing that the bullroarer is a flatulent phallus.' Alan Dundes, 'A Psychoanalytic Study of the Bullroarer', *Man* 11 (1976), p. 220.

19 Tuzin, 'Miraculous Voices', p. 588.

20 Rossing, *Science of Percussion Instruments*, p. 128.

21 See the worldwide lists compiled by the Guild of Carillonneurs of North America at http://www.gcna.org/data/Great_Bells.html (accessed 12 January 2011).

22 Rossing, *Science of Percussion Instruments*, p. 180.

23 George W. Bird, *Wanderings in Asia* (London: Simpkin, Marshall, Hamilton, Kent & Co, Ltd, 1897), p. 318.

24 Satis N. Coleman, *Bells: Their History, Legends, Making, and Uses* (New York: Rand McNally & Company, 1928), p. 117.

25 'Table 4-1 Measured frequencies and observed pitches for 25 heavy bells', in William A. Hibbert, *The Quantification of Strike Pitch and Pitch Shifts in Church Bells* (The Open University: PhD dissertation, 2008), p. 73.

26 'Eastern Bells' in Rossing, *Science of Percussion Instruments*, pp. 164–81.

27 Ibid., p. 138.

28 Ibid., pp. 172–3. If the instrument's hum tone is 22 Hz (F_0), as Rossing's measurements indicate, then the bell's strike tone (which he does not give) should be one octave higher, at about 44 Hz (F_1). Zhang and Hong give a strike tone of 90 Hz (F_2) for the same bell, but this is not necessarily a contradiction, first because the pitch they report is still in-keeping with the harmonic series already suggested, and second because while 'Most observers identify the strike note in a tuned bell as having a pitch at or near the frequency of the strong second partial (prime or fundamental) ... to others it is an octave higher.' (Rossing, p. 137). See S. Y. Zhang, Z. L. Xie and Y. S. Hong, 'Damage assessment and preservation of suspending system of Yongle-Big-Bell', in Federico M. Mazzolani (ed.), *Protection of Historical Buildings* (London: Taylor & Francis, 2009), p. 491.

29 That is, 'unnatural' qualities associated with an electronically generated sine wave.

30 Helmholtz, *On the Sensation of Tone*, p. 72.

31 Hibbert, *Quantification*, p. 42.

32 Rossing, *Science of Percussion Instruments*, p. 178.

33 Ibid., p. 175.

34 Ibid. 'In the case of the King Songdok [sic] bell, the depression ... is 94 cm deep.'

35 Ibid., p. 176.

36 Steven Feld, 'From Ethnomusicology to Echo-muse-ecology: Reading R. Murray Schafer in the Papua New Guinea Rainforest', *The Soundscape Newsletter* 8 (1994), pp. 9–13. See also: Steven Feld, 'Places Sensed, Senses Placed', in David Howes (ed.), *Empire of the Senses: The Sensual Culture Reader* (London: Berg Publishing, 2005), pp. 179–91. 'Sound', he writes, 'both emanates from and penetrates bodies; this reciprocity of reflection and absorption is

a creative means of orientation – one that tunes bodies to places and times through their sounding potential.'

37   As strategy: 'Religious ideas may exploit the mystery inherent in certain odd mental states, but in the process they also define the aroused feelings and give them meanings which bind anxiety in a form that culturally informed actors can deal with and perhaps turn to personal and collective advantage.' Tuzin, 'Miraculous Voices', p. 579.

38   Ibid. Emphasis added.

39   This condition should not be equated with the sublime, which is too overcoded with Romantic sentiment to speak adequately to questions of affect and its escape.

40   For Deleuze and Guattari, a becoming in subjectivity is always a becoming-molecular or –minoritarian. It always involves a deterritorialization of something ostensibly whole (the molar/majoritarian) or a transcendent order (the striated). As such, there is an inherent politics to it. All becomings, they say, must pass through a 'becoming-woman', which is not meant to describe a female essence, but to identify andocentric relations as the first impediment to social change. Man is the majoritarian condition. There cannot, therefore, be a becoming-man. More generally, there cannot be a becoming-majoritarian. By this reasoning, there is no becoming involved in conforming to religious norms. However, the point here is to identify a transitional moment in which those relations are destabilized and subjectivity is volatized. The unpredictable nature of these moments is what lends them their mystifying qualities, but it makes them potentially dangerous to molar regimes.

41   A case of what Massumi calls the 'back-formation' of affect – that is, the modulating influence of culture feeding back into affect. *Parables*, pp. 7–9.

42   Anomalous bodily experience – in the form of visions, auditory hallucinations and other spectral encounters – is arguably the defining feature of mystical experience, forming the empirical basis for claims of unusual closeness to the divine. Tuzin (584) notes epilepsy's reputation as the 'sacred sickness', along with several studies claiming that many well- and lesser-known religious figures through history may have had the condition. Elsewhere, it has been suggested that the hyperreligiosity implied by the mystic body may have afforded some medieval nuns extra degrees of freedom and influence, because male religious leadership, however sceptical, were wary of challenging their claims. See: Elizabeth Alvilda Petroff, *Body & Soul: Essays on Medieval Women and Mysticism* (Oxford: Oxford University Press, 1994); and Emile Zum Brunn and Georgette Epiny-Burgard, *Women Mystics in Medieval Europe*, trans. Sheila Hughes (New York: Paragon House, 1989).

43 Consider the church's centuries-long resistance of the organ, and the mass destruction of European organs during the Reformation. Also edicts against music in parts of Islam, etc.

44 Massumi, *Parables*, p. 191.

45 Tuzin, 'Miraculous Voices', p. 587.

46 Andrew L. Mack and Josh Jones, 'Low-Frequency Vocalizations by Cassowaries (Casuarius spp.)', *The Auk* 120 (October 2003), pp. 1062–8.

47 Tuzin, 'Miraculous Voices', p. 582. For example, On the modified slit-gong/ tube instrument which mimics the cassowary: 'The resultant dull booming is a magnified, though otherwise faithful, imitation'.

48 Ibid., p. 582. Emphasis added.

49 Hans Fischer, *Sound-Producing Instruments in Oceania*, trans. Philip W. Holzknecht (Boroko, Papua New Guinea: Institute of Papua New Guinea Studies, 1986), p. 80.

50 Tuzin, 'Miraculous Voices', p. 582. From this, based on the scaling of organ pipes, we can deduce a fundamental frequency of approximately 40 Hz for the pipes themselves. However, this is 'greatly enhanced and distorted' when the pipe is blown into the cavity of a modified drum.

51 Ibid.

52 Tuzin speculates that infrasound is the main cause of the perceptual effects he describes. It may well be, to a certain extent, but it need not be for his argument to hold. The instruments he describes would generally seem to produce sound primarily within the subbass range, perhaps dipping into infrasound at times. While much has been made of the mystery inherent in infrasound, we have already seen that the lowest end of what is typically considered the audible range is marked by perceptual breakdown and multisensory papering over. Moreover, Broner has argued that the range between 20 and 100 Hz may in fact produce the broadest range of perceptual effects. With this in mind, and where appropriate, my discussion will use the term 'low-frequency sound' where Tuzin uses 'infrasound'.

53 Ibid., p. 586.

54 Ibid., p. 582.

55 Ibid.

56 While I was researching the behavioral effects of infrasonic waves, the frivolous thought occured to me that if only the cult leaders could schedule their ritual conclaves to coincide with quiet-before-the-storm periods, their audience would be in a state specifically receptive to the religious truths proclaimed in these events. It then struck me (like a thunderbolt!) that this is indeed the situation, though it comes about through no specific planning by the cult

leaders. Upon reading this, Fitz John Poole informed me that among the Bimin-Kuskumin many ritual performances are deliberately timed to coincide with highly predictable mountain thunder. (Ibid., p. 588n. 2)

57   For the former, see: Margaret J. Evans and W. Tempest, 'Some effects of infrasonic noise in transportation,' *Journal of Sound and Vibration* 22/1 (8 May 1972): pp. 19–24; Stephen Rosen, *Weathering: How the atmosphere conditions your body, your mind, your moods – and your health* (New York: M. Evans, 1979); and Michael A. Persinger. *The Weather Matrix and Human Behavior* (New York: Praeger, 1980). The latter is an ongoing concern in the *Journal of Low Frequency Noise, Vibration and Active Control*, edited by Tempest. Also see Tempest's *Infrasound*, and Malcolm J. Crocker (ed.), *The Handbook of Noise and Vibration Control* (London: Wiley, 2007).

58   Ibid., p. 588.

59   Chris Scarre and Graeme Lawson, 'Preface', in Scarre and Lawson (eds), *Archaeoacoustics* (Cambridge: McDonald Institute for Archaeological Research, 2006), p. vii.

60   Many archaeoacoustic researchers are wary of this perception, citing archaeoastronomy as an example of a field in which such tendencies were allowed too much reign, to the detriment of the reputation of the whole. Chris Scarre 'Sound, Place and Space: Towards and Archaeology of Acoustics' in *Archaeoacoustics*, pp. 6–7.

61   Ibid. Scarre proposes two guidelines for evaluating evidence: 1. 'Patterned repetition' – the recurrence of relevant features, of groupable types, across sites, to an extent that coincidence becomes the less likely explanation; 2. 'Closeness of fit' – recognition of the anomalous if it nevertheless coincides, in compelling ways, with evidence from other sites. Reznikoff proposes similar guidelines in 'The Evidence of the Use of Sound Resonance from Paleolithic to Medieval Times' in the same collection. These principles will help guide the following discussion.

62   Iégor Reznikoff and Michel Dauvois, 'La dimension sonore des grottes ornées', *Bulletin de la Société préhistorique française* 85 (1988), pp. 238–46.

63   Ker Than, 'Stone Age Art Caves May Have Been Concert Hall', *National Geographic News* (2 July 2008) (accessed 17 March 2009).

64   As to probability: if one admits a possible margin of inaccuracy of, say, 10 cm for the location of maximum resonance, the likelihood of locating the dot accidentally at the right location would be 100 to 1 for a tunnel 10 m long and 60 to 1 for one 6 m long. This yields odds for both tunnels combined of 6,000 to 1.

But when findings from multiple locations are considered together, 'the odds of all these correspondences having come about purely by chance would reduce to something of the order of a million to one.' Reznikoff, 'The Evidence of the Use of Sound Resonance', pp. 79–80.

65 Ibid.

66 The exploratory ethic is never abandoned; it persists in all sonic practice that proceeds intuitively.

67 Chris Scarre surveys investigations of Mesoamerican pyramids, churches, ancient henges, monastic vaults and other sites in 'Sound, Place and Space: Towards an Archaeology of Acoustics', in Scarre and Lawson (eds), *Archaeoacoustics*, pp. 1–10.

68 Not unique to the area, prehistoric mound structures of different sorts can be found on every continent. Passage tombs can also be found elsewhere in Europe.

69 For discussions of holey space as a strategy of *ungrounding*, repurposing the earth, and subverting surface relations, see Deleuze and Guattari, *A Thousand Plateaus*, pp. 413–15. For a more occult interpretation, see Reza Negarestani's work of 'theory-fiction'. *Cyclonopedia: Ccomplicity with Anonymous Materials* (Melbourne: re.press, 2008), pp. 41–68.

70 Robert G. Jahn, Paul Devereux and Michael Ibison, 'Acoustical Resonances of Assorted Ancient Structures', *Journal of the Acoustical Society of America* 99 (1996), p. 649.

71 Neil P. McAngus Todd, Sally M. Rosengren and James G. Golebatch, 'Tuning and Sensitivity of the Human Vestibular System to Low-Frequency Vibration', *Neuroscience Letters* 444 (2008), pp. 36–41.

72 John Askill gives 145 Hz as the average fundamental frequency of the male speaking voice and 230 Hz for women. In musical terms, the bass range of the singing voice is 82–294 Hz (E_2 to D_4), baritone is 110–394 Hz (A_2 to G_4) and tenor is 147–523 Hz (D_3 to C_5). John Askill, *The Physics of Musical Sound* (New York: D. Van Nostrand Co, 1979), p. 148.

73 Jahn, Devereux and Ibison, 'Acoustic Resonances', in Scarre and Lawson (eds), *Archaeoacoustics*, p. 654.

74 Elsewhere, Devereux has followed Tuzin and Persinger in speculating that the 110 Hz frequency band may have an influence of theta-wave brain activity – associated with hypnagogic states, vivid mental imagery and auditory hallucinations – making it an especially powerful facilitator of ritually useful altered states. He cites an internal report by Ian Cook of the Neuropsychiatric Institute at UCLA on EEG tests that measured brain activity associated with

exposure to a 110 Hz audio signal. Paul Devereux, 'Ears and Years: Aspects of Acoustics and Intentionality in Antiquity', in Scarre and Lawson (eds), *Archaeoacoustics*, pp. 27–9.

75   Jahn, Devereux and Ibison, 'Acoustic Resonances', p. 652.

76   Aaron Watson and David Keating, 'Architecture and sound: an acoustic analysis of megalithic monuments in prehistoric Britain', *Antiquity* 73 (1999), p. 334.

77   Ibid., p. 336.

78   John R. Shannon, *Understanding the Pipe Organ: A Guide for Students, Teachers and Lovers of the Instrument* (Jefferson, NC: McFarland, 2009), p. 12.

79   Jean Perrot, *The Organ from its Invention in the Hellenistic Period to the end of the Thirteenth Century*, trans. Norma Deane (London: Oxford University Press, 1971), p. 50.

80   Ibid., pp. 160, 163.

81   Ibid., pp. 15–16. 'The term used to describe the pipes is αὐλοί (auloi), the αὐλοί being a reed instrument, a type of oboe producing a rather penetrating tone. ... This was probably because these instruments were not designed to pass by unnoticed. Ktesibios' hydraulic organ, with its abundant supply of highly compressed air, was certainly capable of producing quite a thunderous volume of sound.' (p. 33); Perrot is especially well equipped to comment on the sound of the hydraulis as the author built his own, following instructions contained in Vitruvius' *De Architecura* (ca. 15 BC), pp. 142–53.

82   Ibid., pp. 17–22. And elsewhere: 'The Organ described by Heron, in his work "Pneumatika," differs in no essential point for that described by Vitruvius. It had, however, only a single stop or rank of pipes, while the later Organ of Vitruvius had four, six, or eight ranks, marking a decided advance in tonal appointment.' George Ashdown Audsley, *The Art of Organ Building, Volume 1* (1905; Mineola, NY: Dover, 1965), p. 12.

83   Perrot, *The Organ*, p. 62.

84   Poul-Gerhard Andersen, *Organ Building and Design*, trans. Joanne Curnutt (1956; London: George Allen and Unwin Ltd, 1969), p. 105. Wright expands on this interchangeability of terms:

> Of all the words in the medieval Latin vocabulary, few had a greater number of interpretations than *organum* (pl. *organa*). In a general sense it meant any sort of contrivance or device. When applied specifically to music, it could variously denote an instrument of mechanical fabrication encompassing keys and pipes, the human voice, a sacred song generated by the human voice (often in phrases such as in *hymnis et organis*), or a sacred

song sung according to the precepts of a particular type of polyphonic music (*organum*). Used in a metaphorical sense, *organa* was often employed during the thirteenth through sixteenth centuries as a synonym for the Mass and canonical hours (*organe divinae laudis*). ... Given the variety of applications of the term *organum* in the MIddle Ages, it is hardly surprising that much confusion has been created in the modern mind with regard to the presence and function of the only musical instrument then sanctioned by the Western Church, the organ. (Craig M. Wright, *Music and Ceremony at Notre Dame of Paris, 500-1550* (Cambridge: Cambridge University Press, 1989), p. 143)

85   Perrot, *The Organ*, p. 46.

86   'Muristus has always been surrounded by an aura of mystery. It is not certain exactly when he lived; and his name, not to mention his personality, is a subject of some controversy. ... At all events, the descriptions bearing Muristus' name are adapted from an earlier work, and revised and corrected in the Arab fashion. The writings of the Byzantine author were certainly compiled from those a Greek engineer, probably Ktesibios himself. As I have said before, the graphic resemblance between the names Muristus and Qatasibiyus – that is to say Ktesibios – has been noted.' Perrot, *The Organ*, p. 191.

87   'If nature was a miracle, it was also, according to Hellenistic sources, knowable only by divine revelation. Scientific knowledge was a sacred mystery disclosed only to a chosen few. Thus, much of what survived of ancient science came into the West under an aura of secrecy. Often it came with formulaic injunctions against disclosing it to a vulgar crowd.' William Eamon, *Science and the Secrets of Nature: Books of Secrets in Medieval and Early Modern Culture* (Princeton: Princeton University Press, 1996), p. 15.

88   Wright, *Music and Ceremony*, pp. 148–9; and Perrot, *The Organ*, p. 223.

89   Eamon writes that official science was not interested in *secreta*, which were considered to belong to magic, and were grouped with the mechanical arts as '*techne* rather than *scientia*'. The distinction is essentially that between nomad and Royal Science outlined in Deleuze and Guattari's *A Thousand Plateaus*. Their discussion of 'the secret' as an agent of deterritorialization is also relevant here.

90   Ibid., p. 28.

91   Perrot, *The Organ*, pp. 253–6.

92   Andersen, *Organ Building and Design*, p. 55.

93   Ibid., p. 47.

94   Eamon, *Science and the Secrets of Nature*, p. 89.

95   Waves Audio Ltd uses the same principle in its MaxxBass hardware and software, used to create the illusion of lower bass in recordings destined for small speakers (e.g. televisions, radios).

96   Augoyard and Torgue, *Sonic Experience*, p. 129.

97   The question of combination tones' objective reality was long a subject of debate and that confusion persists in many descriptions of the effect. There are, in fact, two types. One (difference tones) is an effect of distortions produced in the ear canal, while the other (summation tones) is a physical phenomenon existing beyond the ear. S. N. Sen, *Acoustics, Waves and Oscillations* (New Delhi: New Age International, 1990). The discovery of 'mirror' neurons may have implications for the way we understand neuro-affective aspects of the missing fundamental. Mirror neurons are so-called because their job is to neurally 'act out' involvement in observed phenomena (e.g. watching another person grasp an object or kick a ball), as if the observer herself were performing the action – a sort of rehearsal in-the-moment. This has any number of potential implications for collective bodies in sonic experience. With regard to frequencies that are perceptually present, but physically absent, it raises the possibility of the nervous system, beyond the ear, engaging with the 'sonic hologram' much as it would to real physical vibration – that is, the emergence of an operative reality at the level of neurophysiology. See G. Rizzolatti, L. Fogassi and V. Gallese. 'Neurophysiological mechanisms underlying the understanding and imitation of action', *National Review of Neuroscience* 2 (2001), pp. 661–70; G. Rizzolatti and L. Craighero, 'The Mirror-Neuron System', *Annual Review of Neuroscience* 27 (2004), pp. 169–92. Also 'The Corporeal Roots of Symbolic Meaning', in Mark Johnson, *The Meaning of the Body: Aesthetics of Human Understanding* (Chicago: University of Chicago Press, 2007).

98   Pierre Buser and Michel Imbert, *Audition* (Cambridge, MA: MIT Press, 1992), p. 88.

99   Augoyard and Torgue, *Sonic Experience*, p. 130.

100 Ibid. This is the principle behind LRAD Corporation's Long Range Acoustic Device, which is marketed as a non-lethal crowd control weapon that works by producing painfully loud, high-frequency combination tones. Technical details in Elwood G. Norris, 'HyperSonic™Sound', *Acoustical Society of America 133rd Meeting Lay Language Papers* (1997), http://www.acoustics.org/press/133rd/2pea.html (accessed 15 January 2011).

101 Quoted in Perrot, *The Organ*, p. 195.

102 Ibid., p. 223.

103   Ibid., pp. 220–1.

104   Stanley Webb, 'The Organ at Winchester', *The Musical Times* 129/1745 (July 1988), p. 369.

105   C. F. Abdy Williams, *The Story of the Organ* (1903; Detroit: Singing Tree Press, 1972), pp. 30–1.

106   In another translation: 'Like thunder the iron tones batter the ear, so that it may receive no sound but that alone.' Williams, p. 31.

107   Translation in Perrot, *The Organ*, p. 230.

108   Edward F. Rimbault, *The Early English Organ Builders and Their Works* (1864; New York: AMS Press, 1976), pp. 16–18.

109   Williams, *The Story of the Organ*, p. 57.

110   Ibid., p. 59.

111   Andersen, *Organ Building and Design*, p. 108.

112   Williams, *The Story of the Organ*, p. 281.

113   Andersen, *Organ Building and Design*, p. 107.

114   Ibid.

115   Perrot, *The Organ*, p. 221.

116   Wright, *Music and Ceremony*, p. 159.

117   Julian Henriques, 'Sonic Dominance', pp. 451–80.

118   'The punitive spirit of Gregory's whip can still be felt in an eleventh century Customal from St Benigne in Dijon ...' and 'The memory of violence looms powerfully in two of the most influential medieval treatise on the learning of plainchant ...' Bruce W. Holsinger, *Music, Body, and Desire in Medieval Culture* (Stanford: Stanford University Press, 2001), pp. 273–9.

119   Ibid., p. 65.

120   Ibid., p. 30.

121   Ibid., p. 64.

122   Ibid., pp. 1–2. Following George Lakoff (upon whom both Simons and Hufford draw) Holsinger argues that concepts can only be formed through the body ('conceptual embodiment'). 'Metaphorical language is rooted in the body and tempered and constrained by lived, corporeal experience; and metaphors in turn actively shape bodily experience and thought, enlisting sensorimotor interference and allowing us to construct abstract concepts (such as philosophy of music, for example) out of experiences of the flesh.' Ibid., p. 12. In this, there is an echo of Massumi's treatment of the body as an idea. 'Imagination is rational thought brought back to the body. It is a pragmatic, synthetic mode of thought which takes the body not as an "object" but as a realm of virtuality, not as a site for the application of an abstract model or prefabricated general

idea but as a site for superabstract invention.' *User's Guide to Capitalism and Schizophrenia*, p. 100.

123   Here, Holsinger draws on Elaine Scarre's *The Body in Pain*, although he is critical of what he calls her 'overriding focus on language' and the importance she places on giving pain a linguistic voice. Holsinger's analysis is somewhat fraught as well, however. 'Musicality' and 'sonority' are routinely collapsed into one another, and there is very little discussion of sound in any capacity other than its organized participation in music. Moreover, his basis in literary studies becomes evident in his suggestion that attention to the sonorous body could be a supplement to (rather than problematization, or even refutation, of) the all-too-pervasive notion of the 'body as text'. Finally, he concludes with an odd statement to the effect that the 'musical body continues to resonate powerfully in our time' and that there is no better place to find evidence than in twentieth-century writing.

124   Timothy J. McGee, *The Sound of Medieval Music* (Oxford: Clarendon Press, 1998), pp. 32–3.

125   Holsinger, *Music, Body and Desire*, p. 16.

126   As, for example, in the menacing voice and organ drones on the album *Dømkirke* recorded at Bergen Cathedral, Norway during the 2007 Borealis Festival.

127   McGee, *The Sound of Medieval Music*, p. 32.

128   Ibid.

129   Dietrich Bartel, *Musica Poetica: Musical Rhetorical Figures in German Baroque Music* (Lincoln: University of Nebraska, 1997), p. 32.

130   As Bartel argues, it is impossible to identify a singular 'Doctrine of the Affections'. Nevertheless, a prominent work like Johann Mattheson's *Der vollkommene Capellmeister* (1739; 'The Perfect Chapelmaster') certainly helped lend conceptual unity to *Musica Poetica*.

131   Ibid., p. 5.

132   An assessment of relationship between Musica Poetica and Spinoza's Ethics, both as more or less contemporaneous bodies of thought, and as interpreted by Deleuze, is beyond the scope of the present discussion. Spinoza does not appear to have exerted any significant, direct influence on the German theorists of the affections. For Deleuze, Leibniz rather than Spinoza is the figure most essential to an understanding Baroque art and thought.

133   Ibid., p. 33.

134   Bartel, *Musica Poetica*, pp. 34–5.

135   Ibid.

136 Ibid., p. 27.

137 Andersen, *Organ Building and Design*, pp. 239–41.

138 Richard Kassel and Douglas Bush, *The Organ: An Encyclopedia* (New York: Routledge, 2006), p. 526.

139 *Birds, Bells & Thunder*, Peerless Record Co Ltd, UK, date unknown. 'This record explores a little-known, but most attractive and original field of baroque organ music. Next to the usual stops, many instruments possessed so-called "subsidiary registers", added "per l'abellimento et bizaria", which enjoyed great popularity owing to their picturesque effect, even though serious musicians often had to warn against misusing them.'

140 Andersen, pp. 215–19.

141 This ideal was demonstrated by an English organ – whose ranks included two 32-foot, four 16-foot and three 8-foot pipes – at the Great Exhibition of the Works of Industry of All Nations in London, 1851. 'Nothing in this world can be compared to it.' Ibid., pp. 175–6.

142 On cinema organs, see: Rick Altman, *Silent Film Sound* (New York: Columbia University Press, 2004), pp. 321–43. One example of a widely used performance manual is: Edith Lang and George West, *Musical Accompaniment of Moving Pictures* (New York: Boston Picture Co, 1920). Much more recently, David Sonnenschein's *Sound Design*, a standard in the field, includes a table labelled 'Acoustic Expression of Emotional States' that is drawn directly from the work of *Affektenlehre* theorist Friedrich Marpurg (1718–95). David Sonnenschein, *Sound Design: The Expressive Power of Music, Voice and Sound Effects in Cinema* (Studio City, CA: Los Angeles: Michael Wiese Productions, 2001), pp. 107–8.

143 Andersen, *Organ Building and Design*, p. 50.

144 Christhar Mahrenholz, *The Calculation of Organ Pipe Scales: From the Middle Ages to the Mid-Nineteenth Century*, trans. Andrew Williams (1938; Oxford: Positif Press, 1975), p. 5.

145 On Notre Dame de Paris, Wright explains that although the choir was usable by 1178, 'not until the second half of the thirteenth century was construction of the edifice sufficiently complete to permit the erection of a large positive organ in the customary place'. Moreover, around 1,400, the original organ was replaced with a much larger and more powerful one, with a compass extending to about B_1 (62 Hz). The new machine contained about 600 pipes, including a separate Bourdon cabinet, but it was still dwarfed by the organ at Amiens with its 2,500 pipes. Wright, *Music and Ceremony*, pp. 144–7.

146 Perrot, *The Organ*, p. 273.

147   Robert A. Scott, *The Gothic Enterprise: A Guide to Understanding the Medieval Cathedral* (Berkeley: University of California Press, 2003).

148   Gothic structures 'portrayed God as light and the universe as a luminous sphere that radiated outward from God, infusing the body of Christ, who as both God and man linked ordinary humans and the divine. Cathedrals were the vectors through which this process worked.' Ibid., pp. 34–5.

149   Georges Duby, *The Age of the Cathedrals: Art and Society, 980-1420* (Chicago: University of Chicago Press, 1981), p. 99.

150   Scott, *The Gothic Enterprise*, pp. 103–6. Also see Deleuze and Guattari's description of builders moving away from theorematic Euclidean geometry and

> appealing to the specificity of an operative, Archimedean geometry, a projective and descriptive geometry defined as a minor science, more mathegraphy than matheology. ... The monk-mason Garin de Troyes, speaks of an operative logic of movement enabling the "initiate" to draw, then hew the volumes in 'penetration in space', to make it so that the 'cutting line propels the equation'. ... One does not represent, one engenders and traverses. This science is characterized less by the absence of equations than by the very different role they play: instead of being good forms absolutely that organize matter, they are 'generated' as 'forces of thrust' (*poussees*) by the material, in a qualitative calculus of the optimum. (*A Thousand Plateaus*, p. 364)

151   Scott, *The Gothic Enterprise*, p. 121; See also Otto Georg von Simson, *The Gothic Cathedral: Origins of Gothic Architecture and the Medieval Concept of Order*, 3rd edn (Princeton: Princeton University Press, 1988).

152   Ettore Cirillio and Francesco Martellotta, *Worship, Acoustics, and Architecture* (Brentwood, UK: Multi-Science Publishing Co Ltd, 2006), p. 15.

153   Ibid., p. 122.

154   Ibid., pp. 108–9, 132.

155   Ibid., p. 95.

156   Scott, *The Gothic Enterprise*, p. 110.

157   Cirillio and Martellotta have conducted an extensive series of acoustic measurements at Italian churches of every period, including reverberation times at different frequencies and clarity values for speech. Gothic churches scored highest on the former and lowest on the latter. It might be reasonable to suggest that the findings elsewhere in Europe would have been even more pronounced given the authors' comments on Italian architects' tendencies to scale back the defining features of Gothic and defer somewhat to Romanesque methods. Cirillio and Martellotta, *Worship, Acoustics, and Architecture*, p. 23.

158   Deleuze and Guattari, *A Thousand Plateaus*, p. 364.

159   Michael D. Mann, 'Chapter 9 - Vestibular Functions', *The Nervous System In Action* (Michael D. Mann, 1997–2012). URL: http://www.unmc.edu/physiology/Mann/mann9.html (accessed 12 February 2012).

160   Ibid.

161   H. E. von Gierke and C. W. Nixon, *Infrasound*, p. 142.

162   Neil P. McAngus Todd and Frederick W. Cody, 'Vestibular responses to loud dance music: A physiological basis of the "rock and roll threshold"', in *Journal of the Acoustical Society of America* 107/1 (January 2000), pp. 496–500. Emphasis added.

163   The French ethnomusicologist Gilbert Rouget disagrees and takes issue with link between 'inner ear perturbations' and altered states in his widely cited 1985 book *Music and Trance*. Rouget aims to 'demystify' trance, arguing that any trance-like states arising from ritual musical activity are culturally conditioned, semiotic exchanges with no neurophysiological basis. Rouget credits Rousseau with initiating the move away from interest only in the physical properties of sound (which misses the art of it), and 'forg[ing] the way for cultural relativism in music.' Gilbert Rouget, *Music and Trance: A Theory of the Relations Between Music and Possession* (Chicago: University of Chicago Press, 1985), p. 170. In Rousseau's words, 'Each is affected by accents familiar to him; one's nerves will respond only to the degree to which one's mind prepares them for it: he must understand the language before what he is being told sets him in motion' (p. 169). Rouget says Rousseau was right, but was ignored in favour of mechanistic views of sound's physical effects, and he offers no middle ground or possibility of passage between nature and culture. He launches an attack on modern versions of that approach, particularly those studies that have looked to vestibular stimulation, some of which he quite rightly critiques for [assumptions and basis in lab work]. However, his response seems both petulant and disingenuously simplistic, demanding that any factors rooted in nature be universal and perfectly consistent. Ultimately Rouget's semiotics of trance precludes attention to the affective work of musical sound in ritual: 'I hope I have demonstrated by now that nothing authorizes us to think that music – at least insofar as it is being heard, not made, which is the case in possession – plays any direct role in the onset of trance other than by means of its "moral action"' (p. 183).

164   Michael A. Persinger, *Neurophysiological Bases of God Beliefs* (New York: Praeger, 1987), p. 26.

165   In the Catholic Church, speech clarity only becomes a concern following the
      Second Vatican Council in 1960s (along with move towards conducting mass
      in the local vernacular, rather than Latin). Efforts to dampen church acoustics
      in the service of speech (and to the detriment of sonority) only began in 1989.
      Cirillio and Martellotta, *Worship, Acoustics, and Architecture*, pp. 24–6.

166   Ibid., pp. 57, 180. Elsewhere: 'You are willingly mutated by intimate machines,
      abducted by audio into the populations of your bodies. Sound machines throw
      you onto the shores of the skin you're in. The hypersensual cyborg experiences
      herself as a galaxy of audiotactile sensations.' Ibid., -001.

Chapter 4

1   Guattari, *Chaosmosis*, p. 106.
2   Deleuze, *Francis Bacon*, p. 81.
3   Relative speeds are a fundamental concern in Spinoza's conception of ethics and
    affects. Deleuze explains, with reference to the materiality of sonic experience:
    'A body, of whatever kind … is defined by relations of motion and rest, of
    slowness and speed between particles. That is, it is not defined by a form or by
    functions. … The important thing is to understand life, each thing individually,
    not as a form, or a development of form, but as a complex relation between
    differential velocities, between deceleration and acceleration of particles. A
    composition of speeds and slownesses on a plane of immanence. In the same
    way, a musical form will depend on a complex relation between speeds and
    slownesses of sound particles. *It is not just a matter of music but of how to live:
    it is by speed and slowness that one slips in among things, that one connects with
    something else.*' (emphasis added) Deleuze, Spinoza, p. 123.

        Drawing on interpretations of Spinoza, Jane Bennett writes of matter's self-
    organizing vitality, what we could call its private life, as it persists, changes and
    interacts, in infinite ways that escape or exceed human awareness. This vitality
    is, in the most literal sense, the world-creating power of 'dumb matter'. Bennett
    uses the term 'Thing-Power' to describe 'the curious power of inanimate things
    to animate, to act, to produce effects dramatic and subtle.' Bennett, *Vibrant
    Matter*, p. 6. Geology attests to inanimacy's ultimate relativity, showing it to be a
    matter of relative speeds.
4   'Vibration'. See the unseen, http://www.fluke.com/Fluke/usen/solutions/
    vibration/vibration-see-the-unseen.htm (accessed 2 May 2012).

5   'Vibration. See the unseen: Cymbal at 1,000 frames per second', http://www.youtube.com/watch?v=kpoanOlb3-w (accessed 2 May 2012).

6   Hans Jenny, *Cymatics: A Study of Wave Phenomena and Vibration*, 3rd edn (Tacoma, WA: MACROmedia Publishing, 2001), p. 20.

7   Sand shows nodes while liquid shows antinodes: 'different expressions of the same vibratory field.' Ibid., pp. 28–9.

8   Ibid., pp. 21–2.

9   Ibid., p. 103.

10 Ibid., pp. 109–10.

11 Ibid, pp. 91, 98, 266.

12 Ibid, pp. 17–19.

13 Ibid., pp. 244–8, 259. The point, he says, without encroaching on geology or geophysics is that we've identified a 'field of nature which can be described in terms of the wave processes and phenomena in it.' There is no intention to push 'parallels to extremes ... the cymatics of acoustic waves are no proof of orogenesis, nor orogenesis of cymatics.' Much more recently, researchers claim to have found evidence of a 56-million-year 'beat' in the orogenic rhythms of North America. S. R. Meyers and S. E. Peters, 'A 56 million year rhythm in North American sedimentation during the Phanerozoic', *Earth Planetary Science Letters* (2011), doi:10.1016/j.epsl.2010.12.044.

14 Internet searches reveal that cymatics, Schumann resonances, space recordings and other topics covered below, have all been eagerly absorbed by New Age discourses that take each as evidence of a transcendent cosmic order (much as infrasound, radio waves, the Hum and acoustic weapons have figured prominently in Atomic Age conspiracy theories). This association does not, however, mean such things should be ignored. They fascinate because they are weird, because they mystify and suggest systems that shape experience while operating beyond our capacities to perceive them. The trick is to find ways to address them without sliding either in New Age-isms or, equally, into unimaginative debunking.

15 Jenny, *Cymatics*, p. 27.

16 Ibid., p. 20.

17 Deleuze, *Francis Bacon*, p. xxi.

18 See Eleni Ikoniadou's recent book *The Rhythmic Event: Art, Media, and the Sonic* (MIT Press, 2014) for an investigation of comparable themes, but specifically in relation to the rhythmicity of digital artworks (as opposed to this chapter's analogue orientation) and what she terms 'hypersonic sensation'

which, in her definition, 'brings forth the affective emptying of perception's conscious activity and the subsequent emergence of an autonomous, bodiless feeling' (p. 25).

19   Jenny, *Cymatics*, p. 288.

20   Ibid., 289. It is difficult not to notice the similarities between Jenny's conceptual language, and that of Deleuze and Guattari several years later, in part, at least in Guattari's case, through an interest in systems theory. In both, we find talk of 'becomings', immanence, exteriorized relations and refrains across vibratory milieus, self-organization, non-metaphorical analogy, process-minded language and reality's heterogenous excess as an invitation to new modes of thought and perception.

21   Deleuze and Guattari, *A Thousand Plateaus*, p. 309.

22   Peter Marsh's review of *Wind* by Hazard at http://www.bbc.co.uk/music/reviews/qhjw (accessed 6 March 2012).

23   Interviewed in Rob Young, 'Exotic Audio Research', *The Wire* 57 (March 1997), http://www.thewire.co.uk/articles/169/print (accessed 1 July 2011). Douglas Kahn has impressively built on this basic premise, investigating artists' engagements of naturally-occurring wave energies (particularly in the electromagnetic spectrum) in *Earth Sound, Earth Signal: Energies and Earth Magnitude in the Arts* (Berkeley: University of California Press, 2013).

24   Many people do, however, report sound-like perceptions of aurora borealis and other geomagnetic events. Acoustic researcher Unto K. Laine speculates that this may be a result of interactions between electromagnetic energy and acoustic energy in the infrasound range:

> Another hypothetical possibility is that a strong geomagnetic storm is able to ionize the air, or with some other mechanism, able to form ionized clouds of opposite charges in the atmosphere. Ground level measurements of the electric field during bright aurora have revealed large variations. A strong infrasound wave package 'shooting' through these clouds may activate discharging mechanisms and acoustic noise is produced.

> Unto K. Laine, 'Denoising and Analysis of Audio Recordings Made During the April 6–7, 2000 Geomagnetic Storm by Using a Non-professional Ad Hoc Setup', *Joint Baltic-Nordic Acoustics Meeting 2004* (8–10 June 2004, Mariehamn, Åland), p. 11.

25   The recordings and the accompanying booklet are in the public domain at http://www.archive.org/details/ird062 (accessed 1 July 2011).

26   Sagdeev and Kennel describe the discovery: 'The late Fred Scarf of TRW [Space and Technology Group] and his collaborators often played back

the microturbulent-wave electric fields recorded by the ISEE and Voyager spacecraft through an ordinary loudspeaker. To most listeners, shocks would sound cacophonous; to our ears, however, they were a symphony of space.' Roald Z. Sagdeev and Charles F. Kennel, 'Collisionless Shock Waves in Interstellar Matter', *Scientific American* 264 (April 1991), pp. 106–13. Archived at http://www.zoklet.net/totse/en/fringe/fringe_science/shockwav.html (accessed 5 June 2011).

27 Time stretching is a process used in digital sampling which allows a recording to be stretched or shrunk in the time domain, while retaining the same pitch (i.e. frequency content).

28 Liner notes reprinted at: http://www.discogs.com/No-Artist-Voice-Of-Earth-I-NASA-Voyager-Space-Sounds/release/2846894 (accessed 5 June 2011).

29 Thompson, a chiropractor and sound therapy researcher, owns the Brain/Mind label that released the NASA recordings. The label's catalogue also includes a variety of New Age and self-help titles. His professional biography can be found at the website of the Center for Neuroacoustic Research http://www.neuroacoustic.com/dr_thompson.html (accessed 5 June 2011).

30 Audio and notes available at http://www.archive.org/details/Startendtime-theSoundOfTheGroundVibrations During TheCollapseOfThe (accessed 25 July 2010).

31 Quoted in Mark Oliver, 'The Day the Earth Screamed', *The Guardian* (13 February 2004), http://www.guardian.co.uk/artanddesign/2004/feb/13/art.usa (accessed 11 November 2009).

32 Note the reference to 'the drone of the Earth' – the quieter moments in 'StartEndTime' resemble *The Voice of Earth*, but as if from within rather than above. For an expanded discussion of seismic recordings and their creative interpretation, see the 'Sounds of the Underground: Earthquakes, Nuclear Weaponry, and Music' in *Earth Sound, Earth Signal*, pp. 133–61.

33 Peculiar in that the two only appear to have communicated to share and consult on the audio files, leaving Duncan unaware of Cabrera's own work as a low-frequency sound artist (one seemingly far less concerned with personalizing vibration). 'While working on this project, listening to the sources, checking Densil's website, I tried to deduce something about his character, why he'd chosen to record these sounds, why he'd chosen to share them openly with anyone. Aside from a few technical images from his audio research, these recordings were all the evidence there was available to form an impression of who I was working with. They seemed to imply a person as fascinated with the technical processes of making the recordings – designing and building the recording equipment, making the tests, writing the software – as he was in

the results. Clearly he was seeking some sort of contact with someone outside of his immediate colleagues and friends, but he appeared not to be interested in knowing anything at all about who I was.' From: http://www.johnduncan. org/audio2003.html#INFRASOUND-TIDAL (accessed 3 November 2009). For his part, Cabrera has assembled a number of sound installation based on his research, including 1995's 'Pipes and Bells' which involved vibrating metal sheets and four large pipes – between 6 and 12 metres long – as resonators for subwoofers. 'Four channels of pre-recorded sound were fed to the pipes and steel sheets. The sound consisted entirely of extremely deep bass. The overall effect was a quiet but deep presence.' See http://densil.tripod.com/pb.html (accessed 16 July 2009). Details of Cabrera's work can be found at http://web. arch.usyd.edu.au/~densil/ (accessed 16 July 2009).

34 Felix Hess, *Light as Air* (Heidelberg: Kehrer Verlag, 2001), pp. 126–7.

35 David Toop, *Haunted Weather* (London: Serpent's Tail, 2004), p. 192.

36 Geoff Manaugh, 'When Landscapes Sing: Or, London Instrument', http:// bldgblog.blogspot.ca/2005/12/when-landscapes-sing-or-london.html (accessed 12 November 2009).

37 Geoff Manaugh, *The BLDGBLOG Book: Architectural Conjecture, Urban Speculation, Landscape Futures* (San Francisco: Chronicle Books, 2009), p. 163.

38 See http://news.nationalgeographic.com/news/2005/11/1129_051129_ iceberg_sing.html (accessed 21 February 2008). The article refers to Muller et al., 'Singing Icebergs', *Science* 310/5752 (25 November 2005), p. 1299. Hydroacoustics in water and ice has been studied for decades. See, for example, Henry Kutschale, 'Arctic Hydroacoustics', *Arctic* 22, no. 3 (1969), pp. 246–64. Elsewhere, sound artist Andreas Bicke offers two recordings of sound wave dispersion in ice sheets at http://silentlistening.wordpress.com/2008/05/09/ dispersion-of-sound-waves-in-ice-sheets/ and http://silentlistening.wordpress. com/2010/01/17/ice-recordings-updated/. The Alfred Wegener Institute for Polar Research has a live audio stream of Antarctic underwater sound at http:// www.awi.de (accessed 21 February 2008).

39 Audio available at http://www.sciencemag.org/content/ suppl/2005/11/21/310.5752.1299.DC1/Muller.AudioS1.wav (accessed 21 February 2008).

40 Archived at http://www.ashinternational.com/editions/ash_65_hazard_wind. html (accessed 17 November 2010).

41 Scott's inclusion actually works to blur the Poles in the triptych, but in these and subsequent recordings (*Nuuk*, 2004; *Novaya Zemlya*, 2012). Köner's reference points are almost exclusively northern.

42 Efforts to grasp relative periodicities figure prominently in Köner's recordings. He claims they are based in part on his own efforts to enter the logic of the cooling body by subjecting himself to extreme winter cold for extended periods, in order to observe shifts in perception (aural, temporal, etc.) and the slowing of the biological processes. 'He uses this heightening and slowing down of perception to prolong the passage of time to achieve something which, "is like a door, through which one enters new spaces." These can be intermediate areas between the inaudible audible and audible inaudible, as well as associative approaches to undetermined terrain.' Maija Julius writing on *Nuuk* in 'Traces in Vinyl' at http://www.koener.de/maijajuliustracesinvinyl.htm. (accessed 12 November 2009). It is worth noting that, in this affective setting, low-frequency sound's ability to produce sensations of being chilled may become an important part of the artist's toolkit.

43 A Thousand Plateaus, p. 273.

44 Polarity inversion, sometimes called phase inversion, occurs when the left and right wires in a stereo audio cable are crossed. This can result in an unnatural sounding stereo spectrum that is unusually wide and hollow-sounding. Many mixers and audio software packages have an 'invert' feature that can be used to correct such phase problems. However, the technique can also be used as an audio effect to produce a type of presence-absence. See the section called 'Ye Olde Phase Trick' in Paul White, 'Improving Your Stereo Mixing', Sound on Sound (October 2000). Archived at http://www.soundonsound.com/sos/oct<00/articles/stereomix.htm (accessed 16 March 2012).

45 Eshun, *More Brilliant Than the Sun*, pp. 178–9.

46 Hugh Brody, *The Other Side of Eden: Hunters, Farmers and the Shaping of the World* (Vancouver: Douglas & McIntyre, 2000), pp. 42–3. Remember that Spinoza's definition of ethics rests on the question of whether an affection augments or diminishes the capacity of a body to act.

47 In a chapter called 'A Life of Metal', Jane Bennett asks: 'can nonorganic bodies have a life? Can materiality itself be vital ... is there such a thing as a mineral or metallic life?' She draws on Deleueze's short essay 'Immanence: A Life' and its discussion of life as a force that is a-subjective, indeterminate and transversal, in the sense that it cuts across bodies and time. Later:

> A life thus names a restless activeness, a destructive-creative force-presence that does not coincide fully with any specific body. A life tears the fabric of the actual without ever coming fully 'out' in a person, place or thing. A life points to what *A Thousand Plateaus* describes as 'matter-*movement*'

or 'matter-*energy*', a 'matter in variation that enters assemblages and leaves them.' A life is a vitality proper not to any individual but to 'pure immanence', or that protean swarm that is not actual though it is real. (Bennett, pp. 53–4)

48   H. P. Lovecraft, 'At The Mountains Of Madness', S. T. Joshi (ed.), *The Thing on the Doorstep and Other Weird Stories* (London: Penguin, 2001), p. 288.

49   Viscera is

a second dimension of the flesh: one that is deeper than the stratum of proprioception, in the sense that it is farther removed from the surface of the skin, but it is still at a medium depth in that it also intervenes between the subject and the object. It, too, involves a cellular memory and has a mode of perception proper to it: viscerality (interoception). Visceral sensibility immediately registers excitations gathered by the five "exteroceptive" senses even before they are fully processed by the brain. Walking down a dark street at night in a dangerous part of town, your lungs throw a spasm before you consciously see and can recognize as human the shadow thrown across your path. As you cross a busy noonday street, your stomach turns somersaults before you consciously hear and identify the sound of screeching brakes that careens toward you. Having survived the danger, you enter your building. Your hear steps before you consciously feel the tap on your shoulder and identify it as the greeting of a friend. The immediacy of visceral perception is so radical that it can be said without exaggeration to precede the exteroceptive sense perception. It anticipates the translation of the sight or sound or touch perception into something recognizable associated with an identifiable object. (Massumi, *Parables*, pp. 60–1)

50   Goodman writes: 'Where there is a visceral perception initiated by a sound and in a split-second the body is activated by the sonic trigger, then the gut reaction is preempting consciousness.' *Sonic Warfare*, p. 48.

51   In the original: 'We have entered a new regime of the image, one in which vision is visceral and intensive instead of representational and extensive.' Shaviro, *The Cinematic Body*, p. 139.

52   This could be seen as a terminus of the originary becoming-mineral described by Delanda: 'In the organic world, for instance, soft tissue (gels and aerosols, muscle and nerve) reigned supreme until 500 million years ago. At that point, some of the conglomerations of fleshy matter-energy that made up life under-went a sudden mineralization, and a new material for constructing living creatures emerged: bone. It is almost as if the mineral world that had served as a substratum for the emergence of biological creatures was reasserting itself, confirming that geology, far from having been left behind as a primitive stage

of the earth's evolution, fully coexisted with the soft, gelatinous newcomers. Primitive bone, a stiff, calcified central rod that would later become the vertebral column, made new forms of movement control possible among animals, freeing them from many constraints and literally setting them into motion to conquer every available niche in the air, in water, and on land. *And yet, while bone allowed the complexification of the animal phylum to which we, as vertebrates, belong, it never forgot its mineral origins: it is the living material that most easily petrifies, that most readily crosses the threshold back into the world of rocks. For that reason, much of the geological record is written with fossil bone* (emphasis added). Manuel De Landa, *A Thousand Years of Non-Linear History* (New York: Zone Books, 2000), pp. 26–7.

53 Tony Herrington, reviewing Eleh and referring to David Toop, on Thomas Köner, in *The Wire*. Archived at http://www.touchshop.org/product_info.php?products_id=359 (accessed 2 May 2009).

54 At the same moment, a new bass-centric minimalism was emerging on dancefloors, in the form of dubstep, minimal techno and a revived interest in dub techno. Old infrasonic fictions were finding new currency in discussion forums and the electronic music press. Eleh, however, passed largely unnoticed by the new 'bass culture'.

55 One exception is 'In the Ear of the Gods' which employs a spring reverb.

56 From: Eleh, *Meditations & Improvisations: Volume Two* (Important Records, 2009).

57 One of apparently very few Eleh recordings that uses instruments other than electronic oscillators, although their tonal qualities are no different from the others, leaving the listener to guess what role a guitar might have played. The two parts of 'For 2 Guitars and 4 Oscillators' are among Eleh's most monolithic and unchanging pieces.

58 Webster's defines just intonation as 'any musical tuning in which the frequencies of notes are related by ratios of whole numbers'. It is distinguished from equal temperament,

> the tuning system that is by far the most common in the West, which arranges all notes at multiples of the same basic interval. This results in a tuning system where all intervals except the octave will sound out of tune equally in any key – all major thirds will have exactly the same character, for example – but the intervals themselves are detuned slightly. Each interval possesses its own degree of detuning.

Whereas equal temperament works against intuition to rationalize intervallic relations, the vibratory relations in just intonation are immediately sensible when experimenting with tones (as is the case with the Monochord). Following

Goodman and Parisi, we can call it a 'sensual mathematics' – the term
borrowed from information theorist Gregory Chitin, who used it to identify 'a
dynamics of numbering in which conceptual feelings are immediately active
before becoming cognized.' Steve Goodman and Luciana Parisi, 'Extensive
Continuum Towards a rhythmic anarchitecture', *iNFLexions* 2 (January 2009),
http://www.senselab.ca/inflexions/volume_4/n2_parisigoodmanhtml.html
(accessed 2 June 2011).

59   As in the series of releases titled *Floating Frequencies/Intuitive Synthesis*, vols.
I-III. (Important Records, 2006–8).

60   For example, the press release for Floating Frequencies Vol. I advises that
'Listeners are strongly encouraged to sit with ears at speaker level between 8
and 12 feet away from the speakers.' For Volume II, however, 'It is ... highly
recommended that stereo listeners are seated at least 7 feet away from their
speakers, centered, with ears at speaker height.'

61   Again, mention of instruments other than oscillators can be misleading
when the recording itself consists only of drones that resemble the output of
oscillators.

62   Quoted in Matt Wuethrich, 'Eleh', *The Wire* 314 (April 2010), p. 31.

63   Keith Potter, *Four Musical Minimalists: La Monte Young, Terry Riley, Steve
Reich, Philip Glass* (Cambridge: Cambridge University Press, 2000), p. 57.

64   Wim Mertens, *American Minimal Music*, trans. J. Hautekiet (London: Kahn &
Averill, 1983), p. 22.

65   Ibid., p. 16.

66   A 'crisis' only in the sense that it is a moment of rupture in the ongoing process
by which we synthesize the present of experience. Massumi writes:

> A body present is in a dissolve: out of what it is just ceasing to be, into
> what it will already have become by the time it registers that something
> has happened. The present smudges the past and the future. it is more like
> a doppler effect than a point: a movement that registers its arrival as an
> echo of its having just past. The past and future resonate in the present.
> Together: as a dopplered will-have-been registering *in* the instant as a unity
> of movement. That past and future are in continuity with each other, in a
> moving-through-the-present: in transition.

And on the body out-of-phase with itself: 'A body does not coincide with
its present. It coincides with its *potential*. The is potential is the future–past
contemporary with every body's change.' Massumi, *Parables*, p. 200.

67   Sam Davies, 'Eleh – Floating Frequencies/Intuitive Synthesis', *The Wire* 279 (May 2007), p. 57.

68   This is the principle behind the low-frequency oscillator (LFO) in an analogue synthesizer, which uses infrasonic wave to modulate (or give shape to) audible ones.

69   See, for example: Robert Fink, *Repeating Ourselves: American Minimal Music as Cultural Practice* (Berkeley: University of California Press, 2005); Brandon Labelle, *Background Noise: Perspectives on Sound Art* (New York: Continuum, 2008); and Potter, *Four Musical Minimalists*.

70   Although Riley does use the term.

71   That is, by abstracting perception, causing involuntary responses, physical adjustment, etc.

72   Dave Hickey, Introduction to Joe Houston, *Optic Nerve: Perceptual Art of the 1960s* (London: Merrell, 2007), pp. 11–12.

73   Eshun, *More Brilliant Than the Sun*, p. 77.

74   Quoted in 'In Conversation with Maurice de Sausmarez', in Robert Kudielka (ed.), *Bridget Riley: Dialogues on Art* (London: Zwemmer, 1995), p. 76. This is very much a nomad science. Joe Houston notes that retinal artists drew, to varying degrees, on mathematical principles, and developments in science, with some calling their work 'research'. However, Op's effects were almost always arrived at inductively, with theory typically providing only a point of departure or a basic concept. Riley, for example, was resistant to depictions of her work as scientific, claiming only to use 'rudimentary mathematics' combined with 'empirical analysis and synthesis.' Levinson 'had neither a scientific nor a studio art training.' Houston writes 'that in the process of making his multilayered moiré constructions, he was, in essence, "discovering physics" in his own studio.' Joe Houston, *Optic Nerve: Perceptual Art of the 1960s* (London: Merrell, 2007), p. 60.

75   *Descending* (1965) repeats the experiment with triangular lines.

76   J. T. Reason, 'Motion Sickness and Associated Phenomena', *Infrasound*, p. 299.

77   Richard D. Zakia, *Perception and Imaging*, 3rd edn (Oxford: Focal Press, 2007), pp. 161–2.

78   Ibid., p. 161. These effects were explored at length by Albers in his 'Homage to the Square' painting. He also discusses them in a chapter 'Vibrating Boundaries', in *Interaction of Color* (New Haven, CT: Yale University Press, 1963).

79   Quoted in Lynne Cooke and John Elderfield, *Bridget Riley: Reconnaissance* (New York: Dia Center for the Arts, 2000), p. 25. Includes a discussion of

pattern's ability to expose the limits of central or foveal vision as well as peripheral and parafoveal vision. Also: repetition and induced perceptions of movement, uses of luminosity to create perceptions of oscillation in the visual field (p. 19).

80 Steve Goodman, 'Speed Tribes: Netwar, Affective Hacking and the Audio Social', in F. Liebl (ed.), *Cultural Hacking* (Berlin: Springer-Verlag, 2004).

81 Houston, *Optic, Nerve*, p. 60.

82 Auyogard and Torgue (*Sonic Experience*, pp. 87–8) use the term 'remnance' to describe 'the mnestic trace of barely subsided sound signals' which they say are not hallucinatory but bordering on it. The effect is not strictly different from tinnitus, but closer to the aftermath of a loud concert. There is memory involved, but it is cellular as much as anything else. And again, the effect is not strictly cochlear; one can, for example, be left with phantom ripples coursing across the skin after a long session spent in the breeze of a sound system.

83 Erin Manning, *Relationscapes: Movement, Art, Philosophy* (Cambridge: MA: MIT Press, 2009), pp. 6–7, 13–28.

> The concept of preacceleration is a way of thinking the incipiency of movement, the ways in which movement is always on the verge of expression. Bodies invent motion incessantly, creating habits to satisfy the carrying out of these inventions. These habits tell us how to keep our balance as we take one step after another, how to reach the floor with our toes as we crawl out of bed in the morning, how to find the bathroom at night without running into the walls. Proprioception provides us with clues that precede our cognitive understanding of where we are going. Preacceleration: we are going, always already.

This theorization of preacceleration's proprioceptive dimensions resonates strongly with the phenomenon of vestibular felt-motion taken up in Chapter 3. Where the present discussion diverges significantly from Manning's work is in its specific emphasis on material vibration as the catalyst and attractor of movement. A similar distinction could be made with Stamatia Portanova's investigation of choreographed dance and its capture in digital media in *Moving without a Body: Digital Philosophy and Choreographic Thought* (MIT Press, 2013).

84 DJ Spooky quoted in Alan Licht, 'Maryanne Amacher: Expressway to Your Skull', *The Wire* 181 (March 1999), http://www.thewire.co.uk/articles/3220/ (accessed 18 May 2013).

85 La Monte Young quoted in Potter, *Four Musical Minimalists*, p. 66.

86 Licht, 'Maryanne Amacher'.
87 From http://www.melafoundation.org/GuggenheimPress09.html (accessed 11 May 2011). Incidentally, after any lengthy viewing of the bright, fuschia background on the official Dream House website (http://www.melafoundation.org/), one is left with a potentially disconcerting afterimage effect whereby the entire visual field becomes cast in a dull yellow hue.
88 Labelle, *Background Noise*, p. 73.
89 Ibid., pp. 73–4.
90 Maryanne Amacher, 'Music For Sound Joined Rooms', http://www.maryanneamacher.org/Maryanne_Amacher/Amacher_Archive_Project/Entries/2009/10/24_music_for_sound_joined_rooms.html (accessed 11 May 2011).
91 Maryanne Amacher, 'Composing Perceptual Geographies', http://www.maryanneamacher.org/Amacher_Archive_Project/Entries/2009/10/23_Composing_perceptual_geographies.html (accessed 11 May 2011).
92 Ibid.
93 Camille Norment, 'Notes from the Oscillating Dream Space', in John Corbett, Anthony Elms and Terri Kapsalis (eds), *Pathways to Unknown Worlds: Sun Ra, El Saturn and Chicago's Afro-Futurist Underground 1954-68* (Chicago: Whitewalls, 2006), p. 25.
94 http://www.norment.net/studio/art/groove/index.html (accessed 11 May 2011).
95 Louise Gray, 'Cross Platform: Camille Norment', *The Wire* 284 (October 2007), p. 24.
96 http://www.norment.net/studio/art/deadRoom/index.html (accessed 11 May 2011).
97 http://www.norment.net/studio/art/driftglass/index.html (accessed 11 May 2011).
98 Deleuze, *Francis Bacon*, pp. 17–18.
99 Tom Conley, 'Faciality', in Parr (ed.), *The Deleuze Dictionary*, p. 96.
100 Arun Saldanha, *Psychedelic White: Goa Trance and the Viscosity of Race* (Minneapolis: University of Minnesota Press, 2007), p. 100.
101 Ibid., p. 101.
102 Gray, 'Cross Platform.'
103 Ralph Ellison, *Invisble Man* (1947; New York: Vintage, 1990), p. 3.
104 Mark Bain, 'The Live Room: Transducing Resonant Architectures', *Organised Sound* 8(2), pp. 166–7.
105 Quoted in 'Live Room'. Original at http://en.wikisource.org/w/index.php?title=The_New_York_World-Telegram/1935/07/11/Nikola_Tesla,_

at_79,_Uses_Earth_to_Transmit_Signals:_Expects_to_Have_$100,000,000_
Within_Two_Years&oldid=3054744 (accessed 14 January 2012).

106 Mark Bain, 'Sonic Architecture', *Earshot: The Journal of the UK and Ireland Soundscape Community* 3 (November 2002), www.vpro.nl/attachment.db/ Sonic_Architecture2.doc?23220323 (accessed 19 October 2010).

107 Ibid.

108 Bain, 'Live Room', p. 166.

109 Tom Gunning, 'The Cinema of Attractions: Early Film, Its Spectator and the Avant-Garde', in Wanda Strauven (ed.), *The Cinema of Attractions Reloaded*, (Amsterdam: Amsterdam University Press, 2006), p. 384.

110 Ibid.

111 The dbx 120A Subhamonic Synthesizer is often used in film sound design to synthesize an additional layer of low-frequency content one octave below the rest of the soundtrack. The process is explained by Hollywood sound mixer Tom Johnson in the special features of the DVD release of Peter Jackson's 2005 *King Kong* remake. A related but different tool is Waves MaxxBass which uses combination tones to produce the illusion of lower bass where there is none.

112 From the *Sensurround Manual*, reprinted at http://www.in70mm.com/ newsletter/2004/69/sensurround/index.htm (accessed 21 March 2009).

113 Ibid. (emphasis added)

114 Quoted in Bain, 'Live Room', p. 166n. 13.

115 See http://www.thebuttkicker.com.

116 From http://www.djenerate.com. Djenerate calls its version 'Human Induction Technology'. Their BodySonic system has been used in London's Fabric Nightclub, and their BodyKinetic system in Glasgow's Sub Club and New Dehli's Elevate.

117 Bain, 'Sonic Architecture'. Video at http://www.youtube.com/ watch?v=zVFsP9xqhF8 (accessed 15 January 2010).

118 Bain, 'Live Room', pp. 164–5.

119 Ibid., p. 167.

120 Ibid., p. 169.

121 Ibid., p. 166.

122 Ibid.

123 Manning, *Relationscapes*, p. 10.

124 Bain, 'Live Room', p. 163.

125 Ibid., pp. 168–9.

126 Ibid., p. 169.

Chapter 5

1   A very small sampling of bass-referencing track titles, drawn from bass-centric music scenes of the 1980s to 2000s. As Eshun put it: 'the track manifests the title's manifesto'. *More Brilliant Than the Sun*, p. 132. For more, search 'bass' and variants at http://www.rolldabeats.com and http://www.discogs.com.

2   By Eshun's account, 'disco is ... *audibly* where the 21st C begins'. *More Brilliant Than the Sun*, p. -006.

3   Of Jamaican musics, Michael Veal writes that 'With the rise of digital technologies, in fact (and as jazz has become increasingly associated with elitist and academic values), the experimental envelope in much black music has been frequently pushed in the arena of communal dance musics.' He continues: 'The creators of [dub] certainly viewed themselves as experimentalists, as their comments and professional monikers indicate: Scientist, Peter Chemist, Professor, as so on. Their work represented the sonic vanguard of Jamaican music in the 1970s and early 1980s, and it later entered into the production of Euro-American popular music in a de facto avant-garde position ...' Michael Veal, *Dub: Soundscapes & Shattered Songs in Jamaican Reggae* (Middletown, CT: Wesleyan University Press, 2007), pp. 40–1.

4   Whether applied to club musics that are not in any way remarkable for their bass content, or which are at least as notable for other spectral characteristics (e.g. the metal-like mid range noise of much contemporary drum & bass and dubstep). It is also common for event flyers to promise large quantities of 'BASS!' regardless of the sound system's actual capabilities (i.e. frequency range and wattage).

5   An 'occulture' in the literal sense of a collective assemblage that treats bass as a secret of nature and an arcanum – that is, a terrain of secretly held knowledge and techniques.

6   Forms of African-descended drumming (e.g. Buru) have had an important influence as well, both spectrally, and as the basis for some of the 'riddims' (standard rhythmic patterns) used in reggae and related musics. See Norman Stolzoff, *Wake the Town and Tell the People: Dancehall Culture in Jamaica* (Charlotte, NC: Duke University Press, 2000), p. 107.

7   Lloyd Bradley, *Bass Culture: When Reggae was King* (London: Viking, 2000), pp. 157–8. According to Bradley, Byron Lee imported the first electric bass in 1959 or 1960, and their use quickly spread. He describes the appeal of the instrument's more powerful sound which, due to its quick dynamics (compared

to those of an acoustic bass), could also more easily syncopate with drums, thus enabling it to become an effective lead instrument.

8   Interviewed in Veal, *Dub,* pp. 97–8.

9   Quoted in Paul Theberge, *Any Sound You Can Imagine: Making Music/ Consuming Technology* (Middletown, CT: Wesleyan University Press, 1997), p. 198. The first digital sequencers, developed, in the late-1960s, by Peter Zinovieff and David Cockerell of Electronic Music Systems (EMS), were adapted from computerized process control systems used in factory assembly lines. See the documentary *What the Future Sounded Like*, directed by Matthew Bate, Porthmeor Productions (Australia), 2007.

10   Mr. Mixx interviewed in J-Mill, 'Original King', *The Source* 54 (March 1994), p. 21. This special 'Miami' issue of *The Source* also makes repeated reference the influence of the Jamaican sound system as a set of technologies and practices. Early on, the preferred musics were electro and hip-hop rather than reggae, but the city's sound system/car stereo culture is depicted as the necessary precondition for the development of Miami bass.

11   Quoted in Simon Reynolds, *Generation Ecstasy: Into the World of Techno and Rave Culture* (New York: Routledge, 1999), p. 116.

12   Three articles on the subject of layered basslines with a sine wave subbass foundation http://www.soundonsound.com/sos/sep10/articles/qa0910–4.htm; http://www.soundonsound.com/sos/jul10/articles/Dubstep.htm and http://www.kmag.co.uk/editorial/musictech/ten-ways-to-make-a-dnb-bassline.html (accessed 12 March 2012).

13   Peter Shapiro, 'The Primer: the Roland TB-303 Bass Line', The Wire 303 (May 2009), p. 40.

14   Guattari, *Chaosmosis*, p. 47.

15   *A Thousand Plateaus*, p. 345.

16   *Last Angel of History*, directed by John Akomfrah (UK: Icarus Films, 1996).

17   Eshun, *More Brilliant Than the Sun*, p. 187.

18   Mark Dery, 'Black to the Future: Interviews with Samuel R. Delany, Greg Tate and Tricia Rose', in Mark Dery (ed.), *The South Atlantic Quarterly: Flame Wars: The Discourse of Cyberculture* Vol. 92 (1993), pp. 770–1.

19   Eshun, *More Brilliant Than the Sun*, pp. 28–9.

20   Veal, *Dub*, p. 212.

21   Barry Chevannes, *Rastafari: Roots and Ideology* (Syracuse: Syracuse University Press, 1994), pp. 32–3.

22   Erik Davi, 'Roots and Wires: Polyrhythmic Cyberspace and the Black Electronic' (paper presented at 5CYBERCONF, Madrid, 1996), http://www.techgnosis.com (accessed 3 October 2009).

23 Bradley, *Bass Culture*, pp. 309–10.

24 Veal, *Dub*, p. 160.

25 Ibid., p. 211.

26 Bradley, *Bass Culture*, p. 319. Veal, *Dub*, p. 160. Producer Mikey Dread has said that King Tubby 'would figure out an effect he wanted and then design and construct the circuit that would give him that ... if the man don't think a sound sound like he want it, he would go into the circuitry there and then and change it to create the particular effect he want. ... It's because he truly understood sound, in a *scientific* sense, that he was able to do what he did.' Ibid., p. 116.

27 John F. Szwed describes Sun Ra's education ancient in Egyptian, Greek and hermetic texts, and his attraction to the Theosophical teachings of the Russian-born mystic Helena P. Blavatsky. 'Blavatsky had incredible influence at the turn of the century, inspiring Edison to consider the theosophic implications of the phonograph; focusing the mysticism of the Russian composer Scriabin to go on to experiment with synesthetic composition and light organ.' While, 'in the work of one of her offshoots, Rudolph Steiner, he read of a German who attempted to bridge the everyday and the spirit worlds by means of scientific methods.' John f. Szwed, *Space is the Place: The Lives and Times of Sun Ra* (New York: Da Capo, 1997), pp. 108–9. It is worth noting that Steiner was also perhaps the single greatest influence Hans Jenny's conception cymatics.

28 Ibid., pp. 137–8.

29 Szwed (pp. 132–3) notes thematic and cosmological points of similarity. Graham Locke finds even closer links: 'According to both Alton Abraham, a close associate of Ra's in Chicago, and Arkestra tenor saxophonist John Gilmore, there was definitely contact between Ra and members of the Nation of Islam in the 1950s, with Gilmore claiming that the Black Muslims stole several ideas from Ra: "They would sort of antagonise him, in order to get him to talk."' Also see: Michael Muhammed Knight, *The Five Percenters: Islam, Hip-Hop and the Gods of New York* (New York: Oneworld Publications, 2008).

30 Szwed, *Space is the Place*, p. 132.

31 For a discussion of the OVC and its connections to both Sun Ra and Miami Bass/Electro, see the chapter 'Color Out Of Space', in Dave Tompkins, *How to Wreck a Nice Beach: The Vocoder From World War II to Hip-Hop - The Machine Speaks* (Chicago: Stopsmiling Books, 2010).

32 Szwed, *Space is the Place*, pp. 95–6.

33 The term is generally attributed to Anindya Bhattacharyya. Now in common usage, it was popularized by Simon Reynolds who explains: '"Vocal science" is Bat from [uk-dance.org]'s term for this vivisection of the diva, which

effectively transforms the singer into a component of the drum kit.' Simon Reynolds, 'Adult Hardcore', *The Wire* 182 (April 1999), http://www.thewire.co.uk/articles/2033/ (accessed February 2009). Edwards discusses his sampling techniques at http://www.stylusmagazine.com/articles/weekly_article/todd-edwards-the-stylus-interview.htm (accessed September 2007).

34   *Rhythm Science* (Cambridge, MA: MIT Press, 2004) is a book by DJ Spooky That Subliminal Kid and Peter Lenenfeld. The term itself has been in circulation for somewhat longer.

35   Eshun, *More Brilliant Than the Sun*, p. 149.

36   Troutman treated his Talk Box rig like a secret technology, recruiting crew member Bigg Robb to guard it before and after shows. Bootsy Collins renamed it the Secret Magic Babbler, Roger's Snake Charmer, and the Cosmic Communicator. He warned: 'Everyone wants to use it. It is a special gift, and it is forbidden for you to know the secrets. It will remain a mystery.' Tompkins, *How to Wreck a Nice Beach*, p. 138.

37   For example, the synth-based work of Scientist, Jah Shaka, Mad Professor. The Yamaha DX-7 synthesizer is still a common sight in these studios.

38   First heard in the track 'Mentasm' (1991) by the techno act Second Phase. It was used widely in Belgian techno, and then in UK Hardcore, darkside and early-jungle, where it was typically sampled and heavily manipulated (see the work of Bizzy B/Warped Kore, for example). It has more recently reappeared in Lady Gaga's 'Bad Romance' single (2009), while a 2014 release called *Wormhole Shubz*, by the computer music outfit Evol, works through every possible variation of the original Roland Alpha Juno synthesizer patch and includes an interview with the sound's creator.

39   The TX81Z's 'Lately Bass' preset is reputedly meant to mimic the bass patch used in Janet Jackson's 1986 single 'What Have You Done For Me Lately?'

40   Based on the author's spectral analysis of Reese's 'Just Want Another Chance' (1988), Renegade's 'Terrorist' (1993) and Remarc's 'Thunderclap' (1994). By the mid-1990s, multitudes of synth-based reworkings began to appear.

41   'Ragga', referring to digital version of dancehall music that became dominant in Jamaica following the release of Wayne Smith's 'Under Mi Sleng Teng' in 1985.

42   Tracks by T2, Paleface, EJ and DJ Q are typical of the style.

43   There is an echo of the organ builder here: itinerant, known for a signature sound of undisclosed origins, versed in obscure aspects of music technology.

44   Interviewd by Kodwo Eshun in 'Wookie: Civilization and its Discos – Part 1 (2000)', http://www.riddim.ca/?p=216 (accessed March 2010).

45 Cutting engineers play up this reputation at the Secret Society of Lathe Trolls ('A forum devoted to record-cutting deviants, renegades & experimenters'), http://lathetrolls.phpbbweb.com/

46 Stolzoff describes studios with in-house lathes in Jamaica (Stolzoff, pp. 124–30), while London's Ariwa Sounds, run by Mad Professor, advertises '1/4 mastering still available', http://ariwa.com/portfolio/small-fullwidth-portfolio/ (accessed June 2011).

47 Transition's client list is viewable at http://www.transition-studios.com/about-us.html (accessed June 2011).

48 Jason Goz's discography can be found at http://www.discogs.com/artist/Jason+Goz (accessed May 2012).

49 See, for example, the mastering credits on releases from the Tempa, DMZ and Hyperdub labels, from this period, at Discogs.com. Information on Deaf Raves can be found at http://www.deafrave.com/ (accessed June 2011).

50 Ridout describes the vibratorium

> as a model for thinking about the transmission of affect in the theater. ... The familiar idea of a reciprocal 'energy exchange' between performers and audience is developed by way of an Artaudian conception of theater, in which the vibrations of sound and light are manipulated, not for their signifying potential but for the ways in which they might work upon the body of the spectator. The intimacy of this work on the body also binds together the spectators in the sociality of an audience, as the vibratory transmission of affect between bodies requires, or perhaps even constitutes, their being together. ... The Vibratorium is the theater auditorium in those moments when signification and representation have yet to establish their sway: it is where the vibrations get right into you, before you start making sense of them. (Nicolas Ridout, 'Welcome to the Vibratorium', *The Senses & Society* 3 (2008), pp. 221–2)

51 Sarah Thornton, *Club Cultures: Music, Media and Subcultural Capital* (Hanover: University Press of New England, 1996), p. 58.

52 On early wattages and speakers: see Bradley, *Bass Culture*, pp. 36, 317. Contemporary systems can reach 20,000 watts or higher. Stolzoff, *Wake the Town*, p. 197.

53 Stolzoff (pp. 43–5) discusses the work of Hedley Jones, beginning in the late-1940s. His signature amp was 'not only more powerful than commercially available amplifiers, but it featured a technological breakthrough – the capacity to distinguish and enhance the treble, mid-range, and bass frequencies.' Bradley

(p. 118) writes that amplifiers in the UK, at the time, were loud but not 'heavy' ('that don't get you moving'). He interviews DJ Jah Vigo, who explains that English engineers refused to modify them, so sound system operators found someone else who would: 'an African man, an electrical engineer who have a shop.' The unnamed man was, at first, stunned by the request for so much more bass ('That will kill people!'), but he was soon doing a brisk business in custom equipment.

54   Ibid., p. 37.

55   Ibid., p. 118.

56   Ibid., p. 314.

57   Tim Lawrence, *Love Saves the Day: A History of American Dance Music 1970-1979* (Durham, NC: Duke University Press, 2003), pp. 86–90. One, somewhat contradictory, exception to the point above about intensity v. fidelity is The Loft's David Mancuso who, as well as wanting to elicit great amounts of bodily force from his system, also took audiophilic ideals to extremes. His efforts to achieve 'pure' sound included using hand-crafted needle cartridges at a cost of several thousand dollars apiece, and the refusal to introduce a cueing system into his mixer's signal chain (requiring him to mix 'in the air', as he put it).

58   Mancuso and Robert Coleman interviewed in *Maestro*, directed by Josell Ramos, Sanctuary (USA), 2003.

59   Journalist Ralf Niemczyk on early German techno parties in *We Call It Techno!*, directed by Maren Sextro and Holger Wick, Sense Music & Media (Germany), 2008. This is true, even without factoring in what Goodman (*Sonic Warfare*, p. xvi) labels the 'narcosonic' dimension – these combinations of intensities had, quite literally, not been explored before.

60   The 'becoming-body' of dance is theorized in Manning, *Relationscapes*.

61   Julian Henriques makes a similar point about bass and affect in 'The Vibrations of Affect and their Propagation on a Night Out on Kingston's Dancehall Scene', *Body & Society* 16 (2010), p. 78.

62   Mikey Dred interviewed in *Musically Mad: A Documentary on UK Reggae Sound Systems*, directed by Karl Folke, 2008.

63   Lawrence, *Love Saves the Day*, p. 279.

64   Another case of the affectation-driven dancefloor is the recent vogue for '80s'-themed club nights, in the early-2000s. There, the overriding feature is the ironic treatment of certain of the decade's songs and images, decontextualized, and collapsed together largely for their supposed camp value ('cheesiness'). On this dancefloor, at its most pronounced, every song becomes an inside joke, sent and received with an attitude of knowing detachment. Every pose, facial

expression, stylized move, t-shirt and singalong, is couched in a disavowal ('it's good because it's so bad'). In this semiotic economy, ironic distance becomes a useful hedge against being thought to naively enjoy, or be moved, by something 'bad'. This circumscribing dancefloor explicitly works against becomings. It is not that this space is affect*less* (a material impossibility), but that it seems to distrust affect, striving to diffuse its shocks and uncertainties through a mediating layer of familiar signs. At the same time, while its non-committal character distinguishes it from the self-serious crowd at Studio 54, on one level, the two are more deeply linked by the ways that each places greater emphasis on affected poses, manners and meaning-response circuits, than on the eventness of moving bodies.

65   Eric Schloss has made a similar critique of hip-hop scholarship in the 1990s which too readily absorbed the music into the then popular discourses of postmodernity. The near-exclusive reliance on models from cultural studies and literary theory, he says, 'implies that hip-hop has articulated no aesthetic principles of its own' when, in fact, 'the culture's participants have invested a great deal of energy in the development of theoretical frameworks to guide its interpretation.' This, he says, is a 'grievously underutilized resource for scholars.' Schloss, *Making Beats*, p. 67.

66   Guattari, *Chaosmosis*, p. 133.

67   'A becoming-animal always involves a pack, a band, a population, a peopling, in short, a multiplicity.' Deleuze and Guattari, *A Thousand Plateaus*, p. 239.

68   Lawrence, *Love Saves the Day*, p. 25.

69   Ibid., p. 24.

70   Reynolds, *Generation Ecstasy*, p. 5.

71   Ibid., p. 9.

72   Lawrence, *Love Saves the Day*, p. 371.

73   Deleuze and Guattari use the concept of diagramming to describe the way an abstract machine extracts tendencies and potentials from an assemblage. *A Thousand Plateaus*, p. 100. Bringing the matter to questions of the 'lived and relived' experience, Massumi suggests that 'biograms might be a better word.' *Parables*, p. 186.

74   Lawrence, *Love Saves the Day*, p. 225.

75   Eshun cites DJ Shadow who suggests that 'HipHop is ... not a genre so much as an omnigenre, a conceptual approach towards sonic organization rather than a particular sound in itself. *More Brilliant Than the Sun*, p. 197n. 14.

76   It could be argued, for example, that the garage machine doesn't become meaningfully distinct from house, until it being transplanted to the UK where

it mingled with jungle's subbass and broken rhythms to emerge as UK garage. Or, depending on the circumstances, we might also imagine a breakbeat machine that encompasses hip-hop, hardcore rave, jungle, big beat, breaks, breakstep, etc.

77   For example: Afrika Bambaataa's 'Planet Rock' or Phuture's 'Acid Tracks'.

78   These are the dominant modes of analysis in the field, but examples would include: Thornton, *Club Cultures*; Andy Bennett, 'Subcultures or Neo-Tribes? Rethinking the Relationship Between Youth, Style and Musical Taste', *Sociology* 33 (1999), pp. 599–617; Kimbrew McLeod, 'Genres, Subgenres, Sub-Subgenres and More: Musical and Social Differentiation Within Electronic/Dance Music Communities', *Journal of Popular Music Studies* 13 (2001), pp. 59–75.

79   The reality of rhythmic operating systems becomes evident when attempting to mix musics that are notionally quite different but which share a rhythmachinic lineage – for example, 4x4 UK garage, grime, half-time dubstep and 2-step. In the mix, one discover that they share elements of an internal logic. Brought to a common tempo, they simply work together.

80   This became the bed upon which dub's delirious sound design could be built.

81   Grandmaster Flash interviewed in *Once Upon a Time in New York: The Birth of Hip-hop, Disco and Punk*, directed by Benjamin Whalley, BBC Four (UK), 2007.

82   Lawrence, *Love Saves the Day*, pp. 125–6, 146.

83   Interviewed in *We Call It Techno*. 'Straight' refers to a rigidly quantized rhythm in which all metric divisions are perfectly equal. Conversely, a rhythm with 'swing' or 'shuffle' introduces small degrees of irregularity that make it move in a less mechanical way.

84   Mark Fisher, 'Ghosting the Jungle', http://web.archive.org/web/20070106162319/ http://www.factmagazine.co.uk/da/42229 (accessed 18 May 2012). Fisher is referring here to Reynolds' concept of a 'hardcore continuum' that is understood to run through a lineage of likeminded musical moments since Rave. The concept has been debated at length in recent years, and will not be taken up here. The important point, in this instance, is that dubstep can be understand as a moment of retooling, at the drums-and-bass level, of the garage machine.

85   Goodman, 'Speed Tribes: Netwar, Affective Hacking and the Audio-Social', in F. Liebl (ed.), *Cultural Hacking* (Vienna: Springer-Verlag, 2004).

86   'It is thus necessary to make a distinction between speed and movement: a movement may be very fast, but that does not give it speed; a speed may be very slow, or even immobile, yet it is still speed. Movement is extensive; speed is intensive. Movement designates the relative character of a body considered

as "one", and which goes from point to point; *speed, on the contrary, constitutes the absolute character of a body whose irreducible parts (atoms) occupy or fill a smooth space in the manner of a vortex, with the possibility of springing up at any point.'* Deleuze and Guattari, *A Thousand Plateas*, p. 381.

87 Manning, *Relationscapes*, p. 62.

> Preacceleration refers to the virtual force of movement's taking form. It is the feeling of movement's in-gathering, a welling that propels the directionality of how movement moves. In dance, this is felt as the virtual momentum of a movement's taking form before we actually move. Important: the pulsion toward directionality activates the force of a movement in its incipiency. It does not necessarily foretell where a movement will go. (Ibid., p. 6)

88 *More Brilliant Than the Sun*, p. 149.

89 Ibid., p. 14. In digital animation, motion capture technology allows the movements of human subjects, through space, to be digitally sampled and then used to animate computer-generated figures on screen.

90 Davis, *Roots & Wires*.

91 Ibid. Davis suggests that jungle '[resembles] polymetric drumming in allowing dancers to satisfactorily hook into and pass between different rhythmic milieus nested within the same cut. ... [It] induces a remarkably delicious sense of disorientation, as reverbed cymbals and chopped-up snares savagely tug against the bass beat, upsetting the listener's habitual desire to 'fill in' the music with a comprehensible rhythm.'

92 Reynolds, *Generation Ecstasy*, pp. 253–4.

93 Davis, *Roots & Wires*.

94 Fisher, 'Ghosting the Jungle'.

95 Deleuze and Guattari, *A Thousand Plateaus*, p. 356.

96 This use of 'capacitance' is adapted from electrical terminology where it refers to 'the ability of a system to store an electric charge' and 'the ratio of the change in an electric charge in a system to the corresponding change in its electric potential' (*OED*). In some applications, capacitance can be used to modulate the energy in a system. In electronics, a capacitor's role is to store and hold a charge, but also to release it, at different rates and rhythms, depending on its connections.

97 Deleuze and Guattari, *A Thousand Plateaus*, p. 400.

98 'Catasonic' is adapted from Fisher's 'katasonic'.

99 Given how difficult it can be for DJs to mix tracks that are so sparse and rhythmically unsteady, producers tend to work almost exclusively 160 BPM.

100 Dave Quam, 'The Evolution of Footwork', http://www.residentadvisor.net/
     feature.aspx?1235 (accessed 17 December 2010).
101 In dance music production since Rave, 'chipmunk' refers to vocals sped or
     pitched up until they become squeaky.
102 In this sense there is an obvious link to break dancing, but also other
     contemporary dance cultures, like jit in Detroit, and krumping in California.
103 'Chicago footwork interview, Sadler's Wells 25/04/11', by Ruth Saxelby for
     DummyMag.com. http://vimeo.com/23276306 (accessed August 2011);
     From Jack to Juke – 25 Years of Ghetto House, directed by Sonali Aggarwal
     (USA), http://vimeo.com/36275353 (accessed August 2011); Producer/DJ RP
     Boo has said 'The more I see these dancers out here doin' these things, the
     more I feed off of them, and my music gets better', http://www.npr.org/blogs/
     therecord/2010/12/14/131834348/chicago-s-footwork-music-and-dance-get-a-
     transatlantic-lift (accessed August 2011).
104 DJ Rashad has noted sonic similarities to dubstep, and kinetic similarities
     to jungle of the 1994/95 era. 'Chicago footwork interview, Sadler's Wells
     25/04/11'.
105 A similar argument could be made about Grime vocals – normally delivered at
     140 BPM – when backed by half-tempo basslines.

Conclusion

1 Massumi, *Parables*, pp. 245–6.
2 Ibid., pp. 12–13, 245–56.
3 For introductions to each, see: Levi Bryant, Nick Srnicek and Graham Harman
   (eds), *The Speculative Turn: Continental Materialism and Realism* (Melbourne:
   re.press, 2011); and Diana Coole and Samantha Frost, *New Materialisms:
   Ontology, Agency, and Politics* (Durham, NC, Duke University Press, 2010).
4 Levi Bryant, Nick Srnicek and Graham Harman, 'Toward a Speculative
   Philosophy', in *The Speculative Turn*, pp. 3–4.
5 Bennett, *Vibrant Matter*, p. xvi.
6 Eugene Thacker, *In The Dust of This Planet: Horror of Philosophy Vol. 1*
   (Winchester, UK: Zero Books, 2011), pp. 1–9.
7 Encounters with deaf studies suggest promising new directions. See, for
   example: Michele Friedner and Stefan Helmreich, 'Sound Studies Meets Deaf
   Studies', *The Senses & Society* 7/1 (2012), pp. 72–86.

8   The book has lately experienced a renaissance, but that has been driven primarily by renewed interest in Afrofuturism, rather than by Eshun's theorization of moving bodies and musical machines.

9   Actress, Emptyset, Demdike Stare, T++, Laurel Halo, Andy Stott, TCF, Senking, Rashad Becker and Samuel Kerridge, to name just a few.

10 Philip Sherburne, 'Hot Organs: Tracking the Trend', *Pitchfork* (25 February 2015). http://pitchfork.com/thepitch/684-hot-organs-tracking-the-trend/ (accessed 25 February 2015).

11 Synthesizers and drum machines, generally, but then specialized devices, too, like the Novation Bass Station (1993), the Control Synthesis Deep Bass Nine (1994), the E-mu Planet Phat (1997) and Mo'Phatt (2000). See http://www. vintagesynth.com.

12 Deleuze and Guattari, *A Thousand Plateaus*, p. 500.

13 As with Hummers, and those troubled by waves of urban, industrial or military origin.

14 As in the case of sonic weapons or the medieval organ.

15 Two somewhat recent examples: In 2006, Goodman (in his kode9 guise) warned of a looming 'bass fundamentalism' on dancefloors. (Fisher, 'Ghosting the Jungle', 2005) What soon emerged was a plodding, aggressively masculinist, take on dubstep, known pejoratively as 'brostep'. Another case is artist Banks Violette's 2007 show at Team Gallery (NYC), in which loud, low drones and Gregorian-styled chants (by Attilla Csithar and Sunn o)))'s Stephen O'Malley) accompanied installations celebrating the clichés and excesses of male rock culture (represented by liquor bottles, a shattered and charred drum kit, amplifier parts cast in salt, etc.). See: Martha Schwendener, 'Heavy Metal and Light: Always Serve Chilled', *New York Times* (6 August 2007): E1 and E6; Lauren Ross, 'Rock Out', *Art in America* (November 2007), pp. 198–201; Michael Wilson, 'Banks Violette', *Artforum* (September 2007), p. 466. In both instances, bass is saddled with the dull task of signifying power (of a very specific and regressive sort), and there is no sense in which sonic force works to volatize subjectivity. As affective strategies, both are pointedly molar.

Bibliography

Albers, Josef, *Interaction of Color*, New Haven, CT: Yale University Press, 1963.

Altmann, Jürgen, 'Acoustic Weapons – a Prospective Assessment', *Science & Global Security* 9 (2001), pp. 165–264.

Altman, Rick, *Sound Theory, Sound Practice*, New York: Routledge, 1992.

Altman, Rick, *Silent Film Sound*, New York: Columbia University Press, 2004.

Amacher, Maryanne, 'Composing Perceptual Geographies', http://www.maryanneamacher.org/Amacher_Archive_Project/Entries/2009/10/23_Composing_perceptual_ geographies.html (accessed 11 May 2011).

Amacher, Maryanne, 'Music For Sound Joined Rooms', http://www.maryanneamacher.org/Maryanne_Amacher/Amacher_Archive_Project/Entries/2009/10/24_music_for_sound_ joined_rooms.html (accessed 11 May 2011).

Amir, Noam, 'Some Insight into the Acoustics of the Didjeridu', *Applied Acoustics* 65 (2004), pp. 1181–96.

Andersen, Poul-Gerhard, *Organ Building and Design* (1956), trans. Joanne Curnutt, London: Allen & Unwin, 1969.

Anderson, Tim J., *Making Easy Listening: Material Culture and Postwar American Recording*, Minneapolis: University of Minnesota Press, 2006.

Askill, John, *The Physics of Musical Sound*, New York: D. Van Nostrand Co, 1979.

Audsley, George Ashdown, *The Art of Organ Building, Volume 1* (1905), Mineola, NY: Dover, 1965.

Augoyard, Jean Francois and Torgue, Henry, *Sonic Experience: A Guide to Everyday Sounds*, Montreal: McGill-Queen's University Press, 2005.

Bain, Mark, 'Sonic Architecture', *Earshot: The Journal of the UK and Ireland Soundscape Community* 3 (November 2002), http://www.vpro.nl/attachment.db/Sonic_Architecture2.doc?23220323 (accessed 19 October 2010).

Bain, Mark, '*The Live Room*: Transducing Resonant Architectures', *Organised Sound* 8 (2003), pp. 163–70.

Bannister, Matthew, *White Boys, White Noise: Masculinities and 1980s Indie Guitar Rock*, Farnham, UK: Ashgate Publishing, 2006.

Bartel, Dietrich, *Musica Poetica: Musical Rhetorical Figures in German Baroque Music*, Lincoln: University of Nebraska, 1997.

Bennett, Andy, 'Subcultures or Neo-Tribes? Rethinking the Relationship Between Youth, Style and Musical Taste', *Sociology* 33 (1999), pp. 599–617.

Bennett, Jane, *Vibrant Matter: A Political Ecology of Things*, Durham, NC: Duke University Press, 2010.

Bijsterveld, Karin, *Mechanical Sound: Technology, Culture, and Public Problems of Noise in the Twentieth Century*, Cambridge, MA: MIT Press, 2008.

Bird, George W., *Wanderings in Asia*, London: Simpkin, Marshall, Hamilton, Kent & Co Ltd, 1897.

Birdsall, Carolyn and Enns, Anthony (eds), *Sonic Mediations: Body, Sound, Technology*, Cambridge: Cambridge University Press, 2008.

Blakeslee, Sandra and Blakeslee, Matthew, *The Body Has a Mind of Its Own: New Discoveries About How the Mind-Body Connection Helps Us Master the World*, Random House Trade Paperbacks, New York: Random House, 2008.

Blesser, Barry and Salter, Linda-Ruth, *Spaces Speak, Are You Listening? Experiencing Aural Architecture*, Cambridge, MA: MIT Press, 2007.

Bogue, Ronald, *Deleuze's Wake: Tributes and Tributaries*, Albany: State University of New York Press, 2004.

Bogost, Ian, *Alien Phenomenology, or What It's Like to Be a Thing*, Minneapolis: University of Minnesota Press, 2012.

Bradley, Lloyd, *Bass Culture: When Reggae was King*, London: Viking, 2000.

Braithwaite, J. J. and Townsend, M., 'Good Vibrations: The Case for a Specific Effect of Infrasound in Instances of Anomalous Experience Has Yet to be Empirically Demonstrated', *Journal for the Society of Psychical Research* 70/885 (2006), pp. 211–24.

Britt, Robert Roy, 'Controversial New Idea: Nerves Transmit Sound, Not Electricity', *Live Science* (14 March 2007), http://www.livescience.com/humanbiology/070312_nerves_work.html (accessed 17 April 2009).

Brody, Hugh, *The Other Side of Eden: Hunters, Farmers and the Shaping of the World*, Vancouver: Douglas & McIntyre, 2000.

Broner, N., 'The Effects of Low Frequency Noise on People - a Review', *Journal of Sound and Vibration* 58 (1978), pp. 483–500.

Brunn, Emile Zum and Epiny-Burgard, Georgette, *Women Mystics in Medieval Europe*, trans. Sheila Hughes, New York: Paragon House, 1989.

Bryant, Levy, Srnicek, Nick and Harman, Graham (eds), *The Speculative Turn: Continental Materialism and Realism*, Melbourne: re.press, 2011.

Bull, Michael, *Sounding out the City: Personal Stereos and the Management of Everyday Life*, Oxford: Berg, 2000.

Bull, Michael, *Sound Moves: iPod Culture and Urban Experience*, New York: Routledge, 2007.

Bull, Michael and Back, Les (eds), *The Auditory Culture Reader*, Oxford: Berg, 2003.

Buser, Pierre and Imbert, Michel, *Audition*, Cambridge, MA: MIT Press, 1992.

Chevannes, Barry, *Rastafari: Roots and Ideology*, Syracuse: Syracuse University Press, 1994.

Chion, Michel, *Audio-Vision: Sound on Screen*, trans. Claudia Gorbman, New York: Columbia University Press, 1994.

Chion, Michel, *Film, A Sound Art*, trans. Claudia Gorbman, New York: Columbia University Press, 2009.

Cirillio, Ettore and Martellotta, Francesco, *Worship, Acoustics, and Architecture*, Brentwood, UK: Multi-Science Publishing Co Ltd, 2006.

Coleman, Satis N., *Bells: Their History, Legends, Making, and Uses*, New York: Rand McNally & Company, 1928.

Conrad, Joseph, *Heart of Darkness* (1902), London: Penguin, 1980.

Cooke, Lynne and Elderfield, John, *Bridget Riley: Reconnaissance*, New York: Dia Center for the Arts, 2000.

Coole, Diana and Frost, Samantha (eds), *New Materialisms: Ontology, Agency, and Politics*, Durham, NC: Duke University Press, 2010.

Creese, David, *The Monochord in Ancient Greek Harmonic Science*, Cambridge: Cambridge University Press, 2010.

Crocker, Malcolm J., *The Handbook of Noise and Vibration Control*, London: Wiley, 2007.

Davies, Owen, *The Haunted: A Social History of Ghosts*, New York: Palgrave Macmillan, 2007.

Davies, Sam, 'Eleh, Floating Frequencies/Intuitive Synthesis I', *The Wire* 279 (May 2007), p. 57.

Davis, Caroline Franks, *The Evidential Force of Religious Experience*, Oxford: Clarendon Press, 1999.

Davis, Erik, 'Roots and Wires: Polyrhythmic Cyberspace and the Black Electronic', paper presented at 5CYBERCONF, Madrid, 1996, http://www.techgnosis.com (accessed 3 October 2009).

Davis, Erik, *TechGnosis: Myth, Magic and Mysticism in the Age of Information*, London: Serpent's Tail, 2004.

De Certeau, Michel, *The Practice of Everyday Life*, trans. Steve Rendall, Berkeley: University of California Press, 1984.

De Landa, Manuel, *War in the Age of Intelligent Machines*, New York: Zone Books, 1991.

De Landa, Manuel, *A Thousand Years of Non-Linear History*, New York: Zone Books, 2000.

De Landa, Manuel, *A New Philosophy of Society: Assemblage Theory and Social Complexity*, New York: Continuum, 2006.

Deleuze, Gilles, *Spinoza, Practical Philosophy*, San Francisco: City Lights Books, 1988.

Deleuze, Gilles, *Difference and Repetition*, New York: Columbia University Press, 1994.

Deleuze, Gilles, *Francis Bacon: The Logic of Sensation*, Minneapolis: University of Minnesota Press, 2004.

Deleuze, Gilles and Guattari, Felix, *Kafka: Toward a Minor Literature* (1975), trans. Dana Polan, Minneapolis: University of Minnesota Press, 1986.

Deleuze, Gilles and Guattari, Felix, *A Thousand Plateaus: Capitalism and Schizophrenia*, trans. Brian Massumi, Minneapolis: University of Minnesota Press, 1987.

Deleuze, Gilles and Guattari, Felix, *What is Philosophy?* New York: Columbia University Press, 1994.

Demers, Joanna, *Listening Through the Noise: The Aesthetics of Experimental Electronic Music*, New York: Oxford University Press, 2010.

Deming, David. 'The Hum: An Anomalous Sound Heard Around the World', *Journal of Scientific Exploration* 18 (2004), pp. 571–95.

Dery, Mark, 'Black to the Future: Interviews with Samuel R. Delany, Greg Tate and Tricia Rose', *South Atlantic Quarterly* 92 (1993), pp. 735–78. Special issue *Flame Wars: The Discourse of Cyberculture*.

Devereux, Paul, 'Ears & Years: Aspects of Acoustics and Intentionality in Antiquity', in Chris Scarre and Graeme Lawson (eds), *Archaeoacsoustics*, Cambridge: McDonald Institute for Archaeological Research, 2006, pp. 23–30.

Devine, Kyle, *Imperfect Sound Forever: Loudness, Listening Formations, and the Historiography of Sound Reproduction*, Carleton University: PhD dissertation, 2012.

Duby, Georges, *The Age of the Cathedrals: Art and Society, 980-1420*, Chicago: University of Chicago Press, 1981.

Dundes, Alan, 'A Psychoanalytic Study of the Bullroarer', *Man* 11 (1976), pp. 220–38.

Eamon, William, *Science and the Secrets of Nature: Books of Secrets in Medieval and Early Modern Culture*, trans. Norma Deane, Princeton: Princeton University Press, 1996.

Elder, J. A. and Chou, C. K., 'Auditory Response to Pulsed Radiofrequency Energy', *Bioelectromagnetic Supplement* 6 (2003), pp. 162–73.

Ellison, Ralph, *Invisible Man* (1947), New York: Vintage, 1990.

Erlmann, Veit (ed.), *Hearing Cultures: Essays on Sound, Listening, and Modernity*, Oxford: Berg, 2004.

Erlmann, Veit, *Reason and Resonance: A History of Modern Aurality*, New York: Zone Books, 2010.

Eshun, Kodwo, *More Brilliant Than the Sun: Adventures in Sonic Fiction*, London: Quartet Books, 1998.

Eshun, Kodwo, 'Wookie: Civilization and its Discos – Part 1 (2000)', http://www.riddim.ca/?p=216 (accessed 6 March 2012).

Eshun, Kodwo, 'Abducted by Audio', http://www.ccru.net/swarm3/3_abducted.htm (accessed 2 May 2010).

Everest, F. Alton, *Master Handbook of Acoustics*, 4th edn, New York: McGraw-Hill, 2001.

Feld, Steven, 'From Ethnomusicology to Echo-muse-ecology: Reading R. Murray Schafer in the Papua New Guinea Rainforest', *The Soundscape Newsletter* 8 (1994), pp. 9–13.

Feld, Steven, 'Places Sensed, Senses Placed', in David Howes (ed.), *Empire of the Senses: The Sensual Culture Reader*, London: Berg Publishing, 2005.

Fink, Robert, *Repeating Ourselves: American Minimal Music as Cultural Practice*, Berkeley: University of California Press, 2005.

Finucane, Ronald C., 'Historical Introduction: The Example of Early Modern and Nineteenth-Century England', in James Houran and Rense Lange (eds), *Hauntings and Poltergeists: Multidisciplinary Perspectives*, Jefferson, NC: McFarland, 2001.

Fischer, Hans, *Sound-Producing Instruments in Oceania*, trans. Philip W. Holzknecht, Boroko, Papua New Guinea: Institute of Papua New Guinea Studies, 1986.

Fisher, Mark. 'Ghosting the Jungle', http://web.archive.org/web/20070106162319/http://www.factmagazine.co.uk/da/42229 (accessed 18 May 2012).

Fletcher, Neville H. and Rossing, Thomas D., *The Physics of Musical Instruments*, New York: Springer-Verlag, 1991.

Fletcher, N. H., Tarnpolsky, A. Z. and Lai, J. C. S., 'Rotational Aerophones', *Journal of the Acoustical Society of America* 111 (March 2002), pp. 1189–96.

Fletcher, N. H., Tarnopolsky, A. Z. and Lai, J. C. S., 'Australian Aboriginal Musical Instruments - The Bullroarer', paper presented at 'Acoustics 2002- Innovation in Acoustics and Vibration', Annual Conference of the Australian Acoustical Society, Adelaide Australia (November 2002).

French, Christopher C., Haque, Usman, Bunton-Stasyshyn, Rosie and Davis, Rob, 'The "Haunt" Project: An Attempt to Build a "Haunted" Room By Manipulating

Complex Electromagnetic Fields and Infrasound', *Cortex* Advance access at doi: 10.1016/j.cortex.2007.10.011 (2008), pp. 1–11.

Frey, A. H., 'Human Auditory System Response to Modulated Electromagnetic Energy', *Journal of Applied Physiology* 17 (1962), pp. 689–92.

Freud, Sigmund, 'The Uncanny', *The Standard Edition of the Complete Psychoanalytic Works of Sigmund Freud, Volume 17,* trans. James Staachey (ed.), London: Hogarth Press, 1957.

Friedner, Michele and Helmreich, Stefan, 'Sound Studies Meets Deaf Studies', *The Senses & Society* 7/1 (2012), pp. 72–86.

Fuller, Matthew, *Media Ecologies: Materialist Energies in Art and Technoculture,* Cambridge, MA: MIT Press, 2005.

Gavreau, Vladimir, 'Infra Sons: Générateurs, Détecteurs, Propriétés Physiques, Effets Biologiques', *Acustica* 17 (1966), pp. 1–10.

Gavreau, Vladimir, 'Infrasound', *Science Journal* 4/1 (1968), pp. 33–7.

Gavreau, Vladimir, 'Sons Graves Intenses et Infrasons', *Scientific Progress – la Nature* (1968), pp. 336–44.

Gilbert, Jeremy and Pearson, Ewan, *Discographies: Dance, Music, Culture and the Politics of Sound,* New York: Routledge, 1999.

Gilroy, Paul, *The Black Atlantic: Modernity and Double Consciousness,* Cambridge, MA: Harvard University Press, 1993.

Gitelman, Lisa, *Scripts, Grooves, and Writing Machines: Representing Technology in the Edison Era,* Stanford: Stanford University Press, 1999.

Goddard, Michael, Halligan, Benjamin and Spelman, Nicola (eds), *Resonances: Noise and Contemporary Music,* New York: Continuum, 2013.

Goethe, Johann Wolfgang von, *Theory of Colours* (1840), trans. Charles Lock Eastlake, Cambridge, MA: MIT Press, 1970.

Goodman, Steve, 'Speed Tribes: Netwar, Affective Hacking and the Audio Social', in F. Liebl (ed.), *Cultural Hacking,* Berlin: Springer-Verlag, 2004.

Goodman, Steve, *Sonic Warfare: Sound, Affect, and the Ecology of Fear.* Cambridge, MA: MIT Press, 2010.

Goodman, Steve and Parisi, Luciana, 'Extensive Continuum Towards a Rhythmic Anarchitecture', *iNFLexions* 2 (January 2009), http://www.senselab.ca/inflexions/volume_4/n2_parisigoodmanhtml.html (accessed 2 June 2011).

Gracyk, Theodore, *Rhythm and Noise: An Aesthetics of Rock,* Durham, NC: Duke University Press, 1996.

Grusin, Richard (ed.), *The Nonhuman Turn,* Minneapolis: University of Minnesota Press, 2015.

Gregg, Melissa and Seigworth, Anthony J. (eds), *The Affect Theory Reader*, Durham, NC: Duke University Press, 2010.

Guattari, Félix, *Chaosmosis: An Ethico-Aesthetic Paradigm*, Bloomington: Indiana University Press, 1995.

Guild of Carillonneurs in North America, http://www.gcna.org/data/ (accessed 12 January 2011).

Gunning, Tom, 'The Cinema of Attractions: Early Film, Its Spectator and the Avant-Garde', in Wanda Strauven (ed.), *The Cinema of Attractions Reloaded*, Amsterdam: Amsterdam University Press, 2006, pp. 381–88.

Hacking, Ian, *The Social Construction of What?* Cambridge, MA: Harvard University Press, 1999.

Haneke, K. E., Carson, B. L., Gregorio, C. A. and Maull, E. A., 'Infrasound: Brief Review of Toxicological Literature. Infrasound Toxicological Summary', submitted to National Institute of Environmental Health Sciences, National Institutes of Health (USA) in partial fulfillment of Contract Number N01-ES-65402. November 2001.

Harman, Graham, 'On the Horror of Phenomenology: Lovecraft and Husserl', *Collapse IV: Concept Horror* (2008), pp. 333–64.

Harman, Graham, *Towards Speculative Realism: Essays and Lectures*, Winchester, UK: Zero Books, 2009.

Harman, Graham, *Weird Realism: Lovecraft and Philosophy*, Winchester, UK: Zero Books, 2012.

Hegarty, Paul, *NoiseMusic: A History*, New York: Continuum, 2007.

Helmholtz, Hermann von, *On the Sensations of Tone as a Physiological Basis for the Theory of Music*, trans. Alexander John Ellis, New York: Dover Publications Inc., 1954.

Henriques, Julien, 'Sonic Dominance and the Reggae Sound System Session', in Michael Bull and Les Back (eds), *The Auditory Culture Reader,* Oxford: Berg, 2003.

Henriques, Julien, 'The Vibrations of Affect and their Propagation on a Night Out on Kingston's Dancehall Scene', *Body & Society* 16 (2010), pp. 57–89.

Henriques, Julien, *Sonic Bodies: Reggae Sound Systems, Performance Techniques and Ways of Knowing*, New York: Continuum, 2011.

Hess, Felix, *Light as Air*, Heidelberg: Kehrer Verlag, 2001.

Hibbert, William A., *The Quantification of Strike Pitch and Pitch Shifts in Church Bells*, The Open University, PhD dissertation, 2008.

'Hidden Sensory System Discovered in the Skin', *Science Daily* (8 December 2009), http://www.sciencedaily.com/releases/2009/12/091208083524.htm (accessed 13 December 2009).

Holsinger, Bruce W., *Music, Body, and Desire in Medieval Culture*, Stanford: Stanford University Press, 2001.

Houston, Joe, *Optic Nerve: Perceptual Art of the 1960s*, London: Merrell, 2007.

Howes, David (ed.), *The Varieties of Sensory Experience: A Sourcebook in the Anthropology of the Senses*, Toronto: University of Toronto Press, 1991.

Howes, David (ed.), *Empire of the Senses: The Sensual Culture Reader*, Oxford: Berg, 2005.

Hufford, David J., 'An Experience-Centred Approach to Hauntings', in James Houran and Rense Lange (eds), *Hauntings and Poltergeists: Multidisciplinary Perspectives*, Jefferson, NC: McFarland, 2001, pp. 18–40.

Hyperstition, hyperstition.abstractdynamics.org (accessed 11 May 2010).

Ihde, Don, *Listening and Voice: A Phenomenology of Sound*, Athens, OH: Ohio University Press, 1976.

Ikoniadou, Eleni, *The Rhtymic Event: Art, Media, and the Sonic*, Cambridge, MA: MIT Press, 2014.

J-Mill, 'Original King', *The Source* 54 (March 1994), p. 21.

Jahn, Robert G., Devereux, Paul and Ibison, Michael, 'Acoustical Resonances of Assorted Ancient Structures', *Journal of the Acoustical Society of America* 99 (1996), pp. 649–58.

James, William, *The Varieties of Religious Experience: a Study in Human Nature; Being the Gifford Lectures on Natural Religion Delivered at Edinburgh in 1901-1902*, New York: Modern Library, 1902.

James, William and Barton Perry, Ralph, *Essays in Radical Empiricism*, New York: Longmans, Green, and Co, 1912.

Jenny, Hans, *Cymatics: A Study of Wave Phenomena and Vibration*, 3rd edn, Tacoma, WA: MACRO media Publishing, 2001.

Johnson, Mark, *The Body in the Mind: The Bodily Basis of Meaning, Imagination, and Reason*, Chicago: University of Chicago Press, 1987.

Johnson, Mark, *The Meaning of the Body: Aesthetics of Human Understanding*, Chicago: University of Chicago Press, 2007.

Julius, Maija, 'Traces in Vinyl', http://www.koener.de/maijajuliustracesinvinyl.htm (accessed 12 November 2009).

Kahn, Douglas, *Noise, Water, Meat*, Cambridge, MA: MIT Press, 1999.

Kahn, Douglas, *Earth Sound, Earth Signal: Energies and Earth Magnitude in the Arts*, Berkeley: University of California Press, 2013.

Kassel, Richard and Bush, Douglas, *The Organ: An Encyclopedia*, New York: Routledge, 2006.

Keightley, Keir, '"Turn it Down!" She Shrieked: Gender, Domestic Space and High Fidelity, 1948-59', *Popular Music* 15 (1996), pp. 149–77.

Kennedy, Barbara M., *Deleuze and Cinema: The Aesthetics of Sensation*, Edinburgh: Edinburgh University Press, 2000.

Kittler, Friedrich, *Gramophone, Film, Typewriter*, Stanford: Stanford University Press, 1999.

Knight, Michael Muhammed, *The Five Percenters: Islam, Hip-Hop and the Gods of New York*, New York: Oneworld Publications, 2008.

Kudielka, Robert (ed.), *Bridget Riley: Dialogues on Art*, London: Zwemmer, 1995.

Kutschale, Henry, 'Arctic Hydroacoustics', *Arctic* 22 (1969), pp. 246–64.

Labelle, Brandon, *Background Noise: Perspectives on Sound Art*, New York: Continuum, 2008.

Labelle, Brandon, *Acoustic Territories/Sound Culture*, New York: Continuum, 2010.

Lang, Edith and West, George, *Musical Accompaniment of Moving Pictures*, New York: Boston Picture Co, 1920.

Laine, Unto K., 'Denoising and Analysis of Audio Recordings Made During the April 6-7, 2000 Geomagnetic Storm by Using a Non-professional Ad Hoc Setup', *Joint Baltic-Nordic Acoustics Meeting 2004*. Mariehamn, Åland, 8–10 June 2004.

Lastra, James, *Sound Technology and the American Cinema: Perception, Representation and Modernity*, New York: Columbia University Press, 2000.

Lavater, Ludwig, *Of Ghostes and Spirites, Walking by Night* (1572), http://archive.org/details/ofghostesspirite00lava (accessed 16 June 2011).

Lawrence, Tim, *Love Saves the Day: A History of American Dance Music Culture, 1970-1979*, Durham, NC: Duke University Press, 2003.

Leventhall, Geoff, 'A Review of Published Research on Low Frequency Noise and its Effects', UK: Department for Environment, Food and Rural Affairs, May 2003.

Leventhall, Geoff, 'Low Frequency Noise. What We Know, What We Do Not Know, and What We Would Like to Know', *Journal of Low Frequency Noise and Active Control* 28 (2009), pp. 79–104.

Licht, Alan, 'Maryanne Amacher: Expressway to Your Skull', *The Wire* 181 (March 1999).

Lock, Graham, *Blutopia: Visions of the Future and Revisions of the Past in the Work of Sun Ra, Duke Ellington, and Anthony Braxton*, Durham, NC: Duke University Press, 1999.

Lomas, Robert, 'Essay: Spark of Genius', *The Independent* (21 August 1999), http://www.independent.co.uk/life-style/essay-spark-of-genius-1114136.html (accessed 9 November 2011).

Lovecraft, H. P., *The Call of Chthulu and Other Weird Stories*, S. T. Joshi (ed.), London: Penguin, 1999.

Lovecraft, H. P., *The Thing on the Doorstep and Other Weird Stories*, S. T. Joshi (ed.), London: Penguin, 2001.

Lovecraft, H. P., 'The Transition of Juan Romero', http://www.hplovecraft.com/writings/texts/fiction/tjr.aspx (accessed 12 January 2012).

Mack, Andrew L. and Jones, Josh, 'Low-Frequency Vocalizations by Cassowaries (Casuarius spp.)', *The Auk* 120 (October 2003), pp. 1062–8.

Mahrenholtz, Christhard, *The Calculation of Organ Pipe Scales: From the Middle Ages to the Mid-Nineteenth Century* (1938), trans. Andrew Williams, Oxford: Positif Press, 1975.

Malbon, Ben, *Clubbing: Dancing, Ecstasy and Vitality*, London: Routledge, 1999.

Manaugh, Geoff, 'When Landscapes Sing: Or, London Instrument', http://bldgblog.blogspot.ca/2005/12/when-landscapes-sing-or-london.html (accessed 12 November 2009).

Manaugh, Geoff, *The BLDGBLOG Book: Architectural Conjecture, Urban Speculation, Landscape Futures*, San Francisco: Chronicle Books, 2009.

Mann, Michael D., 'Chapter 9 - Vestibular Functions', in *The Nervous System In Action*. Michael D. Mann, 1997–2012, http://www.unmc.edu/physiology/Mann/mann9.html (accessed 12 February 2012).

Manning, Erin, *Politics of Touch: Sense, Movement, Sovereignty*, Minneapolis: University of Minnesota Press, 2007.

Manning, Erin, *Relationscapes: Movement, Art, Philosophy*, Cambridge, MA: MIT Press, 2009.

Marsh, Peter, 'Hazard *Wind* Review' (20 November 2002), http://www.bbc.co.uk/music/reviews/qhjw (accessed 29 July 2010).

Massumi, Brian, *A User's Guide to Capitalism and Schizophrenia: Deviations From Deleuze and Guattari*, Cambridge, MA: MIT Press, 1992.

Massumi, Brian, *Parables for the Virtual: Movement, Affect, Sensation*, Durham, NC: Duke University Press, 2002.

Massumi, Brian, *Semblance and Event: Activist Philosophy and the Occurrent Arts*, Cambridge, MA: MIT Press, 2011.

Mattheson, Johann, *Der vollkommene Capellmeister*, 1739.

McGee, Timothy J., *The Sound of Medieval Music*, Oxford: Clarendon Press, 1998.

McLeod, Kimbrew, 'Genres, Subgenres, Sub-Subgenres and More: Musical and Social Differentiation Within Electronic/Dance Music Communities', *Journal of Popular Music Studies* 13 (2001), pp. 59–75.

Mertens, Wim, *American Minimal Music*, trans. J. Hautekiet, London: Kahn & Averill, 1983.

Meyers, S. R. and Peters, S. E., 'A 56 million year rhythm in North American Sedimentation during the Phanerozoic', *Earth Planetary Science Letters* (2011) doi: 10.1016/j.epsl.2010.12.044, http://www.geology.wisc.edu/~smeyers/pubs/Meyers_and_Peters_2011.pdf.

Miller, Paul D., *Rhythm Science*, Cambridge, MA: MIT Press, 2004.

Mitchell, Tony, *Global Noise: Rap and Hip-Hop Outside the USA*, Middletown, CT: Wesleyan University Press, 2001.

Müller, Christian, Schlindwein, Vera, Eckstaller, Alfons and Miller, Heinrich, 'Singing Icebergs', *Science* 310/5752 (25 November 2005), p. 1299.

Natiez, Jean-Jacques, *Music and Discourse: Toward a Semiology of Music*, trans. Carolyn Abbate, Princeton: Princeton University Press, 1990.

Negarestani, Reza, *Cyclonopedia: Complicity with Anonymous Materials*, Melbourne, re.press, 2008.

Norment, Camille, 'Notes from the oscillating dream space', in John Corbett, Anthony Elms and Terri Kapsalis (eds), *Pathways to Unknown Worlds: Sun Ra, El Saturn and Chicago's Afro-Futurist Underground 1954-68*, Chicago: Whitewalls, 2006, pp. 23–25.

Norris, Elwood G, 'HyperSonic™Sound', *Acoustical Society of America 133rd Meeting Lay Language Papers* (1997), http://www.acoustics.org/press/133rd/2pea.html (accessed 15 January 2011).

Oliver, Mark, 'The Day the Earth Screamed', *The Guardian* (13 February 2004), http://www.guardian.co.uk/artanddesign/2004/feb/13/art.usa (accessed 11 November 2009).

Parr, Adrian (ed.), *The Deleuze Dictionary*, Edinburgh: Edinburgh University Press, 2005.

Pedersen, Christian Sejer, Møller, Henrik M. and Persson Waye, Kerstin, 'A Detailed Study of Low-Frequency Noise Complaints', *Journal of Low-Frequency Noise and Vibration* 27/1 (2008), pp. 1–30.

Perrot, Jean, *The Organ from its Invention in the Hellenistic Period to the end of the Thirteenth Century*, trans. Norma Deane, London: Oxford University Press, 1971.

Persinger, Michael A., *The Weather Matrix and Human Behavior*, New York: Praeger, 1980.

Persinger, Michael A., *Neurophysiological Bases of God Beliefs*, New York: Praeger, 1987.

Pertl, Brian, 'Some Observations on the "Dung Chen" of the Nechung Monastery', *Asian Music* 23/2 (Spring-Summer 1992), pp. 89–96.

Petroff, Elizabeth Alvilda, *Body & Soul: Essays on Medieval Women and Mysticism*, Oxford: Oxford University Press, 1994.

Picker, John M., *Victorian Soundscapes*, Oxford: Oxford University Press, 2003.

Pinch, Trevor and Trocco, Frank, *Analog Days: The Invention and Impact of the Moog Synthesizer*, Cambridge, MA: Harvard University Press, 2002.

Pinch, Trevor and Bijsterveld, Karin, 'Sound Studies: New Technologies and Music', *Social Studies of Science* 34 (2004), pp. 635–48.

Pinch, Trevor, *The Oxford Handbook of Sound Studies*, Oxford: Oxford University Press, 2012.

Pinn, Anthony B. (ed.), *Noise and Spirit: The Religious and Spiritual Sensibilities of Rap Music*, New York: New York University Press, 2003.

Porcello, Thomas, 'Speaking of Sound: Language and the Professionalization of Sound-Recording Engineers', *Social Studies of Science* 34 (2004), pp. 733–58.

Portanova, Stamatia, *Moving without a Body: Digital Philosophy and Choreographic Thoughts*, Cambridge, MA: MIT Press, 2013.

Potter, Keith, *Four Musical Minimalists: La Monte Young, Terry Riley, Steve Reich, Philip Glass*, Cambridge: Cambridge University Press, 2000.

Quam, Dave, 'The Evolution of Footwork', http://www.residentadvisor.net/feature. aspx?1235 (accessed 17 December 2010).

Reynolds, Simon, *Generation Ecstasy: Into the World of Rave Music and Dance Culture*, New York: Routledge, 1998.

Reynolds, Simon, 'Adult Hardcore', *The Wire* 182 (April 1999), http://www.thewire. co.uk/articles/2033/ (accessed February 2009).

Reynolds, Simon and Eshun, Kodwo, 'The Natural Laws of Music: Discussing the State of Music Criticism', *Frieze* 46 (1999), http://www.frieze.com/issue/article/ the_natural_laws_of_music/ (accessed 28 July 2010).

Reznikoff, Iégor and Dauvois, Michel, 'La dimension sonore des grottes ornées', *Bulletin de la Société Préhistorique Française* 85 (1988), pp. 238–46.

Reznikoff, Iégor, 'The Evidence of the Use of Sound Resonance from Paleolithic to Medieval Times', in *Archaeoacoustics*, Chris Scarre and Graeme Lawson (eds), Cambridge: McDonald Institute for Archaeological Research, 2006, pp. 77–84.

Ridout, Nicolas, 'Welcome to the Vibratorium', *The Senses & Society* 3 (2008), pp. 221–2.

Rimbault, Edward F., *The Early English Organ Builders and Their Works: From the Fifteenth Century to the Period of the Great Rebellion* (1864), New York: AMS Press, 1976.

Rizzolatti G. and Craighero, L., 'The Mirror-Neuron System', *Annual Review of Neuroscience*. 27 (2004), pp. 169–92.

Rizzolatti, G., Fogassi, L. and Gallese, V., 'Neurophysiological Mechanisms Underlying the Understanding and Imitation of Action', *National Review of Neuroscience* 2 (2001), pp. 661–70.

Rodgers Tara, *Pink Noises: Women on Electronic Music and Sound*, Durham, NC: Duke University Press, 2010.

Roll, William G. and Persinger, Michael A., 'Investigations of Poltergeists and Haunts: A Review and Interpretation', in James Houran and Rense Lange (eds), *Hauntings and Poltergeists: Multidisciplinary Perspectives*, Jefferson, NC: McFarland, 2001, pp. 123–63.

Ronson, Jon, *The Men Who Stare At Goats*, London: Picador, 2004.

Rose, Tricia, *Black Noise: Rap Music and Black Culture in Contemporary America*, Middletown, CT: Wesleyan University Press, 1994.

Rossing, Thomas D., *Science of Percussion Instruments*, Singapore: World Scientific Publishing Co Ltd, 2000.

Rouget, Gilbert, *Music and Trance: A Theory of the Relations Between Music and Possession*, Chicago: University of Chicago Press, 1985.

Sagdeev, Roald Z. and Kennel, Charles F., 'Collisionless Shock Waves in Interstellar Matter', *Scientific American* 264 (April 1991), pp. 106–13. http://www.zoklet.net/totse/en/fringe/fringe_science/shockwav.html (accessed 5 June 2011).

Saldanha, Arun, *Psychedelic White: Goa Trance and the Viscosity of Race*, Minneapolis: University of Minnesota Press, 2007.

Sarig, Roni, *Third Coast: Outkast, Timbaland, and How Hip-Hop Became a Southern Thing*, New York: Da Capo, 2007.

Scarre, Chris and Lawson, Graeme (eds), 'Preface', in *Archaeoacsoustics*, Cambridge: McDonald Institute for Archaeological Research, 2006, pp. vii–ix.

Schafer, R. Murray, *The Soundscape: Our Sonic Environment and the Tuning of the World*, Rochester, VT: Destiny Books, 1994.

Schloss, Joseph G., *Making Beats – The Art of Sample-Based Hip-Hop*, Middletown, CT: Wesleyan University Press, 2004.

Schopenhauer, Arthur, *On Vision and Colors*, trans. Georg Stahl, New York: Princeton Architectural Press, 2010.

Schwartz, Hillel, *Making Noise: From Babel to the Big Bang and Beyond*, New York, Zone Books, 2011.

Sconce, Jeffrey, *Haunted Media: Electronic Presence from Telegraphy to Television*, Raleigh, NC: Duke University Press, 2000.

Scott, Robert A., *The Gothic Enterprise: A Guide to Understanding the Medieval Cathedral*, Berkeley: University of California Press, 2003.

Sen, S. N., *Acoustics, Waves and Oscillations*, New Delhi: New Age International, 1990.

Sensurround Manual, http://www.in70mm.com/newsletter/2004/69/sensurround/index.htm (accessed 17 June 2011).

Shannon, John R., *Understanding the Pipe Organ: A Guide for Students, Teachers and Lovers of the Instrument*, Jefferson, NC: McFarland, 2009.

Shapiro, Peter, 'The Primer: the Roland TB-303 Bass Line', *The Wire* 303 (May 2009), pp. 40–5.

Shaviro, Steven, *The Cinematic Body*, Minneapolis: University of Minnesota Press, 1993.

Silverman, Kaja, *The Acoustic Mirror: The Female Voice in Psychoanalysis and Cinema*, Bloomington, IN: Indiana University Press, 1988.

Simons, Ronald, *Boo! Culture, Experience, and the Startle Reflex*, Oxford University Press, USA, 1996.

Sinker, Mark, 'Black Science Fiction: Loving the Alien in Advance of the Landing', *The Wire* 96 (February 1992), http://www.thewire.co.uk/archive/essays/black_science_fiction.html (accessed 26 October 2006).

Sonnenschein, David, *Sound Design: The Expressive Power of Music, Voice and Sound Effects in Cinema*, Studio City, CA: Los Angeles: Michael Wiese Productions, 2001.

Sorge, Georg Andreas, *The Secretly Kept Art of the Scaling of Organ Pipes* (1764), trans. Carl O. Bleyle, Buren: Uitgeverij Frits Knuf, 1978.

Sterne, Jonathan, *The Audible Past: Cultural Origins of Sound Reproduction*, Raleigh, NC: Duke University Press, 2002.

Sterne, Jonathan (ed.), *The Sound Studies Reader*, New York: Routledge, 2012.

Stolzoff, Norman, *Wake the Town and Tell the People: Dancehall Culture in Jamaica*, Charlotte, NC: Duke University Press, 2000.

Straw, Will, 'Systems of Articulation, Logics of Change: Communities and Scenes in Popular Music', *Cultural Studies* 5 (1991), pp. 368–88.

Swezey, Stuart (ed.), *Amok Journal, Sensurround Edition: A compendium of Psycho-Physiological Investigations*, Los Angeles: Amok Books, 1995.

Synnott, Anthony, *The Body Social: Symbolism, Self and Society*, London: Routledge, 1993.

Szwed, John F., *Space is the Place: The Lives and Times of Sun Ra*, New York: Da Capo, 1997.

Tandy, Vic, 'Something in the Cellar', *The Journal of the Society for Psychical Research* 64.3, no. 860 (2003), pp. 129–40.

Tandy, Vic and Lawrence, Tony R., 'The Ghost in the Machine', *The Journal of the Society for Psychical Research* 62/851 (1998), pp. 360–4.

Tempest, W. (ed.), *Infrasound and Low Frequency Vibration*, London: Academic Press, 1976.

Thacker, Eugene, *In the Dust of This Planet: Horror of Philosophy Volume 1*, Winchester, UK: Zero Books, 2011.

Than, Ker, 'Stone Age Art Caves May Have Been Concert Hall', *National Geographic News* (2 July 2008), http://news.nationalgeographic.com/news/2008/07/080702-cave-paintings.html (accessed 17 March 2009).

Théberge, Paul, *Any Sound You Can Imagine: Making Music/Consuming Technology*, Middletown, CT: Wesleyan University Press, 1997.

Thompson, Emily, *The Soundscape of Modernity: Architectural Acoustics and the Culture of Listening in America, 1900-1933*, Cambridge: MIT Press, 2002.

Thornton, Sarah, *Club Cultures: Music, Media, and Subcultural Capital*, Hanover: University Press of New England, 1996.

Titze, Ingo R., *Principles of Voice Production*, Upper Saddle River, NJ: Prentice Hall, 1994.

Titze, Ingo R., 'Tibetan Chanting and Harmonic Singing', *The Journal of Singing* 53/2 (1996), pp. 31–2.

Todd, Neil P. McAngus and Cody, Frederick W., 'Vestibular Responses to Loud Dance Music: A Physiological Basis of the 'Rock and Roll Threshold'', *Journal of the Acoustical Society of America* 107/1 (January 2000), pp. 496–500.

Todd, Neil P. McAngus, Rosengren, Sally M., and Golebatch, James G., 'Tuning and Sensitivity of the Human Vestibular System to Low-Frequency Vibration', *Neuroscience Letters* 444 (2008), pp. 36–41.

Tompkins, Dave, *How to Wreck a Nice Beach: The Vocoder From World War II to Hip-Hop - The Machine Speaks,* Chicago: Stopsmiling Books, 2010.

Toop, David, *Rap Attack: African Rap to Global Hip Hop*, 2nd edn, London: Serpent's Tail, 2005.

Toop, David, *Haunted Weather*, London: Serpent's Tail, 2004.

Tuzin, Donald, 'Miraculous Voices: The Auditory Experience of Numinous Objects', *Current Anthropology* 25 (1984), pp. 579–96.

Van den Berg, Frits, 'Low Frequency Noise and Phantom Sounds', *Journal of Low Frequency Noise and Active Control* 28/2 (2009), pp. 105–16.

Vasudevan, R. N. and Gordon, Colin G., 'Experimental Study of Annoyance Due to Low Frequency Noise', *Applied Acoustics* 10 (1977), pp. 57–69.

Veal, Michael, *Dub: Soundscapes & Shattered Songs in Jamaican Reggae*, Middletown, CT: Wesleyan University Press, 2007.

Von Simson, Otto Georg, *The Gothic Cathedral: Origins of Gothic Architecture and the Medieval Concept of Order*, 3rd edn, Princeton: Princeton University Press, 1988.

Watson, Aaron and Keating, David, 'Architecture and Sound: an Acoustic Analysis of Megalithic Monuments in Prehistoric Britain', *Antiquity* 73 (1999), pp. 325–36.

Webb, Stanley, 'The Organ at Winchester', *The Musical Times* 129/1745 (July 1988), p. 369.

Weheliye, Alexander, *Phonographies: Grooves in Sonic Afro-Modernity*, Durham, NC: Duke University Press, 2005.

White, Glenn D. and Louie, Gary J., *The Audio Dictionary*, 3rd edn, Seattle: University of Washington Press, 2005.

White, Paul, 'Improving Your Stereo Mixing', *Sound on Sound* (October 2000), http://www.soundonsound.com/sos/oct00/articles/stereomix.htm (accessed 16 March 2012).

Williams, C. F. Abdy, *The Story of the Organ* (1903), Detroit: Singing Tree Press, 1972.

Wiseman, Richard, Watt, Caroline, Greening, Emma, Stevens, Paul and O'Keeffe, Ciaran, 'An Investigation Into the Alleged Haunting of Hampton Court Palace: Psychological Variables and Magnetic Fields', *Journal of Parapsychology* 66 (2002), pp. 387–408.

Wiseman, Richard, Watt, Caroline, Stevens, Paul, Greening, Emma and O'Keeffe, Ciaran, 'An Investigation into Alleged "Hauntings"', *British Journal of Psychology* 94 (2003), pp. 195–211.

Wright, Craig M., *Music and Ceremony at Notre Dame of Paris, 500-1550*, Cambridge: Cambridge University Press, 1989.

Wuethrich, Matt, 'Eleh', *The Wire* 314 (April 2010), p. 31.

Yenigun, Sami and Glasspiegel, Willis, 'Chicago's Footwork Music and Dance Gets a Transatlantic Lift', (6 December 2010), http://www.npr.org/blogs/therecord/2010/12/14/131834348/chicago-s-footwork-music-and-dance-get-a-transatlantic-lift (accessed 22 August 2011).

Young, Rob, 'Exotic Audio Research', *The Wire* 157 (March 1997), http://www.thewire.co.uk/articles/169/print (accessed 1 July 2011).

Zakia, Richard D., *Perception and Imaging*, 3rd edn, Oxford: Focal Press, 2007.

Zhang, S. Y., Xie, Z. L. and Hong, Y. S.,'Damage Assessment and Preservation of Suspending System of Yongle-Big-Bell', in Federico M. Mazzolani (ed.), *Protection of Historical Buildings*, London: Taylor & Francis, 2009.

Zuberi, Nabeel, 'Is this the Future? Black Music and Technology Discourse', *Science Fiction Studies* 34 (July 2007), pp. 283–300.

Index

Lovecraft and   35
machinic phylum and   202n. 51
nonhuman and   38, 166, 239
popular music studies and   5
recuperation by discourse   84
relationality and   13
of ritual sound   78
of sonic experience   2, 4
sound studies and   8–9
Sun Ra and   160
thinking with   15, 19, 187–90
of thunder experience   74
weird   35, 63 (*see also* material agency;
   sonic body)
Mattheson, Johann   104
Mendelssohn, Felix   105
Mertens, Wim   130
metaphor   6, 19, 27, 51, 53, 100, 197n. 16
Mike Ink   175
Miller, Paul   138
molecularity, *see* spectrality
Morris, Sylvan   154
Morton, Timothy   14
Moulton, Tom   173, 175
Muristus   95
musicology   7, 100
   Deleuzian   191
   ethnomusicology   73, 190
Muybridge, Eadweard   40
myth-science   14–15, 18–20, 27–8, 31, 36,
   107, 157–61, 187–9
   Afrofuturism   200n. 44
   hyperstition and   14
   Sun Ra   159–61, 200n. 44 (*see also*
   Arcanum; The Science; Sun Ra)

new materialisms   188, 200n. 41
Nilsen, B. J.   123, 192
   as Hazard   123
noise: scholarship on   6–8
   anti–noise campaigns   66
nomad science   15, 17, 26–7, 54–6, 92,
   113, 219n. 1, 243n. 74
nonhuman   13–14, 33–6, 125–7
   affect   200n. 41
   agencies   43, 53–4, 188–90 (*see also*
   man–made unknown; material agency)
Norment, Camille   141–2

Obeah   158
occult   92, 127, 153, 158
   occulture   247n. 5
   of technology   156, 159 (*see also*
   Arcanum; man–made unknown)
Oliveros, Pauline   129
Op Art   127–37
operative reality   41–2, 51–6
   hauntings as   55–6
   of Hummers   57
   numinous experience as   79, 81
   synaesthesia and   109–11, 141 (*see also*
   hyperstition)
Outer Limits, The   38–40, 42, 56

pain   29, 57, 64, 98–100, 136, 139, 144,
   181
panic   45–8
Parliament–Funkadelic   160, 162
Pearson, Ewan   5
perceptual abstraction   127–37
Perrot, Jean   91, 107, 227n. 86
Perry, Lee 'Scratch'   159
Persinger, Michael   110, 211n. 37
Philo of Byzantium   90, 92
phylum   202n. 51, *see also* bass
physio-logic   18, 176–83, *see also* logic of
   sensation
pipe organ   13, 90–111
   the Arcanum   91–5
   Baroque   102–6
   building   91–5, 105–7
   comparisons to   82
   Helmholtz and   71
   hydraulis   90
   Ktesibios and   90, 92, 227n. 86
   lowest frequencies   72, 91
   medieval   95–102
   organ-church assemblage   17, 90–111
   pipe names   91
   Wurlitzer   106
Plasticman   165
Plastic People   41, 167, 202n. 1, 206n. 33
popular music studies   5–7, 171, 174,
   190
   electronic dance music studies   5, 31,
   190–1
Powers, Herb (Herbie Jr)   167

Lightning Source UK Ltd.
Milton Keynes UK
UKHW02f1219240418
321542UK00006B/236/P